FERVENT YEARS

THE GROUP THEATRE AND THE THIRTIES

HAROLD CLURMAN

We ... *e practical*
fron ... *—rument of*
unin ... *—ter world.*
ROOSEVELT

A ... OUP

Library of Congress Cataloging in Publication Data

Clurman, Harold, 1901–
    The fervent years.

    (Da Capo paperback)
    Reprint. Originally published: New York: Harcourt Brace
Jovanovich, 1975.
    Includes index.
    1. Group Theatre. 2. Theater — United States. I. Title.
PN2297.G7C5 1983   792′.0973   82-25239
ISBN 0-306-80186-8

This Da Capo Press paperback edition of *The Fervent Years: The
Group Theatre and the Thirties* is an unabridged republication of the
edition published in New York in 1975, here supplemented with a
new introduction by Stella Adler. It is reprinted by arrangement with
Alfred A. Knopf, Inc.

Published by Da Capo Press, Inc.
A member of the Perseus Books Group

Manufactured in the United States of America

To the Memory of my Father and Mother

INTRODUCTION
TO THE DA CAPO EDITION

The force of Harold Clurman's personality found no stronger expression than in *The Fervent Years*, unquestionably the most important book in the American theatre. That force, which I encountered at the birth of the Group, convinced me to join an unknown company without plays and without money.

At that time, I myself was looking for something more than the magnetism of "show business" and the glamor of stardom. Alone, I searched for these elements in my wanderings all over the world. I found them in Europe—in Max Reinhardt, Konstantin Stanislavsky, and Yevgeny Vagtangov. But in America, before the Group, theatre of these dimensions did not exist.

Harold too dreamed of a greater and more compelling American theatre, as he explains in his own foreword to *The Fervent Years*. He saw that super-size was necessary and found it in the person of Jacob P. Adler, who could hypnotize an audience with his colossal quality. This was the essence of theatre Harold sought: monumental stature and universality.

Clurman invited me to hear him speak. His force was powerful, mysteriously so. I could not understand its source. Harold's very voice, unlike Reinhardt's and Stanislavsky's softer tones, expressed a man of overwhelming size. Indeed, it sprang from the universal in himself and in his art. He was eagerly, crazily groping to create a world to match his vision. In comparison to Harold, other theatrical thinkers appeared infantile.

Meeting Odets and Miller, Harold instantly recognized them as brothers. They were, like him, groping to express a vision of America in transition, to express it with power, with dimension.

Another way of stating my point is to describe it as a search for universal size, larger than life, a size possessed by a Lear or a Shylock. However, Harold had to confront not only his own limitations but those of the people who surrounded him. His struggle was very hard. What was interesting was his choice of American plays that tried to clarify "large ideas" for an audience very much troubled and confused, living in a country trapped in transition.

Awake and Sing, of course, was the supreme accomplishment of the Group. The actors in the cast possessed dual nationality, so to speak. First life had knocked them about, and now they played stage characters who—like themselves—also found it nearly impossible to survive. America was just too new for the old souls in the plays. In a real sense, the play was about "displaced people" who were trying to succeed. At that time nobody could bring this theme alive in America...except Harold.

As for Harold's legacy to the theatre, I think it may be lost because he didn't create an heir. Some people, nurtured by Harold's creativeness, will perhaps recognize what they have inherited. When he himself tried to sum up what he believed, he said, "What I want to apply my energies to, because I believe in it, is spreading hope and love of life; to combat despair. I am a person who has to build all the time and the way I have chosen to do it is through the great art of the theatre!"

Whether it's a sonnet, a symphony, a play, a performance, this is what all artists really want to say.

—STELLA ADLER
New York City
September 1982

FOREWORD
TO THE 1957 EDITION

Ours is the only modern country which is in a state of permanent revolution. The central period which this book covers is 1931–41, and a record of that time may now strike one as ancient history.

Nevertheless there are very few things I said in the first edition of this book about which I would now prefer to reverse myself. Among the criticisms, leveled at it when it was first issued—1945— criticisms, I might add, which came chiefly from people close to the Group Theatre itself—a common one was that I had been too negative, too self-deprecating, despondent, one might even go so far as to say pessimistic. "The Group Theatre," my friend Irwin Shaw complained, "was a glorious crusade, not a funeral."

It has heartened me in the ensuing years that students of the theatre—young actors, playwrights, directors—and many others too young to have witnessed any of the events described herein have written me to say that the tale the book recounts has served them as a source of inspiration and as a guide in some of the problems they now have to face. So, it would seem, a history of the past—even the theatrical past—may still serve some present purpose. This is one of the reasons I wished to have the book reprinted.

The body of the book has not been altered by one word; I am willing to stand by most of my past misjudgments since they represented my beliefs at the time. I have, however, added an epilogue, covering the period 1945–55, which expresses some of the things I think today.

FOREWORD
TO THE FIRST EDITION

WHEN the Group Theatre was alive and kicking, many of my associates urged me to write the story of what had always seemed to us a fascinating enterprise. I held that I was too busy coping with the problems of the Group to describe them; that our job was to turn out a body of work before we talked about it; and, most important of all, that a book on the Group, no matter how critically and objectively written, might strike the reader as an apology or as just publicity.

My objections never satisfied my colleagues. They thought these objections represented another example of my oft lamented tendency to procrastinate. I was just too lazy to apply myself or too proud to commission anyone else to do it. There may have been some justification for my friends' suspicions. Yet, looking back, I believe the reasons I gave were true ones.

If, however, the period of our active production, 1931–41, struck me as too early for a history of that activity, the time I choose to write it may appear too late. The world is now almost wholly engaged in a great war either in terms of actual combat or in constant adjustment to it.

If my story of the Group represented nothing more to my mind than a chance to reminisce over past pleasures, to dwell on fond memories of struggle and accomplishment, I should deem the present moment fairly inopportune, and I should demur anew before undertaking the task.

But the Group Theatre, in my view, was a symptom and an expression of a profound impulse in American life, an impulse that certainly did not begin with the Group Theatre, and did not end with it. Because I was one of the people who felt the pressure of that impulse and was able to articulate it, the Group Theatre was founded. But the impulse is still current, though hardly perceptible at the moment in the theatre; and because I believe that impulse to be a major force of our times, it is now, perhaps more than ever, necessary to interpret it afresh.

A consideration that frequently occupies an important place in the discussion of a once outstanding but no longer functioning organization such as the Group Theatre is the matter of its final balance sheet. My own opinion is that, like most living things, the Group Theatre was both a failure and a success. Of those who were connected with its work during the greater part of the time it operated, the majority to this day devoutly affirm its success. Some, however, are violently contrary-minded. The theatre world in general, in so far as it has any consciousness at all, is similarly divided — with perhaps a stronger emphasis on the negative side. But for me, at this point, the question of success or failure, as commonly understood, is actually irrelevant. What alone counts is the *life* of the Group, which derived from sources deeper and wider than Times Square. It is the Group as reflection, image, agent, influence and product of its day that is the essence of my narrative.

In this light I regard the Group Theatre as a kind of outpost on a main line of American experience which not only has not come to an end but has barely begun. If the impulse that gave birth to the Group were to die out, the result not merely would spell tragedy for a handful of artists and workers in and around the theatre, but would constitute something like a fatal wound in the American spirit.

The story I propose to tell, then, is one I hope will prove interesting in and for itself as an account of divers personalities in the general environment of the New York stage. But as the theatre by its very nature — its interrelation of business man, producer, writer, actor, and audience — is a remarkable point of vantage for broad observation, I plan to make the reader perceive in this record the delineation of certain American problems that are of yesterday, today, and the morrow to come.

In other words, the theatre where I happened to find myself for over ten years supplies me now with an admirable focus for the real subject of my story, which is to be found in the whole context of American life in the thirties. Perhaps this recollection of that decade may now serve toward an understanding of the inevitable crises in the days that lie before us. I write this book about the past in behalf of the future.

CONTENTS

PART IV: CONSUMMATION

PART V: NEW PHASE

PART VI: FAREWELL TO THE THIRTIES

ILLUSTRATIONS

PART I

S E E D S

CHAPTER ONE

The Tower of Babel

THE TWENTIES, you remember, was a period of parties. Everybody who was anybody, or anybody who hoped to become somebody, threw as many parties as possible. It was a prosperous time, and it seemed that all distinction between people, all struggle, and all natural unpleasantness were to be liquidated in the polite booze of the party ritual.

In the later years of legal drinking the scintillation of the party as a cultural phenomenon was somewhat dimmed by an admixture of "social purpose," but in the twenties the aim of the party seemed actually concentrated on pleasure. It was the time for fun. It was the time of the good time.

The little people crowded the speakeasies; the somewhat bigger people squeezed into night clubs; the best people gave the real parties at their recently decorated homes. Of these real parties, the most brilliant were given by impresarios, publishers, and leaders of the newest musical and theatrical associations. For example, the home of Horace Liveright, publisher and character, was, by common consent, one of the best spots.

My friend Aaron Copland, with whom I shared student days in Paris from 1921 through the summer of 1924, had become early in 1925 one of the season's favorite musical celebrities. From these parties he used to bring back a kind of sizzling index of names that were hot in the Sunday supplements or the more exclusive weekly and monthly journals. "All of these," he reported with a twinkling irony and some curiosity as to my reaction, "were there. . . ."

Later, though I had little identity, I began to crash these parties myself. That is, I was Copland's friend; I had lived in Paris, studied at the Sorbonne, and didn't look stupid when Proust or the Swedish Ballet were mentioned. Many of the people I had been introduced to at a dozen such occasions never were able to recognize me the thirteenth time.

Today almost all these parties have melted into a single image. When I describe one particular gathering I am not sure that I am not borrowing from my impression of another. At any rate, my permanent vision of the time narrows down to an evening when, I could almost swear, Albert Einstein, Mae West, Paul Robeson, Ferenc Molnár, Carl Van Vechten, Gene Tunney, Elinor Wylie, Albert Coates, a movie star, an unidentified clergyman, several especially attractive players from a current revue, a former newspaper editor, an editor of the *Dial*, a famous modiste, a Continental littérateur, a liberal economist, and a successful bootlegger were all present.

I did not ask myself at the moment, but not long after I began to wonder how all these people had come to be in the same room. Was Mae West brought there to fascinate the economist? Had the clergyman come to convert Molnár? The editor of the *Dial* to study Tunney? There was no reason for this assembly of guests — not even that of business — no reason except that the very idea of such a configuration was fun.

It was entertaining because all these people were personalities. They had *done* something. They had attracted attention, made a noise or a name, had in one way or another supplied a subject for conversation, for curiosity, for controversy, or even for contempt. For any single one of these electric beings to have insistently put forward a personal point of view, to have halted the festivity with an emphasis on his own belief, prejudice, or passion, would certainly have spoiled the show, would definitely have been regarded as unacceptable manners. Everybody — no matter how special or exalted — was present chiefly for purposes of display. Artists, preachers, politicians, went through a kind of routined movement of mild gaiety like the figures on the old Wrigley advertisement in the lights of Broadway. . . .

At about that time Copland and I accompanied Nadia Boulanger (who had taught him and so many other young American composers in Paris) on her first walk up the Great White Way. It was really ablaze in those days, you remember, and not without a certain pride I asked: "What do you think of it?" "It is *extraordinaire,* but not very *raffinated,*" she answered. We laughed because her bad English only served to set off her foreign point of view.

We didn't think of Broadway's lack of refinement. We thought that it was *extra-ordinaire;* inside us something cavorted, jiggled, whirled with those signs, quite apart from our taste for the objects they intended to sell.

There were poets then who glorified the facts, the boasts, the pride of business, and Hendrik van Loon proved through an analogy with the past that, owing to its wealth, the United States was due for a renaissance of art and culture. The characteristic feature of the period — what gave it its glow and excitement — was its energy. Everything was rushing on toward an activity that was certain to be effective — that is, successful. The meaning of things lay in their manifestation, in the sheer burst of their energy. The answer to everything was money. The guarantee that everything was as it should be was pleasure. Pleasure was the color of the time. Its hue alone was as reassuring as a flushed complexion in a young man. No need to inquire further into the state of his health. He looked fine, and in this successful world he was sure to go far, or, at any rate, to go. "Invest in your country, it can't go wrong," was the device proclaimed above Broadway and Forty-third Street.

When I returned from Paris in June, 1924, I did not know that the twenties were the twenties. I knew that the time of my postgraduate dalliance was over. I had to do something to earn a living. I had never had to think of this before, because at home it was considered almost a little crude to think of work as long as the liberal school days were in progress.

This was especially true in my case, because I had never shown any disposition to think about money or to question myself about my career. All that was known of me by my parents was that from the age of six, when I had been taken to see Jacob Adler in *Uriel Acosta* at the Grand Street Theatre, I had a passionate inclination toward the theatre. I recall that whenever I was told I was to go to the theatre, I was asked to take a nap in the afternoon before the show, but my anticipation of the event made sleep impossible.

Between the ages of twelve and sixteen I had organized various neighborhood theatrical ventures, for which I wrote, acted, and directed little plays. Between the ages of six and twelve I had attended the theatres of the East Side, where my father practiced medicine. In a way, this theatrical experience was fortunate, since the Yiddish Theatre, as Lincoln Steffens, Norman Hapgood, and other observers of the period pointed out, "was about the best in New York at that time both in stuff and in acting." The "stuff" was frequently Shakespeare, Tolstoy, Gorky, Andreyev, or charming folk operettas and plays modeled after original works by Sudermann, Hauptmann and other contemporary Europeans. The actors were among the best I have ever seen in many years of playgoing all over the world. Most stimulating of all were the audiences. For to the immigrants in the early years of the century the theatre was the one center of social intercourse. Here the problems of their life, past and present, could be given a voice; here they could get to know and understand one another.

When my parents moved uptown to East 172nd Street, I was still too young to travel to Broadway. I visited all the local stock companies, and I saw the success shows of the day. At the age of fifteen when I got used to going downtown to high school on West Fifty-ninth Street, I switched to Broadway itself.

My first college days — in 1919 — were important days for the American theatre and for American literature. The Theatre Guild had entered upon its historic path. Arthur Hopkins, daring in choice of plays and in his use of a new kind of setting, made almost every one of his productions something one wanted to see. I began going to the opera, and heard Caruso many times. I experimented with symphony concerts, to which I had been led by the influence of Romain Rolland's *Jean Christophe*. I read Waldo Frank's *Our America*, which helped make our country seem a wonderful arena for young adventure. I heard the radiantly handsome Franklin D. Roosevelt make a campaign speech in which he kidded the Republican Presidential candidate, Warren G. Harding.

All the intellectuals seemed to be saying that America was culturally hopeless, but they had a great time saying it. We had a swell time reading it, and no one, I think, believed a word of it. A great many Americans went abroad — mostly to Paris. I did not know it then, but I was in the line of that special exodus. I was carried along in the stream because my father had always spoken nostalgically of a France he had never seen and had inspired me with a desire to make up for his loss.

For the purpose of this book, it is sufficient to say that while in Paris I wrote a thesis at the Sorbonne on the French drama from 1890 to 1914, went regularly to the theatre, saw the Moscow Art Theatre before they left for New York, and attended lectures at Copeau's school at the Théâtre du Vieux Colombier as well as all the Copeau productions. My feeling for the theatre was slowly changing. Through Aaron Copland and his friends, through contact with a large new world of books, through the various æsthetic and moral discussions that always played so large a part in Parisian life, the theatre seemed to become ever less important in my eyes. I enjoyed seeing plays — my flesh had a natural hankering for the atmosphere of the theatre, even when the plays were contemptible — but my mind was left dissatisfied.

At that time I might have put it this way: In the books I read, in the painting I see, in the music I hear, in all conversations, I am aware of the presence of the world itself, I detect a feeling for large issues of human concern. In the theatre these are either absent or diluted, frequently cheapened. The composers and the painters are searching for new words, so to speak, new forms, shapes, meanings. Aaron Copland tells me he wants to express the present day, he wants to find the musical equivalent for our contemporary tempo and activity. Where is the parallel to all this in the theatre? There are little *avant-garde* performances here and there; Copeau speaks seriously about the theatre. Of course, the greatest poets of the past wrote for the theatre. Yet, despite all this, what I actually see on the boards lacks the feel of either significant contemporaneity that I get from even the lesser concerts of new music — not to mention the novels of Gide, Proust, D. H. Lawrence — or the sense of a permanent contribution to my inner experience that I get from some things at the Louvre, from the finale of Beethoven's Ninth, or even from the simple reading of certain classic dramatists. Where is the best thought of our time in the theatre, the feeling of some true personal significance in any of its works? Either there is something inferior in the theatre *per se* or there is something wrong about the practical theatre of today that escapes me. I can't live without the theatre, but I can't live with it. The theatre gives itself lofty graces, claims a noble lineage, but has no more dimension than a bordello!

My æsthetic opinions were only occasionally conscious. I had no fixed philosophy of the theatre, and though I was given to the pastime of theorizing — I had been brought up in an environment where artistic-political palaver was next to meat and drink — I really knew what I was about only through my actions. My action on returning home was to look for a job. With the background I have just described, there seemed little choice but for me to seek it in literary and theatrical fields. The writing world, in my view, had more dignity; the theatre was somehow more available.

Nothing happened at first, except that one day, during a rather routine interview with Brock Pemberton, as I looked around and noted a pile of play scripts on his desk, I said to myself: "I guess this is where I want to work. *In the theatre.*"

I landed a job in October 1924. Between July and October, since I had definitely set my course, I read all the practical and theoretical books on the modern theatre. I read Gordon Craig, but although he echoed some of my doubts as to the theatre's æsthetic validity, I understood him poorly. There was something there, but I couldn't make it out. I had too little experience.

The experience began with the new firm of Macgowan-Jones-O'Neill, who, together with James Light, had taken over the Greenwich Village Theatre and the Provincetown Playhouse. This, to me, was a glamorous beginning.

The play these people were doing was Stark Young's *The Saint.* When the young people who, like me, had been promised work as extras came together, we were addressed by Kenneth Macgowan, the executive head of the organization. He explained that Macgowan-Jones-O'Neill and the Provincetown Players were not a commercial setup; they had little money. Macgowan asked those who could afford to work for nothing to state this on a slip of paper, and those who needed five, ten, or fifteen dollars a week to make a similar declaration. I was still living with my parents and had no particular need of money, and so I noted that five dollars a week would do for my pay. I was a little worried that night for fear that I had been too demanding and that only those who had volunteered to work gratis would be used. But Macgowan-Jones-O'Neill were not money-grubbers, and when the ghost walked, I was rewarded with a ten-dollar wage.

I attended all the rehearsals, though as an extra I was infrequently called. Robert Edmond Jones and Stark Young directed. I did not know anything about direction then, but their work on this production seemed vague and slightly amateurish. Richard Boleslavsky, a truant from the Moscow Art Theatre, was called in to take over the direction. The change proved instructive, because Boleslavsky was a man of the theatre from top to toe. The play ran for something like twelve performances.

This was my debut on the professional stage. What I remember best was a talk given by Robert Edmond Jones to the members of the *Saint* company and to the actors engaged for the whole season. It was all rather solemn. Macgowan, Jones, and O'Neill himself sat in the first row of the small auditorium; the actors were seated in the rows behind them. Macgowan (Kenneth the actors called him, just as the others — somewhat to my surprise — were Bobby and Gene) got up and announced: "Bobby has something to tell you." Jones rose diffidently and spoke in a voice that suggested a slight spiritual grief and a noble yet humble exaltation. This is approximately what he said: "Recently I heard the story of a blind child on whom a successful operation had been performed. When the bandages were finally removed from its eyes, the child looked around in ecstasy and murmured: 'What is this thing called light?' To me, the theatre is like a light that blind people are made to see for the first time. The theatre is a dream that the audience comes to behold. The theatre is revelation. I look about me here, and I do not see light, I do not perceive dream, I do not feel revelation. That is what I want to tell you, Mary, Charlie, Norma — " He walked up the aisle and disappeared. Macgowan asked Gene if he had anything to add. Gene indicated that he didn't. There was a tense pause. That was all. The actors got up and left.

I was rather touched by Bobby Jones's speech. Jones was an artist, one of the very few in the American theatre. Yet I realized immediately that he had made no connection with his actors. They could not be blamed for being embarrassed by his talk. They did not speak his language, and he had been at no pains either to teach it to them or to translate himself into a language that might affect them. What light was he talking about? What revelation was he seeking? Actually he was referring to a private world of his own, which he made no effort to share. Here was no unity of point of view or any attempt to make one. Where was the connecting link? Since, obviously, Jones felt he couldn't function — his dream couldn't be realized without the assistance of those to whom he addressed himself — it seemed to me to be Jones's fault that he was not understood. It was the leader's task to fashion

a common language and a common point of reference with those
whom he hoped to lead.

The Provincetown people liked to keep the same company with
them for all their productions, so they called me to a reading for
a part in one of O'Neill's short sea-plays. James Light thrust a
script into my hand and whispered: "The character is a melancholy Russian. Read!" Before I knew where I was, whom I was
supposed to address, or even who was speaking to me, I heard
lines that I was required to respond to in the manner of a melancholy Russian. I didn't get the part.

For six months then I went from office to office looking for another job. I was particularly anxious to work for Arthur Hopkins.
I wrote him a letter, in which I expressed admiration for his contribution to our stage. I got a note to come down to see him. On
arriving at his office, before I had finished the sentence identify-
ing myself he shook his head and said: "Nothing for you in the
French play." (The French play was *What Price Glory?*) That
was all.

I tried hard to get a job with the Theatre Guild. I almost got
one after I interviewed Miss Helburn, who, impressed by my
background and my mention of Jacques Copeau in Paris, was
ready to make me assistant stage-manager of *The Guardsman*.
She sent me up to see Philip Loeb, who was then the Guild's
general stage-manager and casting director. But Philip Loeb
had been very unfavorably impressed by me. I stammered with
almost morbid shyness, I answered his questions quite indefi-
nitely. He told Miss Helburn he wouldn't have me as his assistant.

But I persisted. I kept coming back. "See me in a week," Loeb
would say, to get rid of me. I was back in a week. "Nothing new.
See me in three weeks." In three weeks I would return. "Nothing
new." "If you haven't a job, can't I just watch rehearsals?" I
pleaded. "I'm afraid that's against the rules. Come back in a
month." Finally I got a call to come to the Guild. Loeb had become impressed — or tired. I was to be an extra in *Cæsar and
Cleopatra*, the play that was to open the new Guild Theatre on
Fifty-second Street.

The Theatre Guild at that time paid its extras nothing for the first four weeks of the play's run and ten dollars weekly thereafter — when and if the play's run exceeded four weeks. With the Guild's growing prosperity, the extras in *Cæsar* were promised ten dollars for the first four weeks and sixteen dollars after that. Actually we received sixteen dollars from the beginning of the run.

As a kind of reward or advancement to the young actors — mostly beginners like myself — the Guild offered the opportunity to appear in a trial performance of some play they weren't sure would come off in a regular production. I was invited to one such special performance of Pirandello's *Right You Are If You Think You Are* by an actor who was to play his first real part in it. His name was Sanford Meisner. Meisner was picturesque in his role, but the leading part was played by a young, pale-faced man of intellectual demeanor. He was very short, intense-looking, with skin drawn tightly over a wide brow. He spoke with a faint foreign accent, had a large head of rather curly hair, and a face that expressed keen intelligence, suffering, ascetic control, with something old, withdrawn, and lofty about it. Though he was well cast for the typical Pirandello hero, he did not seem like an actor, so that something disagreeable though effective resulted from his performance. His name was Lee Strasberg.

I met Strasberg one day when we were all gathered in a room together to try out for a show the Guild was going to do at special Sunday matinees. The cast was to be recruited from the younger Guild actors. Meisner and Strasberg were playing in *Processional;* I was in *Cæsar*. As we waited, we were called singly to another room, where each actor was to sing anything he chose for the composer, Dick Rodgers, the lyricist, Larry Hart, and the director, Philip Loeb. Strasberg preceded me, and I could hear he chose to sing with rather manful effort, but not unpleasantly, a verse of *My Wild Irish Rose*. "A peculiar choice," I thought. But it was better than mine, which, for no good reason, was Don José's Flower Song from *Carmen,* which I didn't really know, and couldn't sing in any case.

Strasberg was chosen to act in some of the sketches; I was

asked to be stage-manager. Meisner was chosen for the chorus. This was the *Garrick Gaieties of 1925*.

During the rehearsals of the *Garrick Gaieties* Strasberg and I became friends. I worked very hard at my job. Phil Loeb appreciated this and took a special interest in me, while Strasberg encouraged and helped me because I had had little experience. Strasberg and I hit it off particularly well because he was more passionate about the theatre than I was, better informed, and already equipped with practical study and work. He had attended courses given by Boleslavsky and Ouspenskaya at a new school called the American Laboratory Theatre where, for the first time, the technique of acting according to the Moscow Art Theatre was being taught to American students. He had also played in a settlement house on the East Side, where Phil Loeb had seen him, liked him, and invited him to the Guild for his first job in *Processional*. At this settlement house he was now beginning to direct one-act and even full-length plays with neighborhood amateurs.

We were drawn together by our common dissatisfactions, our still unshaped ideals. Strasberg talked mostly about acting, upon which he seemed as concentrated as a jeweler over the inner mechanism of a watch. I never dreamed that there was that much to it. I had a broad background in the arts generally, and my complaint was against the nature of most plays: their thinness, lack of depth, eloquence, substantial theme. It didn't matter so much that a play was "well done"; what mattered was what was being done.

No, no, Strasberg argued with astonishing heat and pedagogic finesse, the manner in which a play is done is in itself a content. What I was talking about was literature; what he was interested in was theatre. How much acting is of great quality? I countered. Are we to wait around seeing agreeable mumming in the hope that every once in a while a performance will turn up that will justify so many stupid or negligible plays? I didn't understand, Strasberg retorted when I thought I had him stopped — and the debate continued for hours, afternoons, weeks.

We learned from one another. For my part, I learned to think of theatre not simply in terms of plays performed, but in terms of entities, in which each moment contributes to a total effect that is not to be measured solely by the value of the spoken word. The stage setting, the costumes, the actor's appearance, movement, his silences, gestures, rhythm, his very "aura," and the interrelation of all these elements, make the significance of the play, which on the stage is not merely the written text, but the totality of all these phenomena perceived as a whole.

For his part, Strasberg began to accept the validity of my insistence on the text, not alone as literary material for its own sake, but, at the very least, as a vehicle of human meaning. It was not alone important, I reiterated, that *Hamlet* is a beautiful piece of writing, packed with quotable wisdom, but that it is about something that has meaning for men at all times. The attributes of a play as entertainment make it like any other entertainment. What makes a play different is that it pretends to affect men's hearts, to change their very lives in matters of aspiration, sentiment, conviction. I wanted a theatrical production or, to put it more exactly, a play to make men more truly alive. The theatre was not a bar, as Craig had said, but a famous temple. Art was not a pick-me-up, but a communion.

Through these talks with Strasberg, what had previously puzzled me became clear. I understood now why I loved to go to the theatre, even when I did not respect it in the way I respected the very idea of a concert. When I had been contemptuous of the stage I had generally been displeased by the emptiness of the plays. But I loved to go to the theatre because the presence of the actors — their aliveness, the closeness of the audience, and the anticipation of a communion between all of them in terms of imagination, embodied through their actual movement in tangible space — was the very flower of large social contact, even when the occasion for this contact, in terms of literature, was a silly anecdote. At each performance in the theatre something happened between contemporaries that was a deep pleasure for those who loved the human vibration of people in their common play and enthusiasm. Since this pleasure was so rich, even on the low level of the ordinary show, I clamored for greater occasions, for closer embrace, for a more rooted togetherness.

From the time of the *Garrick Gaieties* and my meeting with Strasberg, my study and observation of theatre practice grew more systematic. While I studied, I talked. Indeed, I preached. What I insisted on at first was an elaboration of Strasberg's point of view — a point of view not original with him, of course, but one which he had made convincing to me.

Its pivotal thesis was that the so-called interpretative elements of the theatre were really creative functions, so that plays were to be seen as artistic wholes, not as scripts adorned by acting and direction. The true value of a production could not be adjudged simply on the basis of the writer's work. Much of Shakespeare on the stage was not only boring but empty, because most stage interpretations of his plays were merely illustrative — that is, devoid of creative content. On the other hand, rather ordinary plays were sometimes transfigured into works of art by great actors and directors. Duse in *La Dame aux camélias* was entirely superior to Dumas *fils;* and the tradition of judging plays on the stage almost entirely in terms of texts was due to the fact that dramatic critics were literary gentry (when they were anything at all), not theatre people.

It followed from this that theatre art itself, suffering in part from the encroachments of the literary tradition, had become pale, and few theatre works were ever on the level of a really good play script. What had to be done was to re-educate the theatre artists themselves.

There was another *Garrick Gaieties* the summer of 1926. I didn't want to stage-manage it. Strasberg took the job. I had saved some money from my various engagements, and I decided to join Copland, who had gone abroad again.

That summer I visited Zurich, to attend an international modern music festival, and I stopped off to see some plays and theatres in Munich. One night Copland and I stopped in at the great Hofbräuhaus of Munich. As we entered a side entrance, the huge throng of beer-bloated, smoke-stewed, heavy-seated Germans frightened us so that we actually beat a hasty retreat. I could not say why, I am not sure now, but I strongly suspect that Munich and its famous beer-hall were then already in the grip of the rising

Nazi movement. I was totally apolitical at the time: the trouble over the Versailles Treaty (about which I had heard derisive remarks in Berlin and Vienna during the years 1922–4, the Teapot Dome and Republican Administration scandals (though they had been the subject of many jokes in the very popular first *Grand Street Follies*), even controversies over the Soviet regime were all remote to me.

We spent the summer in Guéthary, a little Basque village between Biarritz and Saint-Jean-de-Luz, where I read more books on the theatre, wrote some articles, and studied Werfel's play *Juarez and Maximilian*, which I knew the Guild was to produce the next season. The theatre at home was always on my mind now. I cut my trip short and returned to Fifty-second Street.

I was engaged to play a few small parts in *Juarez*. By writing an interpretation of the play which the Guild published in its house organ, I attracted more attention to myself than my negligible position in the cast warranted. In the early rehearsal period I studied some of the play's historical background; I was therefore considered an authority, because Philip Moeller, the director, was quite ignorant on the subject.

Work on this production made a lasting impression on me. It was magnificently cast: Alfred Lunt, Clare Eames, Margalo Gillmore, Arnold Daly, Dudley Digges, Edward G. Robinson, Henry Travers, Philip Loeb, and Morris Carnovsky were some of the actors engaged for it. The result, as a whole, was thoroughly undistinguished. I tried to understand why.

It was an interesting play in which a good many actors wandered about. The director, despite his enthusiasm, had only a vague literary feeling for it. He had no organic sense of what the play's theme really was; the characters were so many rhetorical dummies to him. The world that made either the play's people or the play's milieu, and the dramatist's reason for choosing this particular material, were all outside the director's inner experience. For the actors the play was even more abstract than for the director. The play had been made no more alive to them than an essay or a faded theatrical print. Alfred Lunt, who in many respects was

well equipped for his part, had no real understanding of it; he
was undirected from the outside, and at sea within. Here, then,
were good actors, a script of some merit, a director not without
sound instincts; yet all together they produced a dud.

During the rehearsals I couldn't help releasing my restlessness
by talk on the sidelines. The ear I found most attentive to my
conversation was that of Cheryl Crawford, a sturdy girl from
Akron, Ohio, and a recent Smith graduate. She was the assistant
stage-manager of this production. When I said something about
Lunt's "general emotion," the phrase amused her. We got to talking together a lot.

Two important things happened at this juncture. I went downtown to see Lee Strasberg rehearse his amateurs at the Chrystie
Street Settlement. He was working with them in a manner that
struck me as altogether original. I did not know it then: he was
following a method that he had been taught at the American
Laboratory Theatre. I watched with keen interest.

At that time the Guild had instituted a school, in which they
hoped to develop some fresh acting talent for the future. My
friend Sanford Meisner was enrolled there. After a while he confessed that he was not altogether satisfied with his training. Perhaps he needed additional work. I recommended that he get a
part in Strasberg's production at the Settlement.

Strasberg was putting on John Masefield's translation of Racine's *Esther*. To see how Meisner was getting on and how Strasberg worked, I became a frequent visitor at the Settlement
rehearsals. I remember one day watching a Guild rehearsal in
which Helen Westley was having great difficulty with a scene.
The author and director were making no progress. Strasberg, who
sat beside me, finally whispered: "I could get it out of her," meaning that he knew how to deal with the actress's problem in this
scene and could produce the desired result. This confidence on
Strasberg's part piqued me. He spoke as if he possessed a magic
key, a secret of some kind. That is why Strasberg's methods of rehearsal particularly interested me.

Another important step was my enrollment in a course for di-

rectors given by Boleslavsky at the Laboratory Theatre. After
Juarez and Maximilian I had a choice of taking this course or of
going into a new organization as an actor in its first production.
This organization was called the New Playwrights' Theatre, the
new playwrights being mainly John Howard Lawson, Mike Gold,
John Dos Passos.

At their first rehearsal the director addressed the company as
follows: "This is a theatre of the Left. Don't ask me what that
means, but let it go at that; it's a theatre of the Left. The play
we are going to do is John Howard Lawson's *Loudspeaker*. This
play is a farce — has a lot of laughs that we have got to get. Let's
get going and get them." When I discovered that, besides this
lightmindedness, the company was going to pay me no more than
eighteen dollars a week for a fair-sized part, I quit, and took the
Lab course in direction.

Another thing that happened at the Laboratory Theatre which
was to play a crucial role in my life was my meeting with my future wife, Stella Adler, youngest daughter of my childhood stage
hero, Jacob Adler. She was a member of the Laboratory company, where she worked when she wasn't too busy with her regular engagements. She had already been on the stage for years
(with her father, in vaudeville, and on Broadway), but she had
come to the Lab, like Strasberg before me, to make fresh in-
quiries.

The Theatre Guild was going to do Copeau's dramatization of
The Brothers Karamazov, and Copeau himself was engaged to
direct. I wrote a piece on Copeau that the Guild used as a publicity article. Though I was not formally engaged for this production, Copeau invited me to stand by to help him occasionally
when his English went dry, and "to learn from his mistakes."

Copeau's presence in New York acted as a catalytic agent in
bringing Strasberg and myself together with the thought of forming a theatre of our own. Strasberg, even two years before, had
casually spoken of "our theatre," but it was a kind of hypotheti-
cal theatre he referred to, whereas now, though the idea of actually doing anything concrete about it might still seem fantastic,

the thought of "our own theatre" had somehow become more definite.

Copeau's influence exercised itself not only at the rehearsals, but through his talks at the Lab. Copeau said nothing we hadn't previously heard, but his sharp presence gave his words greater reality. Copeau told the story of one of the first talks he gave during his first visit to America in 1917, when he had brought over his company for propaganda purposes on behalf of the French government. A dramatic critic at the conclusion of the evening was heard to remark: "I thought I was coming to hear a talk on the theatre; instead I find myself at the Salvation Army." There was a moral cast to Copeau's approach to the theatre that might have been discomfiting to a dilettante, but that was good for us.

Copeau's attitude was creative also, but we believed we were on the road to learning a sounder technique for the actor. The technique we were learning was, of course, that of the Moscow Art Theatre, the so-called Stanislavsky "system." But, besides a fascination with the technique of acting, a more fundamental feeling was growing in me, a feeling related to but not born of the theatre. It was a sense of the theatre in relation to society.

CHAPTER TWO

First Steps

THE THEATRE and society. There was no question that we were concentrated on the theatre, pondering over all the outstanding productions, searching foreign and domestic periodicals for special articles and new illustrations, going to see all the European productions that the favorable foreign exchange made it possible to import. Gilbert Miller brought over Max Reinhardt's company to the Century Theatre, and we saw the master's production of *A Midsummer Night's Dream, Danton's Death, Everyman,* and

others. We not only studied these productions, we debated them
with passion. We sought out exotic examples of theatre craft. We
visited the Chinese Theatre in the Bowery, and led our friends
down to Grand Street to see the Sicilian, Giovanni Grasso, who
exemplified a violent emotional acting that positively stunned us.
We tried to determine whether Raquel Meller, at whose debut
extravagant New York had paid ten dollars a seat, was truly an
actress or merely a "personality."

All this was done with eagerness and deliberation. The facts
about our society, however, came to me accidentally, as it were.
I found that I had made certain observations, experienced certain
reactions, only when I came to talk about them. There were no
ready-made opinions in my head, no *a priori* conceptions of what
I was to find.

It did not matter, at first, that Babbitt himself was somehow
unhappy within his extreme contentment; it hardly spoiled our
sense of well-being that tragic notes sounded whenever a poem,
a story, or even a play were removed from the restricted Man-
hattan area. It hardly occurred to us when a picture of middle-
class life revealed hysteria, stupidity, or mechanical gagaism that
these were not altogether encouraging signs. When Lawson wrote
his *Processional,* he called it a "jazz symphony," and though it
dealt with the Ku Klux Klan and bloody class war, we thought
of the play only from the viewpoint of its artistic style, which we
approved for its novelty or disliked for its pretension. We never
dreamed of saying: "This is our world, and it bodes no good."

When we saw the film *Potemkin,* it thrilled us because it was a
movie with guts, an advance in cinema technique. We hardly
asked ourselves what conditions produced it or why it was possible for a backward people to make a picture we admired more
than our own. Plays about the nullity of the average man, like
Elmer Rice's *Adding Machine,* were high-brow amusement. The
most typical — and perhaps best — realistic comedy of the period,
George Kelly's *Show-Off,* portrayed the hero as an incurably
sanguine numbskull, a geyser of platitude and inanity mouthing
the slogans of every chamber of commerce with grotesque com-
placency. The whole country loved it. When the reformed Nie-

tzschean, Ben Hecht, in *The Front Page,* came through with a
real box-office success, it was to convert heartbreak, suicide, civic
skullduggery, social callousness, into side-splitting farce.

It was a time of boisterous individualism. Everything and
everyone whizzed by on an isolated, trackless course. It was a
world of fireflies charting itself as a constellation of planets. No
matter who you were or what you did, you were thought of in
terms that properly belonged to the realm of gangsterdom.

I dwell on the Luna Park rather than on the more sober aspects
of the period, because the former were actually dominant. Everything seemed to be affected by them. There were the League of
Composers concerts. No matter what was played, how much in
earnest the partisans of the new music were, or how outraged its
detractors, the atmosphere of the concerts had something giddy
about them. They were a sort of æsthete's prom.

There was the *Dial,* a very cultivated periodical, which ex-
amined even the most trivial phenomena from the vantage-point
of the centuries. Its managing editor's most original book was
composed of a series of articles in which Irving Berlin was made
to seem more esoteric than a treatise on Palestrina, and Mickey
Mouse became a subject for advanced psychological research.
There was *Vanity Fair,* in which the intelligentsia played the
clown in motley; ideas were wrapped in colorful packages and
put on sale like Christmas gifts. The world seemed to have a jag on.

The counter-current could hardly be distinguished from the
rest. The New Playwrights — dubbed the "revolting playwrights"
by Alexander Woollcott — wanted something, but it wasn't very
clear what. They were financed by Otto Kahn, arch-Mæcenas of
the day. First they produced two plays on West Fifty-second
Street. When these plays flopped, they moved to the Cherry Lane
Playhouse in Greenwich Village. Their productions were undisciplined, amateurish, lyrical, frivolous. When John Howard Lawson, the most gifted of these playwrights, was shown an article I
had written that attempted to establish a rational basis of work
in the light of an analysis of the art of the theatre, his sole comment was: "What do you mean, 'art of the theatre'?"

Another reaction to the times came from those rather intense spirits who felt the need for warmer human contact. They were mostly at a loss to formulate these needs; so the sexual act, as a kind of unblessed sacrament, became the symbol for them of personal salvation. This sentiment presumably found literary expression in the works of D. H. Lawrence. But Lawrence was too subjective and ambiguous to articulate any recognizable doctrine. . . . There were the divers talents that gathered around the great photographer and pioneer of modern art in America, Alfred Stieglitz. Many people clung to him as if in his perpetual parables lay a saving creed. But if there was any method in him, it might only be deduced from his impulses and record of action, not from the symbol of his personality, which tended to foster a type of worship rather than any specific steps apart from the separate contributions of a few individual artists.

Between 1921 and 1927 society's headlong rush looked as if it would never end. Between '27 and '29, a slowing down became perceptible, notes of doubt, fear, loneliness, stole into the picture. Spengler's *The Decline of the West* was published, and many Americans were pleased to become morose over this prophecy of historical futility. Joseph Wood Krutch, dramatic critic for the *Nation,* after writing a book celebrating the sexual impotence of Edgar Allan Poe, issued a black report on our general impotence, which he called *The Modern Temper.* The very successful Robert Sherwood was convinced and much perturbed by it. Not to be equally depressed was for many almost a sign of Philistinism or guilelessness.

On the other hand, those who could be accused of neither, began to assess the credit and debit of our spiritual ledger. Puzzled, but staunch, they set forth to investigate the meaning of our past, studied our history with the purpose of shaping our future. Van Wyck Brooks was perhaps their godfather. Lewis Mumford was typical of these men. His books on *The Golden Day* and *Herman Melville* revealed this motive, though they struck me as over-poised, insufficiently disturbed. Waldo Frank wrote a *Rediscovery of America,* in which he likened the contemporary American world to a jungle, and suggested that "with tragic need, America needs groups."

A sort of summation of the intellectual trends of the time in both their positive and their negative phases was unconsciously presented by the Theatre Guild. It put on plays the way lists of guests were drawn up for parties. In one season the avid subscriber might chuckle over the mid-European urbanity of a Molnár, or become annoyed with the prophetic rhapsody of Lawson's *Processional,* grow drowsy over the dewy comedy of A. A. Milne, or enjoy safety through the sprightly classicism of Bernard Shaw.

On the serious side the typical voice of the period in the theatre was that of Eugene O'Neill. It is significant that his plays, first produced in Greenwich Village, came to be the prize of every dissident group there, then of the more forward-looking Broadway managers, finally of the Theatre Guild itself. The twenties took heart in O'Neill's gloom. It proved, despite all the clamor and shouting, that we were keeping our wits about us. In any case, O'Neill struggled valiantly with his soul, with the riddle of the universe, with the chaos of the helter-skelter torrent. His work twisted and turned, writhed in a kind of nocturnal anguish, woke and smiled a bit, proclaimed fresh faith, fell asleep again, and dreamed fitfully anew. Since the early thirties there has been silence. How the issue has been resolved still remains a mystery.

Of course, what I have been describing is only the surface of society, or at least its polished mirror. If I don't linger on political aspects of the time — as far as I could see, to any decent person it mattered little who resided at the White House or what anyone was doing in Congress — it is almost a comment in itself. I suppose the labor organizations, after the depredations of the Palmer raids and the late Wilson reaction, were regrouping themselves in out-of-the-way corners, but from where I stood they were invisible. No one in my circle of acquaintances ever mentioned them.

While I was following the usual path of minor workers in the theatre — going from this engagement to that, in and out of New York — I answered the call of a real-estate man, Sidney Ross by name, who was thinking of going into theatrical production and was seeking an aide of some kind. Mr. Ross had made a lot of money during the war and more in the postwar boom. He wasn't

sure what he wanted me to do for him, but he was "interested."
Theatre people and artists attracted him. At the top of the apartment house he owned on Riverside Drive and Eighty-fifth Street,
there was a long sort of roof-garden hall where he threw parties for
celebrities he vaguely knew.

Mr. Ross one day asked me point-blank what I would like to
do. "I have a plan," I answered. "I will return here tomorrow with
a friend and we will present our plan." That night I called Lee
Strasberg, met with him at Child's restaurant on Fifth Avenue and
Forty-ninth Street. I told him that Sidney Ross had nothing yet
to offer, but we could use his roof as our rehearsal hall, we could
begin doing a play with a group of actors of our choice, and we
might show sufficient promise to make Ross or some others finance
us as a new theatre group.

The next day Ross listened to us. We would find a play, rehearse it, and show it to him. He would then be in a position to
judge whether he wanted to do anything further.

I had heard that Waldo Frank had written a new play. I introduced myself to him and explained my project. We were not
promising a production; we were merely seeking our way. Would
he lend us his script for rehearsal purposes? He gave me his script
to read and to work on if I wished.

It was called *New Year's Eve*, a morality play about contemporary America, the purport of which was that man had to face living
realities rather than be guided by the nomenclature of institutions and dogmas. It wasn't a good play, but it bore the distinction
of a literary man who was in great earnest.

Besides Carnovsky and Meisner, I called on several young actors
whom I had not met in the course of my Guild experience, and a
young actress who had been a member of the American Laboratory Theatre company. In addition still another recruit was suggested by John Hartell, painter and art instructor at Cornell —
a recent graduate who had joined the new Playwrights' Company. I went to see Franchot Tone in Lawson's latest play *International*. He struck me as being rather stiff in his role, but I was
sure that he had had practically no direction in a play that was

most confused. I invited him to come up to our first meeting at least. He came and brought with him a dazzlingly attractive girl.

The time was early in 1928. To this young group — Carnovsky at twenty-nine was the oldest person present — we outlined our ideas and made our proposal. The latter was simple: we wanted to work on a play for which we had no formal production plans, but the work would be instructive to the actors, and a new theatre might be born of our modest efforts.

The ideas propounded were less modest. Young actors, Strasberg and I declared, had no opportunity at the Theatre Guild, or elsewhere, to be trained while they were rehearsing. It was taken for granted by the Guild, as well as by commercial managers, that every actor was ready to perform as required, but the actor's individual problem as a growing craftsman was neglected. There were two reasons for this neglect: theatre organizations, like other business firms, were concerned solely with marketing their product; furthermore, the problem itself was neither realized nor understood by most managers or directors. In our group we would pay careful attention to the actor's development. Rehearsals themselves would constitute a schooling.

Moreover — and this in a way was to be our real innovation — since our technique was, at least officially, taught not only at the Laboratory Theatre but occasionally at the Neighborhood Playhouse, we expected to bring the actor much closer to the content of the play, to link the actor as an individual with the creative purpose of the playwright. In most theatres the actor is hired to do a part: he was expected to make it live on the stage, but as an individual he stood outside the play or the playwright's vision. His art and the playwright's were presumed to be connected only technically. In our belief, unless the actor in some way shared the playwright's impulse, the result on the stage always remained somewhat mechanical.

How did the actors respond to this? Tone's comment was characteristic: "If you can do what you say, it'll be fine!" We asked for no more.

For seventeen weeks, while the actors were engaged in regular

jobs, we rehearsed for four or five hours a day. We showed Waldo
Frank his play at a run-through without scenery, make-up, or
costumes. He felt it was "alive." He advised Sidney Ross to put
us on our feet. Ross asked us what we wanted now. We suggested
that he set our little company up in a country place for the summer, where we would rehearse another play. If he liked it, we
would then proceed to New York — and put it on at some small
house such as the President Theatre (on Forty-eighth Street near
Eighth Avenue), which had a capacity of three hundred seats.
Ross and I spent several Sundays in the country looking for suitable sites for our summer campaign.

But it was not yet to be. At the last minute he changed his
mind about the practicality of the plan. After all, except for
Carnovsky, we were unknown. He was still interested, however, if
we had an alternate, less expensive plan.

We then chose to do a new play by the poet Padraic Colum
with the same understanding that we had had with Waldo Frank.
The play, called *Balloon,* was a delicate fantasy on the big world
of success, and the small world of the poet's heart. It was a slight
comedy, but it had unusual freshness and could have been made
enchanting on the stage.

After six weeks we gave a run-through for an invited audience
of about a hundred people. Mary Colum (the author's wife, herself a critic and poet) declared it was better than a production
at the Abbey! But, concretely speaking, nothing happened. Our
experiment was finished.

Would anything really come of our first flight? I saw no practical way of proceeding; I felt that if we should undertake another
step it would have to be of a more "official" character. Strasberg
and I, as far as the theatre world was concerned, were minor
actors who talked a lot to whoever would lend an ear. We had no
standing. So we went on with the business of job-hunting. We
met our actors socially; even held little informal meetings at our
apartments. Waldo Frank encouraged us and dropped oracular
hints about our future, which his intuition suggested would be
important.

One night, while I was seeing *Strange Interlude* for the second time, I met Miss Helburn, who asked me to come to her office the next day. The Guild was thinking of taking on a new play-reader. Would I read and report on some plays for the Guild? I agreed. It was January 1, 1929.

I got to know the Guild and its board pretty well. The six directors were people of dissimilar temperaments and even of somewhat different tastes. It would be a little unfair to each of them to discuss them as if they were all the same. But as a body they seemed to me to be people of no basic artistic personality. In other words, they represented a general high level of taste in the coming-of-age period of the American theatre, but with no single guiding tendency of their own. They had a collegiate stamp on them, compared to the hearty roughnecks of the epoch of Al Woods, William Brady, and David Belasco. They had traveled abroad and had been slightly overwhelmed by what they had seen there. They understood that the cynicism and melancholy of the Continent was riper and richer than the still green American drama. They were admirers rather than makers. They were imitators rather than initiators, buyers and distributors rather than first settlers or pioneers. They were very much in the vein of their day — most representatively from 1919 to 1929. They were in the very center of that current; and they were carried along in it, not only by the appropriate artistic proclivities, but by their merchant sense. They were symbolic of a Greenwich Village grown prosperous. They were destined to become an institution.

Their platform, from the first, was to do distinguished plays according to the best professional standards. Their function was to bring plays previously regarded as uncommercial to a big middle-class audience. In this function they succeeded admirably. And by organizing their audience through the subscription method they made a first-rate contribution to American theatre practice. People who later complained that the Guild had belied its early ideals spoke lightly. It is a fact that no American theatre organization ever brought to the boards so many worth-while scripts.

But it seemed to me, after I had worked with them awhile, that they had no blood relationship with the plays they dealt in. They set the plays out in the show window for as many customers as possible to buy. They didn't want to say anything through plays, and plays said nothing to them, except that they were amusing in a graceful way, or, if they were tragic plays, that they were "art." And art was a good thing. The board members were in favor of culture. As a result they chose plays of the most conflicting tendencies, and produced them all with the same generalized Broadway technique, though in better taste than the average. All the productions were rather pretty (with a kind of disguised middle-class stuffiness) and they nearly always lacked passion or pointedness. They did Molnár and Sil-Vara excellently, because these were much closer to their own yearnings, but on their stage Pirandello or Werfel became colorless or complacent. Plays like Sidney Howard's *The Silver Cord* were satisfactorily treated, but most of O'Neill and Shaw became chiefly decorative and fake-impressive. The productions had no special tang or recognizable style such as might issue from the strongly marked quality of an artist to whom the plays had personal significance — a situation one discovered occasionally in even bad European productions. The Guild's tone was almost always undifferentiatedly correct or standard, according to the nearly latest models, because back of it was no individual drive, only a dilettante acceptance of something someone else — eminently worthy — had first created.

I was severe with the Guild because I was young and because it no longer satisfied the demands of the generation that was to burst forth in the thirties. This generation took for granted that O'Neill had greater stature than Clyde Fitch, and that it was better to act quietly like Dudley Digges than to vocalize like some of the old-timers. It was looking for something more, for something else.

During my first year as Guild play-reader Miss Helburn called me to her office to tell me that the board wished to produce certain exceptional plays at special Sunday performances for subscribers. The production would be put under the supervision of the three department heads of the organization: Herbert Biber-

man, stage-manager, Cheryl Crawford, casting director, and myself. As play-reader I suggested a Soviet play, *Red Rust*.

Red Rust had an engaging quality of youthfulness. The production given it, under Herbert Biberman's direction, was lusty
and fresh. In casting it I had brought in as many of my friends
from the Riverside Drive epoch as possible: Franchot Tone, Lee
Strasberg (as actor), and a number of the Lab Theatre contingent. There was no organic connection between the production
of *Red Rust* and the later Group Theatre. The choice of a Soviet
play represented no ideologic bias on anyone's part. The play
had novelty — it was the first play from the Soviet Union to reach
these shores — and it had a strong note of self-criticism in it,
though the audience, like myself, tended to enjoy the play for
its exuberance, which was partly in the script and more markedly in the cast.

Red Rust was rather favorably received, and was given as a
regular production under the auspices of the Theatre Guild
Studio, as Biberman, Crawford, and I had decided to call our
subsidiary setup. Soviet sympathizers showed themselves for the
first time on Broadway. Their existence in such numbers was a
revelation to me. I remember being startled at the applause when
the *Internationale* was sung before the curtain on opening night.
The liberal intelligentsia, which had a goodly representation at
that time on the large list of Guild subscribers, welcomed the
play not for its message (it hardly had any) but for its tonic
swing, which came as a relief in the Guild's now academic routine.

After *Red Rust*, the Theatre Guild gave up its Studio project.

The value of the *Red Rust* episode for me was that it provided
me my first managerial training, that it helped keep me in contact with the actors I hoped to cultivate, and that through it I
got to know Cheryl Crawford well. Cheryl Crawford was a practical person, I thought, a person shrewder, more tactful in many
ways, than either Strasberg or I. She had had executive experience
at the Guild, and seemed to know how to deal with such people
as the Guild board. With all this, she was capable of being roused
to fine action when she was confronted with a sound idea or a
noble motive. She had determination, moral perception, a desire

to learn and grow. She was immediately caught by my analysis of the theatre situation, struck by my passion, intrigued by my praise of Strasberg's ability as a stage director.

Soon little informal meetings began to take place. Four or five of my friends would get together, and I would discourse on the need for fresh discussion of the theatre, for real communication between theatre people, which was only symbolic to me of the need for communication between Americans generally. "People don't seem to talk to one another enough," I said. "We are separate. Our contacts are hasty, utilitarian or escapist. We must get to know ourselves by getting to know one another."

These words stirred something in Cheryl and in the others. It is possible that they had never heard the like before. They were lonely in a sense, and they hadn't quite known it. If they knew it, they never thought of overcoming their loneliness through their work. But here I was, intimating that these personal matters were not extraneous to the theatre or its technique, but were at the very heart of my interest in them. What did I mean? They weren't sure, but it seemed very important for them to find out.

At this juncture I had, to my surprise and almost against my will, fallen in love. The lady in question was Stella Adler, poetically theatrical, reminiscent of some past beauty in a culture I had perhaps never seen, but that was part of an atavistic dream. With all the imperious flamboyance of an older theatrical tradition — European in its roots — she was somehow fragile, vulnerable, gay with mother wit and stage fragrance, eager to add knowledge to instinct, spiritually vibrant, as if forever awaiting the redemption of a faith as realistically substantial as it was emotionally exalting. Here was the very flesh of my secret yearning. Here was the personification of something I wanted to integrate with my whole sense of life, someone who was indeed a living symbol of so much I treasured in life.

I went to see Stella Adler backstage where she was playing. I talked vehemently — almost mystically — about the theatre. I was poor (it was just before my regular Guild job), headlong, headstrong, and rather chaste. I was probably peculiar, but very persistent. We saw each other a good deal; I "rushed" her. I belonged to another world; that is, I was of the theatre, but more bookish. I had very little worldliness, masculine *savoir-faire*, form, or elegance — all qualities that she rightly prized. We got on fitfully. I supplied the storm and she the surprise. She ran away and I ran after. I ran away and she called me back. She was unkind and I was foolish. She warned me of difficulty and I wouldn't heed. I promised some magnificent release for her that I hardly understood myself; and she wondered. I was going to have a theatre some day; and she believed. We ran round and round till it was difficult to know who was chasing or following whom. It all meant something!

One night when Aaron Copland came home from a summer abroad, I told him all that had happened. I felt pent up, overwrought by my love, intent on bringing my first years in the theatre to an issue, anxious to seize the essence of all I had experienced since my homecoming five years before. Everybody is so clever in New York, I said. Ability, even talent, flashes at every turn and corner of the city. This was a fantastic world we were living in, electric with energy, feverish with impulse, gigantic with invention. It was a world full of sharp curiosity, quick assimilation, enormous activity, mountain-high with reward. But it was a meaningless world, just the same, a downright silly world. It was terribly attractive: had the fairest flesh, the most resplendent contours, the most bedizened dress imaginable. But it had no insides; it was empty. Or if it wasn't empty, its contents were in such a perpetual boil that nothing emerged from it except an eruption of brilliant particles that turned cold and dead when they hit the earth. Nothing tied the fast-moving forces together, no governing principle, no aim, no deep and final simplicity. The gyration and tremor made it all an overwhelming burden that no human spirit could survive. Everything had been rendered both too easy and too difficult. One was rushed giddily through brightly bursting substance that had no real texture; it ended by making one tired as if one had been struggling with a colossus. The American man was alone, and he made his woman, who clung to his neck as he twisted and whirled, equally lonesome and more hysterical. There was no quiet here. Man couldn't find himself. He was perpetually on the go to a place he didn't know for a pleasure he couldn't enjoy, for a purpose he didn't seek. Man no longer understood his own nature, his own dreams, even his own appetites. And despite the fact that he was constantly agitated, he was actually passive. He let everything be done to him. His consent was his habit, not his choice. He was dizzy with his own jitteriness. He could not rest, stop, or feel his own motion, for it had become identical with life. If the motion were to cease, it would be as if all were to cease. He was prepared for nothing else. . . . I'm sick of this dervish dance they've got us doing on steel springs and a General Electric motor. When it stops — as it must — there will be dissolution and devastation; everything will become as frightfully blank as today everything is fiercely congested. Perhaps to rush out of line is to invite disaster. If so, let it come. If enough of us try to form another line according to our true nature, ours may become the right line, one which others may follow and walk on more peacefully and gracefully. We must help one another find our common ground; we must build our house on it, arrange it as a dwelling place for the whole family of decent humanity. For life, though it be individual to the end, cannot be lived except in terms of people together, sure and strong in their togetherness.

On and on I raved, clear and turbulent, mixing metaphors, categories, vocabularies, confident that out of this chaos I might achieve an order of meaning and ultimately of action. Copland listened silently. Finally I couldn't help noticing that his eyes had filled with tears and that he was suppressing a sob. "What's the matter?" I cried, bewildered. He positively couldn't say. He thought about it, and the next day he remarked that he had wept because he realized I was in for a load of trouble.

CHAPTER THREE

Getting Together

IT was Cheryl Crawford who now urged me to prepare for the
future by seeking actors who might be selected for our permanent
company. I would talk to them, excite their enthusiasm, and
generate the momentum that would transform what had been a
somewhat vague program into a going concern. When our company had been chosen, when our aims had become concretized
through association and discussion, she might be able to enlist the
Guild and others as sponsors for the new theatre.

The first people we called on were, of course, those with
whom we had already worked: Tone, Carnovsky, Meisner, and the
others. Down at the Civic Repertory Theatre there was a promising character actor, J. Edward Bromberg, who might be interested. Mary Morris from the Macgowan-Jones-O'Neill days should
be summoned. Stella Adler would now be willing to listen to me,
and there were those people from the Lab — Ruth Nelson, Eunice
Stoddard — we had cast in *Red Rust*, as well as a number of
youngsters — Phoebe Brand, Dorothy Patten — in the current
Guild productions. From Broadway, Margaret Barker, who was
playing an agreeable role in *The Barretts of Wimpole Street*,
should be considered. These and more we would call together.
We would explain — that is, I would, for I did most of the talking
at that time — that we proposed a new approach to the theatre,
that we wished to get acquainted with all those actors who might
come to share our approach, that we wanted to lay the foundations of a new theatre. As for practical matters, the manner of our
functioning, we would take them up only after we had established
a common ground of understanding through our meetings together. We had no plays, no money; the meetings were to be entirely "unofficial."

The first meeting was held in my room at the Hotel Meurice on West Fifty-eighth Street in November 1930. Since my room was too small, later meetings were held at Miss Crawford's apartment on West Forty-seventh Street, and when her apartment became too crowded, owing to the increasing number of people who showed up, we repaired to a large room at Steinway Hall which some friend of a friend provided without cost. These meetings, held every Friday night at half past eleven, continued from November till May 1931 with hardly an interruption from week to week.

A curious thing happened from the first. Instead of telling the prospective actors of our theatre what advantages would accrue to them through an association with us: that we believed in a permanent company which would guarantee them continuity of work and, consequently, security of livelihood, that we believed in developing the actor — not merely in hiring him — thus ensuring greater versatility — instead of all this, which would have been eminently to the point, I chose an almost metaphysical line which led away from matters of the theatre. Cheryl Crawford, for this reason, told me she thought my first talk had been "lousy." Gerald Sykes, a literary friend, who was present at the first talk, came from the meeting with the conviction that "such passion can't arise from concern with the theatre alone."

An article in dialogue form I had written in 1929 had begun this way:

THE LAYMAN: If you will omit the evangelical tone, you may
    talk to me about the theatre.
THE THEATRE MAN: Fanaticism is not only inevitable with us;
    it is almost indispensable.

I had observed elements of fanaticism in Copeau, in Craig, in Stanislavsky — indeed, in almost every first-rate man of the theatre. But in me this fanaticism — which antagonized some of my listeners though it attracted others — was intimately bound up with the nature of my message, which extended beyond the limits of the theatre or a desire to make good in it. I was well aware of the fact that there had been other permanent companies in the recent theatre (the Neighborhood Playhouse and the Civic Repertory had them). As for training actors, at least two other organizations proposed to do this. In fact, every one of the reforms our theatre might bring had been announced, at least, by a previous organization.

My approach emphasized the theatre's reason for being. New technical methods, no matter how intriguing in themselves, had a very minor value unless they were related to a content that was humanly valuable. To what human beings, one might ask, were theatre ideas to be valuable. First, to the theatre artists themselves — to actors, since they were the theatre's crucial factor; actors were citizens of a community before they took on their dubious connection with "art." Second, theatre ideas were to be important to an audience, of which the actors were a focus, for it is the audience (seen as a "community") that has given birth to its artists. The criterion of judgment for what is good or bad in the theatre — be it in plays, acting, or staging — does not derive from some abstract standard of artistic or literary excellence, but from a judgment of what is fitting — that is, humanly desirable — for a particular audience.

The unity of theatrical production, about which Craig had spoken at such length, was a unity that does not spring, as Craig presumed, out of an abstract sense of taste or craftsmanship, but out of a unity that is antecedent to the formation of the theatre group as such. It is a unity of background, of feeling, of thought, of need, among a group of people that has formed itself consciously or unconsciously from the undifferentiated masses. In the Broadway theatre, productions are cooked up haphazardly for money-making purposes in the hope that they will appeal to a large enough number of customers to make them pay. This produced positive results when the elements thrown together were based on the rather primitive appetites of a large number of people. Action melodrama, a leg show, a conventional musical, or a knockabout farce was generally more satisfactory from the standpoint of completeness or unity of style than were the more ambitious efforts of the highbrow theatre. Jed Harris's production of *Broadway* or the Ziegfeld *Follies* were capital because all the ele-

ments that composed them matched each other and were well related to the audience that paid speculator's prices to see them.
The same could not be said for many of the "fine things" I had
seen done at the Guild and other of our "better organizations."

A technique of the theatre had to be founded on life values.
The whole bent of our theatre, I reiterated time and again, would
be to combine a study of theatre craft with a creative content
which that craft was to express. To put it another way, our interest in the life of our times must lead us to the discovery of those
methods that would most truly convey this life through the
theatre.

If man was to be the measure of all things in our theatre, if
life was the starting-point, and an effect on life the aim of our
effort, then one had to have a point of view in relation to it, one
had to define an approach that might be common to all the members of the group.

It was this that added a dimension to the talks and to the whole
atmosphere around the Group, that was to become its distinguish-
ing mark, its strength, its impediment, and its wound. Certain it
is that there was added to all the technical discussion of the actor,
the director, the scene-designer, the audience, and the problems
of casting and administration a new note, an attitude that lifted
these subjects from the realm of narrow craft to that of a general
concern with our lives and the life of our times.

For this reason photographers like Paul Strand and Ralph
Steiner, a musician like Aaron Copland, an architect like William
Lescaze, and many others not directly connected with the theatre
found these meetings, and the subsequent development of the
group that emerged from them, both stimulating and relevant to
their own fields of interest.

Despite their "fanaticism," these talks were no general assaults
on the ineffable, no attempts to penetrate the mystery of life. They
dealt precisely and particularly with American life, with conditions in the theatre that mirrored their equivalent outside; they
dealt with American character as we saw it depicted in plays or
as we knew it from our own experience. The point of view evolved

was indirectly rather than dogmatically stated, an attitude and sentiment rather than a platform.

Mordecai Gorelik, who was to design so many of our productions, often said with more than a trace of irony that the Group's favorite theme was "What shall it profit a man if he gain the whole world and lose his own soul?" It is true this theme was the oblique keynote of much of what I said in criticism not only of certain American ideals and customs but of everything that pertained to the practice of our profession. Though we had a combative air, we were lovers at heart.

Since we were theatre people, the proper action for us was to establish a theatre in which our philosophy of life might be translated into a philosophy of the theatre. Here the individual actor would be strengthened so that he might better serve the uses of the play in which our common belief was to be expressed. There were to be no stars in our theatre, not for the negative purpose of avoiding distinction, but because all distinction — and we would strive to attain the highest — was to be embodied in the production as a whole. The writer himself was to be no star either, for his play, the focus of our attention, was simply the instrument for capturing an idea that was always greater than that instrument itself. The playwright too could be worked with, the power of his play could be enhanced by the joint creativity of the theatrical group as a whole, which saw in the play a vehicle to convey a motif fundamental to the theatre's main interest. The director was the leader of the theatrical group, unifying its various efforts, enunciating its basic aims, tied to it not as a master to his slave, but as a head to a body. In a sense, the group produced its own director, just as the director in turn helped form and guide the group.

It did not matter at first that each person who attended these meetings put his own special interpretation on them, lent them the color of his own dreams. There were some who were nonplussed by the generalities, others who were shocked by the arrogant boldness of my expression, still others thought me a theorist, which signifies in theatre parlance a practical do-nothing. One

lady flatly stated: "The man is crazy," for she had never seen anyone so carried away by the expression of ideas. The playwright
Lynn Riggs was worried by my emphasis on the contribution of
actor and director: he was afraid this boiled down to a contempt
for the writer's work. Some of the people came once or twice
never to return again. I rarely besought them to alter their course.
One actor, a young man who had played secondary roles in two
Guild productions, confessed to me, after perhaps ten meetings,
that he was just beginning to understand what I was talking about.
His name was Clifford Odets.

The Guild board got wind of these meetings. The theatrical
trade papers, *Billboard* and *Variety,* announced — tabloid-fashion
— that "revolt" was brewing in the Guild's ranks. Miss Helburn
questioned me. I explained the nature of these meetings and told
her that when we had definitely chosen our people, we planned
to address the Guild board, as they might want to help in what
we were doing. We would present our ideas to the Guild in a
paper; and we would make suggestions as to what they might
do for us.

Cheryl Crawford drew up a report, listing the actors and playwrights interested in us, giving also some of our thoughts regarding the financially modest basis on which we could be subsidized
as a Guild "Studio." In addition to this, I submitted a general
statement. The Guild never commented on it; in fact, I never
knew whether it was actually read. It was not unsympathetic,
however. When Cheryl Crawford asked the board to release a
play they held an option on — Paul Green's *The House of Connelly* — they were prompt to do so. More than that, they allowed
us to engage Franchot Tone and Morris Carnovsky, who were
then under contract to them, and they added the gift of a thousand
dollars toward our expenses in rehearsing the play that summer.

For that is what we decided to do: to go away to some country
place with twenty-eight actors and rehearse two plays till they
were ready for production in New York. We would pay no salaries, but we would provide meals, living quarters, laundry expense. The three directors — that is what Cheryl Crawford, Lee

Strasberg, and I now constituted ourselves — had chosen a company from among the people we had come in contact with during our winter meetings. A good many — indeed, a majority — remained with us for years, some to the very last days of our functioning.

We had chosen our actors before we knew what play we would do. They were *our* actors, and they would have to suit our plays. That is what we directors were there for. Nor did we have any money to finance our ambitious plan. We only had the will to carry it out. When the Guild agreed to let us have *The House of Connelly* and a thousand dollars, they were our only concrete assets.

Maxwell Anderson had attended some of our meetings because his friends Morris Carnovsky and Phoebe Brand, who were playing in his *Elizabeth the Queen*, had invited him. He was accompanied by his wife-to-be, whose stage name was Mab Anthony. Her eagerness to join the new group and his own thoughtfulness made him follow our meetings with interest.

He submitted a play to me for criticism. It was a play in verse about the early days of the Russian Revolution — a play he never sought to have produced. My reaction was frankly negative. After telling him so, I asked him to help finance our first summer. He agreed at once. He gave us fifteen hundred dollars, and later in the summer several hundred more. My friend Dorothy Norman, whom I had met through Alfred Stieglitz, contributed another five hundred. Mary Senior, introduced to me by Aaron Copland, likewise added to our funds.

Then Cheryl Crawford, who was resourceful in such things, thought of running a symposium at the Guild Theatre on the subject "What Chance Has the Theatre?" It took place on April 25, 1931. The *New York Times* announced that "the proceeds of the Symposium will go to a new theatre group which will work on plays this summer to be presented in the fall" — the first mention in the press of our future group.

Finally, Edna Ferber, having heard of us, told Cheryl Crawford she would contribute five hundred dollars if her niece, Janet Fox, could join in our summer work. Miss Fox was asked to come up to meet us shortly before our departure. Miss Fox was rather abashed by all these intense young people. She lost her desire to go away with us. Miss Ferber said we might have the five hundred dollars just the same.

Cheryl Crawford and a girl Friday she had chosen to help her had gone out and found a site for our summer work. It was in Brookfield Center, Connecticut, about five miles from Danbury. It consisted of a number of small homes, some of them two-room bungalows, others a little larger, a main dining-room, a good-sized barn that had been cleaned and refloored so that we might use it as a rehearsal hall.

The actors were sent brief invitations to leave with us within a few weeks. This was the only contract they had; they never asked for another.

PART II

BEGINNERS

CHAPTER FOUR

Honeymoon

SOME of us owned cars; others were borrowed. On the morning of June 8, 1931, twenty-eight actors, some wives, two children, the three directors, and a few friends left from the front of the Guild Theatre on Fifty-second Street for Brookfield Center, Connecticut.

When we arrived and quarters had been assigned, I was amused to find that the first visible activity of the newly gathered company turned out to be an indoor baseball game on the main lawn. It had been started by Franchot Tone, who, he explained to me later, thought it a good way to overcome the natural self-consciousness of the occasion. The average age in our company at this time was twenty-seven. I noticed that Stella Adler looked out from her window somewhat sadly, almost frightened. These people were strangers: they did not behave like actors. To her, the place was like a camp for overgrown high-school kids.

There was little time, however, for introspection. After dinner, at about eight thirty, we all met in the rehearsal hall. This was to be a kind of opening exercise in which the three directors were to give the assemblage an emotional send-off. No record was made of our speeches, but that the meeting had a certain atmosphere of high dedication I am sure. In fact, for a few moments Lee Strasberg was unable to speak at all. He began twice and faltered. A man of intense feeling and an even more intense effort to control his feelings, he was deeply conscious, he said, of the responsibility of our task — his task, since it was he who had been chosen to direct our first play.

The meeting was short, although a few actors tried to add some words of their own to the occasion. One of them, William Challee, had difficulty in articulating his ideas or even his words, but I believe he stammered something about the feeling of being among "brothers." It was about ten when the actors left the hall. No one thought of sleep. The conversation was rather hushed, and in no time a number of phonographs were hauled into the open to play music of an elevated character. These little manifestations of our new life were as mysterious to me as they would have been to any visitor who might have happened on the scene. I had started something, but once begun, this life would gather a momentum of its own from which I was to learn many things.

Next morning, we collected in the main living-room to hear Cheryl Crawford read Paul Green's *The House of Connelly*. In presenting to our actors this play about the decadence of the old South and the emergence of a new class from among the poor tenant farmers, my emphasis was on the basic struggle between any new and old order. The actors immediately made the obvious parallel between this play and Chekhov's *The Cherry Orchard*, just as many other very different plays were later to be discussed by the reviewers in terms of the same Chekhov — parallels and analogies that are academic, empty, and useless. But at this time — and perhaps the only time in our history — concern over the play gave way to the actors' far greater absorption in it as a vehicle for the strengthening of their craft.

Lee Strasberg was the natural choice for the director of our first production. Cheryl Crawford had been a little shocked at first by my insistence on this, as her background was obviously much closer to the play than Strasberg's, but I was concerned with the formulation of a technique of acting and production, a specific training that might be shared by the entire company. For this, Strasberg, with his experience (off Broadway) and his peculiar gifts as a teacher, was best adapted. It was from no pedagogic dogmatism, however, that I insisted on the establishment of a single unified method for the company. It was a question of artistic necessity. You couldn't actually say what we wished to say in the theatre by simply having a troupe of actors give "good performances." Talent, contrary to the accepted doctrine of Broadway, is not enough. Talent is accident; craft, in the use of talent, is a matter of some consciousness, of training. Talent might be sufficient for the individual actor; it didn't lead to the solution of the problem of a whole production, which is the relating of a number of talents to a single meaning. "For the elements of a theatrical production to be shaped into a true artistic organism," I had written, "it is not sufficient for them merely to be 'good.' They must be homogeneous, they must belong together, they must form an organic body." That day in June 1931 Strasberg began to make of the twenty-eight actors an "artistic organism" with its own special character and aims.

While Strasberg rehearsed the Paul Green play, I began privately instructing in the methods employed at rehearsal those to whom Strasberg couldn't devote sufficient time or those less familiar with them than others. Beyond this I gave an almost daily talk on both the specific work we were doing and the problems we were facing or going to face in our lives as actors and people working on Broadway.

Not all these problems were technical or artistic. Many were personal. The treatment of many artistic problems, we thought, was often superficial because it limited itself to these problems alone for fear of infringing on more intimate matters. I tried to clarify the actor's life problems by associating them with matters requiring objective understanding. This was not done without some resistance and confusion. But the impetus was there, and willy-nilly it carried us along, perhaps farther and harder than any of us realized or intended. Everything was done in the name of the theatre and its art, but our conception of this art made almost nothing foreign to it. From consideration of acting and plays we were plunged into a chaos of life questions, with the desire and hope of making possible some new order and integration. From an experiment in the theatre we were in some way impelled to an experiment in living.

I must warn the reader not to imagine from the foregoing that we spent the summer wading in emotional mud-puddles. In the early days of our formation Aaron Copland had asked me if, in dealing so intimately with our actors, I wasn't afraid of the well-known fruits of familiarity. I asked Strasberg what he thought of the question. Strasberg answered that we were making a group, not hiring a company, and that a certain closeness to the very pulse of the individuals composing the group was essential to real leadership in it. We respected the individual — without such respect there can be no true culture or progress in our time — but the individual needed help and an objective aim beyond himself to avoid an isolation that would end by confusing and diminishing him. In my talks I frequently pointed out the tragic waste of talent in the American theatre by listing people like the Barrymores, Laurette Taylor, Emily Stevens, Margaret Lawrence, Jeanne Eagels, who, in one way or another, had all been defeated for reasons by no means as purely "individual" as was commonly supposed. Our personal approach to the actor, then, did not consist in an immodest prying into succulent privacies, but was an attempt to get to the fundamental realities that affected him.

Our actors followed their directors because they felt their true selves were being considered and coped with — something that had rarely occurred in the theatre before. But they by no means took everything on faith. One of my earliest memories with an actor of this company was of Morris Carnovsky asking me: "What is this hocus-pocus?" when he was first introduced to the procedure of our acting method.

About our rehearsal method, and the famous Stanislavsky or

Moscow Art Theatre system from which it derived, a great mystery was made in those days, and much nonsense was written and spoken. The reason for this was that while we considered the system vital as a method of training, a way of organizing the study of parts, and above all as a means of achieving concrete results in the interpretation of plays, there was no way of demonstrating its value except to actors at rehearsals, rather than through lectures, commentaries, or critical debate.

The truth of the matter is that the system should never have been made a subject of conversation, a matter of publicity or Sunday articles, for it does not concern the audience or, for that matter, the critic. The system is not a theory, but a way of doing something with the actor. As mine is not a book of theatrical technique, I do not intend to deal with the subject beyond the need of making certain aspects of my story clear.

The aim of the system is to enable the actor to use himself more consciously as an instrument for the attainment of truth on the stage. If we had been satisfied that such truth was achieved in most productions, there would have been little purpose in troubling ourselves over the system, for it was not something taught novices, but rather a method employed in all our productions with experienced actors. We were not satisfied with most of even the best previous productions, which seemed to us to show more competent stagecraft than humanity or authenticity of feeling. With few exceptions, what we saw in most shows was "performance," fabrication, artifice. Theatrical experience was, for the greater part, the antithesis of human experience; it bespoke a familiarity with the clichés of stage deportment rather than experience with direct roots in life. It seemed to us that without such true experience plays in the theatre were lacking in all creative justification. In short, the system was not an end in itself, but a means employed for the true interpretation of plays.

The two particular aspects of the system emphasized during the first summer were the aspects most sensational to people new to its use. One was improvisation. This required the actors to do extemporaneous scenes based on situations emotionally analogous to those in the play, but not actually part of the play's text.

A further step in improvisation was the acting of the play's scenes in the actor's own ad lib. speech. The purpose of improvisation was to make the actor face each of the play's situations spontaneously — that is, without the support of the play's actual lines, which often serve merely to disguise from himself his own lack of relation to the basic matter of the play.

The second, and most striking, feature of the system, as we knew it then, was what Strasberg called an "exercise" — short for "an exercise in affective memory." "Affective memory" may be defined as the "memory of emotion," which, historically speaking, is the root discovery that led Stanislavsky to the elaboration of his system. In this "exercise" the actor was asked to recall the details of an event from his own past. The recollection of these details would stir the actors with some of the feeling involved in the original experience, thus producing "mood." These "exercises" were used to set the mechanism of the actor's emotion rolling, so to speak. When the actor was in the grip of this mood — although that is not what we called it, nor was it the purpose of the exercise to capture it directly — the actor was better prepared to do the scene calling for the particular mood that the exercise had evoked.

It is necessary to say at once that, besides the hilarious tales that were later recounted concerning these "exercises" — it was reported, for instance, that our actors prayed before going on the stage — they can and did provoke much serious theoretical discussion. But whatever its validity or error, the fact is that this procedure was used by us for the first four years of our work, and it unquestionably produced results — of all kinds.

The first effect on the actors was that of a miracle. The system (incorrectly identified by some actors as the use of the exercises) represented for most of them the open-sesame of the actor's art. Here at last was a key to that elusive ingredient of the stage, true emotion. And Strasberg was a fanatic on the subject of true emotion. Everything was secondary to it. He sought it with the patience of an inquisitor, he was outraged by trick substitutes, and when he had succeeded in stimulating it, he husbanded it, fed it, and protected it. Here was something new to most of the actors, something basic, something almost holy. It was revelation in the theatre; and Strasberg was its prophet.

The actors not only rehearsed morning, noon, and night, but they went swimming in a near-by pool, played, kidded, fell in love. Everybody was stirred up by the central fact of the new turn in their professional life. Everything was keyed high. A summer logbook in which a different actor every day was to report the events of the previous day resolved itself into a perpetual pæan of praise to the new theatre and to the perspective of a redeemed future. It didn't matter that the meals were pretty bad (the wily White Russian who had rented us the place and ran it, was making sure he was going to realize a comfortable profit). Tempers sometimes grew short because of the food, but, generally speaking, the inconveniences attending this type of community living played no great role in our consciousness. To Carnovsky and to many others everything was perfect. Art Smith confessed that he felt like a beggar who had suddenly been handed a fortune. It is true that he had gone through very hard times, but he was not talking now of food and drink. Here was companionship, security, work, and dreams.

At night, after rehearsal, the company usually trooped to the main living-room, where milk and crackers were served as supper refreshment. Here Sandy Meisner sometimes played the piano with humorous rapture; some nights hot debates over the fine points of the evening's rehearsal took place; at other times some of the men played cards for small stakes.

The card games soon became a comedy pastime, as the youngest of the actors was a boy so guileless that he could not help providing amusement. It became the frequent pleasure of the card-players to arrange to beat him after having managed to deal him almost unbeatable hands. Naturally he kept losing after heavy betting, while his bewilderment over his invariable bad luck mounted to the point of dizziness. The whole group would gather round to see how long it would take the poor fellow to realize what was happening. But no matter how overt the fixing of the hands became, he never suspected.

Lee Strasberg and I had heard about this entertainment and we came to watch it. After a while — though it was very funny, particularly since the hoax was executed with consummate *sangfroid* and deftness by Franchot Tone — I grew a little uncomfortable. I turned to Strasberg and asked: "Shall we interfere in this?" His eyes blazed. "We should interfere in everything."

I don't remember that we did interfere, nor was it true that we ever tried or wished to interfere in everything, but nevertheless what Strasberg expressed over this trifling incident was fairly representative of a spirit, derived from the premises of our basic approach, which gradually came to dominate all our activity.

Though the first summer was the honeymoon of our life together, and very few grievances came to disturb it, little rifts had begun to show, tiny but telling. For example, some of the actors began to be troubled by Franchot Tone's attitude. He was, of course, one of the original 1928 group. Since then he had had the opportunity to feel his oats. He had played leading parts on Broadway, he was in demand, and the other actors sensed in him a general resistance that at times manifested itself toward the directors and at other times toward the influences prevailing among the group. Actually he was suffering from a variety of growing-pains, but our work as such was not in question.

He was lonely. Though he had been raised in easy circumstances, and had been popular at college, he was not a good mixer. He was shy, with a tendency toward suspiciousness when ill at ease. He particularly suspected that he was not liked because, being more privileged than others, he was regarded as somewhat inferior in character. There was perhaps a mite of truth in his suspicions, but, for my part, I believed they lay chiefly in his distrust of himself. The tension that gripped him made him rude, almost insolent. He was unconsciously revenging himself on us, testing both himself and us. Thus he demonstrated little courtesy to Strasberg, although he had a real admiration for him. Franchot, intelligent and sometimes psychologically keen, said to me: "In the old days" — he referred to Riverside Drive — "we talked only when we didn't work. Now we work only when we don't talk!" I was somewhat taken aback by the remark and repeated it to

Strasberg. He agreed at once: "Yes, we talk a lot because we are not simply rehearsing a play; we are laying the foundation for a theatre. Our theatre is more than just a matter of getting one or two plays produced."

The actors, I repeat, watched Franchot with increasing misgivings. Why was he allowed to get away with little breaches of politeness and discipline? He rarely came to the afternoon talks. He lumbered into rehearsals, sat aloof, whittled away at the side of the barn as he rehearsed. No one reprimanded him. Was he a favored child among the directors? Was he to be treated as a star? Was Lee afraid of him? These disturbing questions were never openly put because the actors had an abiding confidence in the directors' good sense in handling the problem — if it was a problem.

On the Fourth of July, Franchot alone had decided to celebrate by shooting off fireworks. He began rather early in the day. Perhaps this was his childhood custom, perhaps it released his tension, perhaps it was his protest against what seemed to be the indifference of the others to the proprieties of this holiday. Solitary, with darkened brow, he went from place to place over the grounds and set off his firecrackers. Carnovsky and others were fond of music and played recordings of Mozart at every opportunity (except one man who played Caruso records, and Puccini). Carnovsky, no longer able to tolerate Franchot's acoustic vandalism, came out on the porch and cried: "Franchot, for God's sake, I can't stand the noise." Franchot turned and yelled: "And I can't stand your noise" — referring to Mozart and the rest. He stamped off yelling: "I am an American." He left precipitantly for New York to join gayer companions.

Paul Green, whom Strasberg and I had never met, arrived after rehearsals of his play had been in progress for several weeks. *The House of Connelly* had originally been written with the tenant farmer girl, Patsy, strangled to death at the end by the two old Negro maidservants of the Connelly house — remnants of the slave past — who were presented as Fates, *Macbeth*-fashion. This ending we thought false: a stock device to round off a rather somber play. It struck us as historically and humanly untrue and in conflict with what we felt to be the theme of the play. The vacillating hero, a scion of the old South, had to be given his chance to redeem his land and his life with the aid of the tenant girl, who loved him. The resistance of the black servants was something that had to be overcome through Patsy's firmness, rather than yielded to through a memory of the function of Fates in literary drama.

Paul was not altogether sure, partly because, though basically a sound, affirmative nature, he has never been able wholly to overcome a pessimistic drag on his spirit, a bafflement before evil. Our own sense of the perfectibility of man, or at least, the inevitability of the struggle against evil, not only made us impatient with the play's violent ending, but roused Paul's own verve and decision in our direction.

Maxwell Anderson spent part of the summer with us, attended a few rehearsals, worked, and carried on friendly arguments with me about contemporary drama. Max gave parties at his house, a minute from our grounds. He liked the youth and earnest buoyancy of our actors, and was a good host.

Waldo Frank arrived for a brief visit. I invited him to give one or two talks. Mary Morris, being somewhat older than the rest of us, confided a certain uneasiness to Waldo. She was worried, she said, about the directors' arrogance, especially Strasberg's and mine. We spoke with violent self-assurance that took little account of the possibility of error or the simple fact that many of the things we proclaimed with such heat were commonplaces familiar to most adults. We spoke to everybody as to pupils who had to be instructed, sinners who had to be saved, mental babies who had to be whipped into growing up. What could she do about it? Waldo probably explained that some of our excesses were due to inexperience and to temperaments and even backgrounds that made a certain amount of personal storminess almost inevitable.

I told Strasberg all this. In a few days he took over my hour for afternoon talks. He wished to speak frankly, he said, on a subject that perhaps had some importance. Calmly and judiciously at first he proceeded to explain that we were beginners; that what we were trying to do in the theatre was something that had hardly ever been attempted in America before, and that all beginnings were characterized by a lack of smoothness — indeed, were usually marked by a very definite crudeness that had its offensive aspects to people who did not understand them, but represented the stirrings of new life, a kind of upheaval under the surface of society. If the effect was somewhat shocking, so much the worse for those who could not appreciate the value of the shock. At this point Strasberg began to illustrate very vividly the faults Mary had complained about. With ill-concealed impatience he pointed out that we were the first people to realize this and that, the first to understand that and the other, the first to set forth such and such, and that he, Lee Strasberg, in the realm of theatrical study, had been the first to discover X, Y, and Z.

I confess I thought much of what he said that afternoon was true, and that there was great virtue in his saying it, but later events proved that Mary's reaction was not confined to herself. We caused ourselves considerable harm by our appalling lack of grace.

There were many more visitors that summer. The photographers Paul Strand and Ralph Steiner arrived, took pictures, and remained to be strongly impressed by our activities and our spirit. Mordecai Gorelik, the scene-designer, dropped in to observe us, although he had not been engaged to do the settings for our play. Luther Adler, leery, he said, of all idealistic efforts in the theatre, came to see his sister and to flirt with available girls. Stella had previously told Strasberg and me that Luther's place was with us, but he had other plans.

Very few young playwrights turned up. Besides Maxwell Anderson and Paul Green, there was only Gerald Sykes, a young man from Covington, Kentucky, who had joined us to share our experiences and perhaps to find a medium for his literary gifts. I suggested that he work on a Soviet play called *The Man with the Portfolio,* which needed adaptation.

This play was not at all suited to our needs, but we were eager to have one script in addition to *Connelly* to give some of the people who had only bits in that play a chance at something better. I was to direct *Portfolio*. The attempt was abortive because the play was inappropriate, the adaptation weak; and I was still unready to direct any play.

All I remember in connection with the Russian piece is that, in anticipation of its production, I had read a number of Soviet novels and seen some Soviet newsreels. What struck me in all this material was the sense of a people at war even in their most casual cultural and professional activities. Actually I understood nothing of the Soviet Union's significance.

Despite the fact that we contemplated doing a Soviet play, there was very little political discussion among us during the summer of 1931. Of radicalism there wasn't a spark.

It might be asked why, for all my talk about the need of facing our times and of finding affirmative answers to the moral and social problems of our day, politics received so little of our attention. One answer may be that my education and inclinations had been chiefly æsthetic. Besides this, however, I have always had a reluctance to delve into problems while they still remained outside the range of my actual experience. I am troubled only by those questions to which I can see an immediate reference in the lives of people close to me. The fact that a subject is intellectually or even practically important leaves me cold unless some need arising from my own environment prompts me to study it. My own life — which after 1931 included my contact with the people I had chosen as co-workers — was my basic guide, and our experience together was to provide my education.

The crash of 1929 had already come, and though I had lost a bit of money in it (in an effort to help my parents), it had made no strong impression on me. When I first read the headlines announcing the Wall Street debacle, my first thought was a complacent "I told them so." It is true I had had a presentiment of a crack-up after 1926, but this arose from a general reaction to the world around me, not from any economic prescience. More curious is the fact that not only I but none of my colleagues ever spoke of the crash at this time. None of us apparently was directly involved.

Our chief problem the first summer was the unification of our people. The elements for such unification were present in a common artistic ideal, a common search for a way of life. But people are contradictory within themselves. Besides Stella Adler and Franchot Tone, who were perhaps the most strikingly individualistic personalities of the group, the two most truly labyrinthine characters were probably Lee Strasberg and myself.

Though the foundation of my belief was the interdependence of people, the need for a common faith and co-operative action, I was so uplifted by this idea and the need for its dissemination that a good deal of the prophet's self-conceit must have been plainly evident in all my words and behavior. It was, I imagine, a rather naïve conceit, but it could become annoying. Many who perceived it managed to forgive it, because they felt it to be a rather childish foible.

No one admired me at that time more than Cheryl Crawford. Once she called me to her room to tell me she wished to resign as co-director of *Connelly*. I had suggested that she take on this job because I believed she would be very useful in dealing with the two colored actresses who played important roles in it. She wanted to resign from the direction of *Connelly* because her contribution was small, and she felt herself more of an appendage to the production than Strasberg's colleague. I appreciated her position, but I urged her to go on with her work. What was suffering most was her ego, I said, and that hurt was trivial compared to what she would contribute, and learn, by sticking to her job. She stayed on as co-director.

Nothing actually occurred during the summer to cause any alarm, except perhaps to Cheryl, who noticed little signs of strain between her two male partners. The adoration of the actors for Lee Strasberg seemed to have the effect of inflating his ego with what struck me as a sense of total mastery. I did not mind this at first. Indeed, I thought it natural, since I felt that Lee must have suffered much from all sorts of real and imagined neglect,

and he had been under a severe strain during his late wife's ill-
ness. Now he was reaping the harvest of spiritual compensation
that his extraordinary talents deserved. "Let him feed his fill on
the love he is now earning," I said to myself. In time there would
be a normal adjustment.

It did not seem to happen that way. There came into his humble
demeanor something tight and autocratic, driving and fierce. He
would alternate between a childish self-indulgence in people's
good opinion of him and an almost sadistic fury when he was
balked. It was sometimes difficult to tell where the artist's sense
of perfection ended and where personal complications set in.

One Sunday afternoon the members of the company were invited to a near-by country home. On their return to rehearsal
that evening, Lee waited till they were all seated, paused omi-
nously, and asked: "Do you feel tired?" Most of the company
answered that they didn't. Lee paid no attention to the answers,
but said with frozen control: "There will be no rehearsal tonight.
You had such a good time today that you are in no condition to
rehearse." The company was a little stunned and marched out
meekly, because Lee's face at such moments became a relentless
mask.

On the surface this was simply Lee's way of making a point
the actor would not soon forget. The actor couldn't come to rehearsal casually: he had to be physically and mentally prepared.
From the viewpoint of theatrical discipline this was altogether
correct. Apparently some of the actors had had a few more high-
balls than their sober director deemed judicious, and he wanted
to teach them that alcoholic conviviality was not the proper
preparation for rehearsal. Yet there was something so tense and
bitter in his manner that I couldn't help thinking that some scratch
had been inflicted on his ego during the course of the afternoon.
Whether this was so or not, one or two asked me later to explain
Lee's harshness. They were hurt, and I tried to soften the effect
Lee had made by pointing out the lesson he had wished to draw
from the episode. Lee heard that I had spoken to these people
and had perhaps mollified them. "You will please not speak to
my actors," he flashed.

I decided to have a talk with him. Had he lost confidence in me? What was the meaning of his baleful glances and subsequent taciturnity? Lee denied practically everything. Yes, at times he had been annoyed by my laxness in organizational matters. Also he had been hurt during the previous winter by my having conferences with Cheryl without him. And recently at almost every joint session of the company I had put myself in the position of presiding director. This was almost usurpation of power. Yet all this, he admitted, was picayune. He went so far as to apologize for his having spoken of "my actors."

I had irritated Strasberg; and from time to time I would shock others as well. Years later Clifford Odets told me that I had come into his room about midnight — he shared the room with the actor painter Clement Wilenchick — and had unburdened my spirit on many subjects, intellectual and personal. Then I got up, said: "There's no one I can talk to around here," and left!

Writing in our logbook toward the end of the summer, I pointed out that it surprised me how few of the people, in their enjoyment of the summer's activity, reflected on the difficulties ahead. We had come on the scene to improve the theatre, to relieve some of its ills; perhaps, too, we hoped to make some contribution to American life generally. But our task was not an easy one. All of us wouldn't necessarily be made happy because we had set ourselves these high purposes. Our job was a hard one, I wrote then, and in the ensuing years I reiterated the warning. I spoke as if we were going into battle, and presaged casualties, but to the others, "battle" meant only alarums and excursions, fanfare and drumbeat.

The night before our last in Brookfield Center we gave a runthrough of *Connelly* which a few visitors, among them Winifred Lenihan, then director of the Theatre Guild school, attended. There was, of course, no scenery, no costumes, not even a stage. Rarely has a company of players been so captured by its own mood of sincerity and dedication. More even than the play's lines or situations demanded, the actors poured forth a concentrated stream of fervor, that was like the pent-up rivers of all their young

life's experience and the aspirations awakened and released
through the summer's efforts. The company was exalted by its
own transformation.

Miss Lenihan's reaction was that, although there were fine
scenes in the play, the whole thing was "too slow." Two or three of
our company were affected by this comment, and they repeated
the old saw: "too slow." But most of us knew that "too slow" was
not the salient feature to be singled out. Robert Edmond Jones
in a letter we received next morning spoke in quite different
terms.

The last night at Brookfield Center I alone spoke. It was my
salute to the future. First I dismissed the kind of evaluation of
our work, whatever its source, that expressed itself in such gems
of discernment as "too slow." (I did not know then that in later
years almost the entire critical vocabulary of most reviewers in
regard to stage direction was to relate to the matter of pace and
timing. What was slow was bad, what was fast was good.) Second I expressed my own high estimate of Strasberg's accomplishment and of the company's progress. Third, and most important,
I spoke of the resistance that we might encounter in New York,
not so much through mischief as through indifference. This resistance would not embitter us, but would serve as a challenge.
Our heat would melt the city's ice. I quoted "Beanie" (Margaret
Barker), who had answered a manager's offer of a part by a refusal. The manager had asked: "How long do you think you'll be
busy with your present engagement?" She had replied: "If our
play is a success — twenty years. If not — twenty years."

CHAPTER FIVE

Hallelujah!

AMONG our summer pastimes were little informal conclaves to
discuss what name we would give our theatre. Waldo Frank had
written to suggest *Atlantic* (that is, New World) *Theatre*. Morris

Carnovsky semi-seriously submitted that the cactus might be adopted as our trade-mark, because it was an American plant, grew in the desert, was hard to kill, and sustained its prickly life for a long time!

At the last moment, when the company got back to New York, on August 17, the three directors decided amongst themselves that since they had always referred to "our group," they might as well accept the inevitable, and call their company The Group Theatre.

For all our tall talk, we were virtually adrift in New York. True, Cheryl Crawford was still "Assistant to the Board of Managers" at the Theatre Guild, and I the Guild's play-reader, but we had no position as a group. This might be remedied if the Guild chose to finance our first production.

The Guild board came to see our run-through of *The House of Connelly*. The board was rather vague in its reaction at first. Each member seemed to be waiting for the others to commit themselves. Miss Helburn conceded that the production succeeded in creating a mood, that it had emotional substance. But the board as a whole was not sure that Carnovsky could pass as a Southern gentleman. Paul Green defended Carnovsky, of whose performance as Uncle Bob he was very fond. Some objection was made to Mary Morris as Mrs. Connelly, but Lee Strasberg went white as he asserted that he wasn't going to tamper with the ensemble. (The play had been rehearsed for twelve weeks.) Nearly every one on the Guild board protested our happy ending. Some of them spoke as if we had violated an æsthetic law. Nothing was decided that night.

The next day we had the Guild's verdict. It would back our production and make it a regular subscription offering if we removed Mary Morris and Morris Carnovsky from the cast and if we restored the tragic ending. If we declined to do this, they would put up only half the sum required ($5,000), if we could raise the other half; and the production would not be a regular subscription performance, though the subscribers would be invited to see the play at reduced prices.

We did not even discuss the first proposal, but immediately

agreed to raise our half of the total cost of the production. We did not tell either Mary Morris or Morris Carnovsky, however, what the Guild had suggested in regard to them. About a year later I did mention the matter in a speech to illustrate some of the conditions that faced us in the theatre — conditions we were to encounter again and again, which we resolutely fought. The actors, spared some of this knowledge, came to regard these constant battles as easy victories and rather took them for granted.

Our half of the money for *The House of Connelly* was raised, largely by Cheryl Crawford, who interested an executive at Samuel French (the play's publisher) as well as Eugene O'Neill, who, I believe, didn't read or see the play, but who felt that Paul Green and a new group merited a hearing, and Franchot Tone. There was now no hindrance to our proceeding directly to production.

When all arrangements had been concluded, the Guild announced the forthcoming event by releases to the press and by the usual billboard in front of the theatre in which we were to do the play. We had instructed the Guild that no individual actor was to be featured in advertisements, as this was contrary to our policy. The actors were therefore shocked, on arriving for rehearsal one day, to see that several of them — those best known to the Guild publicity department — were listed ahead of others, even, as it happened, when some of these players were playing less conspicuous parts than those less well known. The actors immediately vented their dissatisfaction over this. Lee Strasberg must have been caught unawares by the small tempest, for he lost his head. "If this means so much to anyone," he shouted, "he knows what he can do — leave!"

I was astonished that the actors should have felt so strongly about something so easily corrected, that Strasberg should have reacted so sharply to the company's touchiness, that so negligible an occurrence should cause big words like "principle" to be called into play. Nothing in my previous study of the theatre had prepared me for this. Soon, however, we were able to persuade our publicity people to bill all our actors in alphabetical order, a policy we continued almost to the end.

A very important matter, of course, was the question of salaries. Up to this time no discussion of this point had ever been brought up by anyone. The actors never doubted that the directors, in whose hands the matter lay, would handle it fairly. For the first season it was decided that Franchot Tone and Morris Carnovsky, who were legally still under contract to the Guild, should be paid their regular salaries. This was $300 weekly. The other salaries ranged from $30 to $140 weekly.

Our plan was to pay the actors their full salaries as long as any Group production stayed on the boards, regardless of the kind of part they were doing in a particular play. The basis of the salary standard was not an individual part but an actor's general value to the Group company, plus, as far as it was possible to consider them, some regard for the actor's responsibilities — marital status, number of children, and so forth.

Thus, for example, Bromberg received the same salary — $140 — for the bit he played in *Connelly* as for the lead he played later in the season. Margaret Barker, who was hardly more than a walk-on in our second production, received the same salary then as she had in *Connelly*, in which she played the lead — a higher salary than that of Phoebe Brand, who, an extra in *Connelly*, was the heroine of the next production. In other words, being assigned a better part in a Group production did not necessarily entail receiving more money. The actor's value was determined by his status in the Group as a permanent organization committed to the production of a number of plays every season.

Next season, in order to raise some of the lower salaries and because we could not afford to go as high as $300 a week, we reduced the top salary to $200, which affected only Tone and Carnovsky. Both consented to the reduction, though Franchot, as a matter of intellectual integrity only, submitted that he did not approve of the Group's leveling tendencies.

The directors paid themselves a salary of $50 a week, and divided the $1,500 allowed by the production budget for a director's fee among the three of them, regardless of which one of the three was actually to direct a particular production. This meant that the

directors stood somewhere in the middle brackets of the Group's
financial listing — and sometimes, for reasons that will appear, below that position. This extraordinary fact was no quixotic demonstration of the directors' selflessness. It seemed to be dictated by
the general situation. The actors sometimes became aware of the
peculiarity of an organization in which the leaders were less well
paid than some others; they even protested mildly. But the only
way to increase our pay would have been by doing so at the
expense of some of the actors. Hardly any of them felt they
were being overpaid!

Every season, indeed, we had requests for raises, which were
usually granted, since they were justified. A few requests for
more money were not based so much on need as on morale; an
actor wanted to be assured — through money — that he was not
artistically inferior to another. I must confess that these requests
provoked an unreasonable irritation in me.

The organization profits were not to accrue to the directors.
In the event of a considerable profit, a bonus would be declared
for all. The underlying theory of our financial setup was that the
larger part of any profit would be turned over to a sinking fund
for the continuance and broadening of our activities.

Our first program read: "The Group Theatre (under the Auspices of the Theatre Guild) presents — " The official announcement that preceded the opening merely said: "This theatre is an
organization of actors and directors formed with the ultimate aim
of creating a permanent acting company to maintain regular New
York seasons."

The opening took place the evening of September 23, 1931, at
the Martin Beck Theatre on West Forty-fifth Street, New York
City. It was the only Group Theatre opening I ever watched from
beginning to end. Most of the others I never attended at all.

Cheryl Crawford, Lee Strasberg, and I stood in the rear of the
auditorium, a little worried and let down because the actors that
night were not up to their usual pitch. Their nervousness in this
instance tended to lower their vitality. I could not tell how the
play was going; the audience was subdued. When the final cur-

tain descended, I felt the actors had proved themselves fine-spirited people whose accomplishment I would forever cherish beyond the mere value of their talent or success. Tears came to my eyes, and I began to shout "Bravo" before I was sure that anyone would join me in applause. The applause and cheering were general. Not till four years later would there be anything in opening night receptions to equal this.

The company, Paul Green, some friends or Group Associates, as they became officially known, made for an actor's apartment somewhere on West Forty-seventh Street. We had come to celebrate our achievement. This was the only opening-night party free of the tension that came later when we began to appreciate the power of the press in relation to the New York theatre.

At two A.M. word from Cheryl Crawford came over the phone that some reviews had already appeared, and that they were un-qualified raves. A loud cheer broke out among us. Clifford Odets and I taxied over to Times Square to buy the morning papers. We read such praise as we hardly dared imagine. We rushed back to the expectant company, and Lee Strasberg read the reviews aloud.

Here is what some of them said: "Paul Green has his match in these young players. They are not only earnest and skillful, but inspired. They play like a band of musicians. . . . Their group performance is too beautifully imagined and modulated to concentrate on personal achievements. There is not a gaudy, brittle or facile stroke in their acting. For once, a group performance is tremulous and pellucid, the expression of an ideal. Between Mr. Green's prose poem and the Group Theatre's performance, it is not too much to hope that something fine and true had been started in the American theatre." Another reviewer spoke in comparisons that we had not instigated: "They [the Group] must have convinced the fascinated audience that their way is the only way to prepare a play for all the play is worth. . . . I cannot remember a more completely consecrated piece of ensemble work since the Moscow Art masters went home." Still another reviewer, after describing "the rafter-rocking cheers which are all but un-known at first nights nowadays," pointed out that "the truest rea-son for these cheers was not Mr. Green's play. Instead it was the

simple fact that in this Group Theatre jaded Broadway seems
finally to have found the young blood and new ideas for which
many of us have been praying."

I tried to embrace Strasberg, but a certain rigidity in his posture
made it difficult. His attitude bespoke an unwillingness to be
moved by the superficial rewards of an enthusiastic press. I
clapped him on the back. "Now," I said, "we shall be able to get
everything," by which I meant the financial support to carry out
our program.

In later years, when it seemed our early work had been quite
forgotten, I came to believe that the real significance of *The House
of Connelly* as a production had been neglected. *The House of
Connelly* was something new in the American theatre. In its details the production was far from perfect. Some of the actors were
hard to hear; at least two important roles were pretty threadbare
in feeling and execution; the first scene was badly set and lighted;
no claim could be made to verisimilitude in type or accent; and
occasionally, as Brooks Atkinson warned, the actors may have
"forced their souls too much."

The value and importance of the Group's first production was
not that it had better actors or even a better director, not that it
was composed according to a more serious method or took more
time to prepare, but that its technique and intention were aimed
toward the creation of something different in kind from the usual
expert production. In completeness, technical proficiency, showmanship, there may have been many better productions on our
stage before this; there were hardly any of this precise nature.
The Group people had succeeded in fusing the technical elements
of their craft with the stuff of their own spiritual and emotional
selves. They succeeded in doing this because, aside from their
native character or habit, they were prepared by the education
of their work together before and during rehearsals.

All this would have made nothing but a loud noise if Lee Strasberg hadn't been among us to shape the production in his particular way. Lee Strasberg is one of the few artists among American theatre directors. He is the director of introverted feeling,

The Group Theatre company, at one of Harold Clurman's afternoon talks, Brookfield Center, summer 1931. Harold Clurman at extreme left, wielding stick; Clifford Odets, in shorts, with back to camera; Stella Adler at right, seated on rocking chair; Franchot Tone, extreme right.

Scenes from *House of Connelly* by Paul Green, 1931. (Direction: Lee Strasberg and Cheryl Crawford. Setting: Cleon Throckmorton.) Ruth Nelson and Franchot Tone.

Eunice Stoddard, Stella Adler, Morris Carnovsky, Mary Morris, Franchot Tone.

of strong emotion curbed by ascetic control, sentiment of great intensity muted by delicacy, pride, fear, shame. The effect he produces is a classic hush, tense and tragic, a constant conflict so held in check that a kind of beautiful spareness results. Though plastically restricted, his work through the balance of its various tensions often becomes æsthetically impressive, despite its crushed low key and occasional wild transitions to shrill hysteria. Above everything, the feeling in Strasberg's production is never stagy. Its roots are clearly in the intimate experience of a complex psychology, an acute awareness of human contradiction and suffering, a distinguished though perhaps a too specialized sensibility.

The almost inevitable mention of the Moscow Art Theatre in relation to our first production was in some respects unfortunate. For the importance of *The House of Connelly* as a production lay in the fact that it was an American production — that is, a play and a performance that sprang from circumstances and conditions peculiarly indigenous at that time. To speak of Russian influence, as some did, because we had learned certain things of general technical or artistic value from the best practitioners of contemporary theatrical art was as pointless as it would be to view Sherwood Anderson's novels or Edgar Lee Masters's verse as offshoots of Dostoyevsky's work.

While our aims and technique made a strikingly favorable general impression, they produced certain negative reactions not only in the spectator (as in the case of one reviewer who found our cast "either sleepy, hysterical, or both") but in the Group itself.

Several actors and actresses were apparently hurt as much as they were helped in the course of their "treatment." For one thing, they overstrained. This was not something Lee Strasberg called for; they were often cautioned, even reproved about this. It did not matter that we made relaxation the fundamental technical prerequisites for all acting. There was something in our environment that was not conducive to relaxation. The intensity with which we attacked many of our problems, our anticipation of struggle against the current, held a dangerous attraction for some

of our people. Those who were seeking — unconsciously sometimes — for solutions to inner problems that had previously been
neglected thought they found in our emphasis on "true emotion"
a key to their salvation. For this reason they flung themselves on
it with too great a will. Their idealism often reached the border-
line of a violent amateurishness.

In later years certain observers with an antipathy for the Group
accused the organization of inducing neurosis in normal people;
others, less severe but no less critical, asserted that the Group attracted the unbalanced. There is much to be said on this score.
But for the moment let us admit that while, abstractly speaking,
the Group represented a drive toward wholeness, a psychologically and morally integrated attitude to life, it was, by virtue of
the fact that it considered anything but the purely professional
matter of putting on plays, a special kind of organization. The
complete, the universal, the strong individual, balanced by a feeling for the social unit, were Group ideals and, one might say,
entirely "classic." But to set up such ideals at all, and to pursue
them with any seriousness under the conditions obtaining on
Broadway, might be regarded as eccentric in itself.

Any equivalent group — no matter what its purpose or motivation — would necessarily contain within itself certain iconoclastic
elements, since such a group arises from some sense of dissatisfaction as well as from positive and constructive impulses. Thus
it will attract people under pressure of some kind, troubled, not
quite adjusted people, yearners, dreamers, secretly ambitious.

One particular point must not escape our attention. Whether it
knew it or not, the Group was behaving according to a tradition
that is far more deeply American than is usually recognized. We
might answer the gibe about our strangeness by recalling Thoreau's "If a man does not keep step with his companions, it is
perhaps because he hears a different drummer."

Our sources, and with them our strength and our failings, lay
in the place and time in which we worked, in the original backgrounds of each of our people. Margaret Barker, daughter of
the dean emeritus of Johns Hopkins Medical School, Franchot
Tone, son of an eminent chemist in Niagara Falls, Dorothy Pat-

ten, whose father was a very prominent citizen in Chattanooga, Art Smith, who had been a lumberjack in the West as well as a bohemian in Paris, Walter Coy from college in Seattle, Ruth Nelson, product of a theatrical family and a long convent training, Eunice Stoddard of a thoroughly correct New York family, Clifford Odets, out of prosperous small business in Philadelphia and the Bronx — these backgrounds, and that of all the others, are, I repeat, more pertinent to our story than any discussion of foreign æsthetic theories or influences.

We had been very sensible about one thing. We had not asked for huge sums of money before we had demonstrated our ability to carry out our ideas. The reception accorded us in *The House of Connelly* warranted my optimism regarding our future prospects.

We did not want backing for shows. We wanted our theatre to be supported. We did not propose to put on a series of single productions, but to build a theatre: develop actors, playwrights, scene-designers, directors. We were seeking a conscious audience to follow the program of a theatre that would grow with the years and make a permanent contribution to our social-cultural life in the manner of certain State theatres abroad, or of the Moscow Art Theatre, which was sustained by private funds before it was incorporated into the Soviet system, or of the Reinhardt theatres in their heyday.

To this end I wrote an article, published in the *New York Times* on December 13, 1931. It was the first public expression of our program and faith. It announced almost at the outset that "The [Group] organization has the temerity to believe — *particularly* in a time of economic stress — that its aims should be a matter of real public concern." The salient feature of the article — the theme to which I was to return time and again through the years — was: "The Group Theatre is not yet fully established — it still rests on a makeshift foundation. *Of course it would not be impossible — though difficult and wearing — to go on from production to production in this way. But whatever the nature of our productions or the success they might win, this would not be establishing the*

Group Theatre so that it could carry out the real object it has set
itself. To do this it needs an endowment of $100,000." (Not itali-
cized in the original article.)

The figure — $100,000 — was an arbitrary one. In the course of
a few seasons we raised more than that sum. But the point to be
emphasized is that we raised it in dribs and drabs for individual
productions. Never was any substantial sum set aside at one time
for a carefully planned program on a long-term or at least a seasonal basis.

The money we raised was given to us, in effect, as gamblers'
"investments," never as money to support an institution of some
permanent value. The function and use of these two types of
money are antithetical. An "angel" who has contributed the backing for a production that proves successful has no interest in gambling on the next production, which may prove less fortunate. The
person who would be interested in endowing a theatre would realize that the box-office failure that follows the success may be
just as much a part of the theatre's program as the success, and
sometimes prove more important to the theatre's future.

In seeing people about money I encountered a universal fear
which the 1929 crash and the increasing depression inspired in the
hearts of all business men at the time. One gentleman, typical of many I interviewed, said very sympathetically: "If you
can get your venture on its feet in such times, you are sure to go
on for a long while." But, like the others, he gave us no money.

We took actual steps for a legal incorporation of our Group
Theatre, by which the three directors became the officers and
owners of corporation property. There was some sort of stock
issued, and a few friendly souls bought shares at $100 par, more
in an effort to help us than in the hope of profit. I believe only
Cheryl Crawford knew the meaning of our gestures — they could
hardly be called transactions. Lee Strasberg was unconcerned, and
I was anxious to get them over with as a perhaps necessary evil.

Though no one leaped forward to become the patron of the
newly formed organization, our appearance caused some little stir
in the world that interests itself in the theatre. Not the least in-

terested in our emergence was the radical wing in New York intellectual life. It did not particularly approve of *The House of Connelly*. (In contrast to the reviewers in Baltimore who thought Paul Green rather angry on the subject of the old South, the radicals thought he sentimentalized it.) But we were "out of line" with the commercial theatre, and certain of our statements smacked of "progressive tendencies."

Lee Strasberg and I were invited to a symposium on "Revolution and the Theatre" held at the John Reed Club, a literary, artistic circle of the period. I was thrown off balance just before I began to speak because the chairman introduced us as middle-of-the-roaders as compared with the Right of the Theatre Guild and the Left of certain workers' groups that apparently were then in the making. I did not know what it meant to be a middle-of-the-roader in this connection.

When I got up to speak I pointed out that certain plays like *The Moon in the Yellow River*, recently done by the Guild, were often praised for their charm or some similar attribute, but that they were actually commentaries on our time and could only be understood in that light. What I was really driving at was that a play didn't have to deal with obvious social themes in order to have social significance. People who were concerned with such topics as "revolution and the theatre" tended to seek social significance only where it was advertised, so to speak; and to do this might be to overlook some of the important work that our time might produce.

Though my presentation of this slight thesis was lame, I was not prepared for the heavy battery of sarcasm, even derision, that followed. Everyone wanted the floor to tear me to pieces at once. I had spoken no word of politics, so I failed to understand some of the terms of abuse, several of which were entirely new to me. I was a "liberal," possibly even a "social fascist." Someone got up and placed me in the category of the "undistributed middle class."

Here for the first time I heard a slogan that was quite popular in these circles for another two years: "The theatre is a weapon!" As it was expounded here, this slogan had for me the earmarks of a caricature of all I had said in my Group talks. The tone these amateurs used infuriated me. I began to shout — something I could do with the best of them — and announced that I hadn't come to be instructed by "these people"! To my astonishment, it was my bad temper that was most appreciated and applauded. I did not realize then that we were entering a period of controversy. It was my first lesson in the temper of the thirties.

Though business was only fair, we behaved as if our play was enormously successful, for the quality of the response more than compensated us for the lack of profits. At any rate, we were able to return their original investment to our various "angels." To our simple souls, this was achievement enough.

When I was asked what we were going to do after *The House of Connelly*, I replied: "I do not know how we are going to go on, but I am sure we will." The future was sure because we had the will to make one.

In those days I had the equivalent of a "God will provide" attitude, which I was some time in losing. I plunged ahead with artistic and ethical considerations that interested me as part of the Group's essential task. Cheryl Crawford was swept away by this "bit-in-the-mouth idealism," as she once called it, but it caused her considerable worry none the less. As a practical person (her father had been in the rubber business) she couldn't help feeling that Strasberg and I were a bit too cavalier about the facts of life (money!). I "agreed" with her, but couldn't help my bad upbringing, in which (though my parents had never been people of means) money played so subsidiary a role. Lee Strasberg was almost vexed by Cheryl's pressure and, in effect, rationalized our behavior as a concern with essentials — that is, our work.

Lee prepared a long analysis of the merits and shortcomings of our first production. This was a way of learning from our mistakes and making ready for future tasks. It was a practice that we continued till 1937, when certain ill effects resulting from it began to manifest themselves.

In addition to this I undertook an analysis of each actor's individual problem. One lacked discipline — it made his work spasmodic; another was intolerant — it limited his emotional scope;

another was timid — it stood in the way of his portraying the heroic; and so on.

One of my intimate talks was with Clifford Odets. During the winter in which I gave my lessons of "indoctrination" I had had very little contact with him. One evening after one of my talks he accompanied me along Fifth Avenue on my way home. We walked in silence for a while, when suddenly he murmured something about knowing a man who had grown a beard because he had a weak chin. A peculiar duck, I thought to myself, not in reference to the man described, but to the speaker.

During the summer he had mooned about some of the girls, but struck me as being rather shy of them. He carried on raucous philosophical dialogues with Joe Bromberg. Between matinee and evening performances in the theatre, he would sit in the wings and improvise pathetic chords on the piano. He was given to outbursts of song or sound, forceful but indeterminate as to origin or content — an idiosyncrasy that strongly resembled one of my own. The only mental trait I had noticed revealed itself one evening when we were dining together. Odets worried lest Strasberg and I were bent on making our actors "normal" human beings. It was precisely through his abnormality, Odets insisted, that the actor functioned. This tendency to nurse his own oddities, combined with a shadowy life he seemed to be leading and an occasional sally into highly charged but vague verbiage in the form of letters and sundry pieces of writing, might have led me at the time to set him down definitely as a strange young man.

Shortly after the *Connelly* opening he had submitted to me a play of his own, entitled *910 Eden Street*. It dealt with a house in Philadelphia he had lived in, full of confused and unhappy young people. I hardly thought of it as a play, or of its author as a potential playwright. It was a personal document, such as others brought me from time to time.

In the wings of the Martin Beck Theatre, Odets sat down to hear my reaction to his play. What I said, as far as I can remember now, had to do with only one aspect of the play. It gave evidence of an internal injury in the writer, I said. Something in his past life had hurt him. He was doubled up in pain now, and

in his pain he appeared to be shutting out the world. His perception was disturbed because everything was seen in relation to
his hurt. He had to learn to stand up straight and see the world
more objectively.

After the more than creditable showing we had made with
The House of Connelly, we thought it a good time to approach
the Theatre Guild once again to request its support. Some of
the acclaim accorded the Group reflected favorably on the Guild,
since we were frequently referred to as its offspring.

We met with the Guild board. I opened the sitting by stating
what seemed to me the incontrovertible fact that the Guild's productions were always more successful — even artistically — with
plays like *The Guardsman, Liliom, Caprice, The Second Man,*
than with *Goat Song, Jaurez and Maximilian, The Brothers Karamazov, The Moon in the Yellow River.* This I ascribed to the fact
that the Guild's actors, though perhaps the best in the country,
were not prepared by their background to do such plays. The
new times were going to bring plays even farther removed from
the older actors than those I enumerated. These new plays would
demand a new type of company. The Group Theatre supplied such
a company.

This approach to the Guild seemed to me the most matter-of-
fact possible. I made no headway with it. Strasberg supplemented
my words with what he thought were equally pertinent observations, but made no more progress than I. Despite the Guild's
sympathy, coldness and resistance were perceptibly growing.
When I said that the Group was trying to establish a Theatre
rather than just a production organization, I was challenged. A
Theatre, I said, was a homogeneous body of craftsmen to give
voice to a point of view which they shared with the dramatist,
whose work might be described as the most clearly articulated
and eloquent expression of the Theatre's conscience. When I tried
to elaborate on this, Philip Moeller interrupted with the question,
"What is so new about that?" "Basically my idea is as old as the
Greek Theatre; there have been true Theatres in every country
on the Continent — but there just doesn't happen to be any in

ours." But as soon as he had won the admission that our idea was not "new," Mr. Moeller ceased to listen.

Not understanding the resistance, I grew angry, and from that moment the meeting became a free-for-all. From the whirl of loose words that followed, I remember my belief that a theatre might work with and perhaps even influence its dramatists being challenged by Lawrence Langner with a question that was calculated to stump me: "Do you think you would have anything to tell Eugene O'Neill?" I didn't hesitate a moment. "Certainly," I answered.

We failed none the less. We failed not because the Guild had disagreed with us: intellectual considerations were only what they talked about, not what motivated them. We should have been less "basic" and much more personal. We should have shown them how they could help us, influence us, earn our gratitude. What we were asking them in effect was to be our patron. We gave no evidence of feeling that we needed them in our work.

Still, the Guild trusted our abilities well enough to contribute $5,000 to our next production. This play, originally entitled *Son of God*, we called *1931 —*.

This was the first time the contradiction between the producer and the critic in me came into conflict. From everything I had said one would imagine I would have no hesitancy in accepting this play. Its subject — unemployment — was certainly urgent enough. But, aside from theoretical considerations, I had a resistance to reportage and journalism in the theatre. The play's point of view was not particularly cogent, and its actual text suffered from dryness and thinness.

While I was still speculating on the merits of the question, Cheryl said to me: "It is our theatre's duty to produce such a play." Cheryl's instincts in these matters were frequently sound; I yielded.

While *The House of Connelly* was still running we put *1931 —* into rehearsal. Franchot Tone again contributed $1,000, the Elmhirst Foundation gave us $2,500, a young lady, Bertha Gillespie, graduate of the Yale School of Drama, appeared as if by magic and put up another $5,000. The final $1,000 was delivered by Herman Shumlin, who thought the play, which he predicted would not make a cent, ought to be put on. We were launched on our program of "continuous activity."

CHAPTER SIX

Growth

1931 —, by Claire and Paul Sifton, the Group Theatre's second production, was rehearsed for eight weeks, opened at the Mansfield Theatre on December 10, 1931, and closed in nine days.

A failure, then, a total failure. One reviewer captioned his notice with the statement that the *year* 1931 would be remembered, but not the play. No doubt he was right, yet the production had more importance than any official record would indicate.

"Seldom has a bad play stunned an audience quite so completely as *1931* —," the *New York Times* reported. In its second review the same paper added: "*1931* — is sufficiently forthright in the theatre to upset a playgoer's natural complacence and to make the life of these times more intelligible and vivid. . . ."

On the other hand, Percy Hammond expressed something of the play's value in a negative but, to my mind, very interesting manner. Referring to the lines of unemployed, hungry, and homeless in the play's later scenes, "It was a depressing sight," he wrote, "and I was melancholy last night as I left the theatre to walk through Broadway to this desk. But on my way I was confused by other long lines of men at the Paramount, the Rialto, and Loew's. None of them was cold and hungry. They were warmly clothed, and they had the price of admission. No symptoms of destitution were present." Perhaps the economic crisis, unemployment, and hardship, like Mark Twain's death, had been grossly exaggerated.

John Mason Brown, who disliked the play, compared its naïveté to that of an "old morality play." But it is precisely from the crude old morality plays, despite their lack of enduring quality, that much of the finest English drama was born. The touchstone of importance in relation to such material depends on how the particular morality is wedded to the living experience of author, actors, audience. From the standpoint of the "taster," with a museum or pastry-shop psychology, such crude documents from the life of the times are rather unappetizing. From the creative standpoint — that is, to those who are concerned in the making or doing of things that produce life — rough first efforts like *1931* — are most valuable.

Works of art never spring full-grown, like Minerva from the head of Jupiter, out of nowhere. In the theatre we are still a nation of beginners. If those seeds of life in the theatre, often misnamed "experiments," are not fostered, nothing better is ever likely to follow. *1931* —, which Mr. Brown and others shunned, helped bring about plays over which they were quite enthusiastic four years later.

The audiences at *1931* — were far more taken with the play than the press. We couldn't fail to notice a kind of fervor in the nightly reception of *1931* — that was intense with a smoldering conviction uncharacteristic of the usual Broadway audience. All the business we did, however, was balcony business. When we announced the play's closing we received a great many letters pleading with us to keep it open — the play would surely catch on. We knew this wasn't so, but if we had had the money, we should have liked to keep the play open for at least that audience which still wanted to see it.

Strangers came backstage in a peculiar state of determination, asking what they could do for our organization, for the play. The play made them want to do *something*. Some of these people, we later learned, set up discussion groups, clubs, new little-theatre circles. Unions and other special organizations called us on the phone to tell us they would buy blocks of seats for future performances if we kept the play open.

The last night of the play the balcony was packed. Each night the audience had grown more vociferous. But that night there was something of a demonstration in the theatre, like the response of a mass meeting to a particularly eloquent speaker. As the actors — surprised and moved — were taking the curtain calls, a man in the balcony shouted: "Long live the Soviet Union!" Franchot Tone, on the stage, shouted back, "Hurrah for America!" Both outcries might be described as irrelevant, but evidently there was something in the air beyond theatrical appreciation.

Like the reviewers themselves, we were unprepared for the very thing we helped call to life. In the program for our second production I had published a short statement under the title: "What the Group Theatre Wants." The last sentences in this statement read: "In the end, however, the development of playwrights, actors, repertory and the rest are important only as they lead to the creation of a tradition of common values, an active consciousness of a common way of looking at and dealing with life. A theatre in our country today should aim to create an Audience. When an audience feels that it is really at one with a theatre; when audience and theatre-people can feel that they are both the answer to one another, and that both may act as leaders to one another, there we have the Theatre in its truest form. To create such a Theatre is our real purpose."

The production of *1931* — had made us aware, for the first time, of a new audience. It was an audience to whom such a play as *1931* — was more valuable than the successful *Reunion in Vienna*. It was an audience that later kept the Theatre Union going for a few seasons, helped sustain the Federal Theatre Project in experiments as diversified as the production of T. S. Eliot's *Murder in the Cathedral*, Lawson's *Processional*, in "documentaries" like *One Third of a Nation* and *Power*, in classics like *Dr. Faustus* and *Macbeth*. It was potentially the audience for a national theatre.

Our production of *1931* —, I say, helped awaken this audience. We sensed its stirring, but we did not yet fully appreciate its value. Mordecai Gorelik, who designed the sets for *1931* —, tried to call our attention to it. But he had an impatient manner and an extremist approach — or so it seemed to us. It appeared that he wanted us to abandon Broadway at once to reach the audience that couldn't afford Broadway prices. Broadway, he thought, was hopeless. We were impatient with his impatience. Gorelik became instrumental in forming a new theatre unit, which came to be known as the Theatre Collective — one of the first off-Broadway groups of the time. The Theatre Collective in 1933 revived *1931* — in the fond hope that below Times Square it would fare better than it had above it. This hope was not fulfilled.

All around us — outside of us — this new audience began to organize itself in small, at first imperceptible ways. But it took another two years for this gestation to manifest itself as a kind of movement in the theatre and in our social-cultural life.

Theatrically speaking, too, the production of *1931* — was notable. Many reviewers reacted to this aspect of the occasion, but they made the mechanical and æsthetically rather false distinction between "a bad play" and "a fine production." On the stage *1931* — glowed with stern beauty, sensitive, vibrant, full of heartache and mute love.

The process whereby a written play is absorbed into the whole context of a theatre production is something that not only most reviewers but many playwrights hardly understand. We had some striking examples of this in *1931* —.

One night, ten days before the opening of the play, Lee Strasberg singled out an extra in this production to show him how to make the emotion of one of the climactic crowd scenes real to himself. Usually when crowds are expected to create the uproar of a riot scene on the stage, the extras are told to be sincere and to make a big collective noise. Strasberg would not have it so. There was really no such thing as an extra in a play; and a crowd reaction — even off stage — had to be as true as anything in the play. To this end he patiently attempted to explain the technical means by which the mass upheaval at the play's final curtain could be transformed into a moment of individual reality for this actor. A half-hour or more of very quiet work went on while the company of thirty-five sat around and watched with keen interest.

Suddenly, like a shot, from the back of the house came the outraged cry of the author: "If you want to give lessons in acting,

do it somewhere else. We've got to open the show in ten days and
the production isn't ready." Strasberg, strangely self-possessed,
turned and said quietly: "I am responsible for the opening of the
play, which will take place at the scheduled time. As for what
is going on here now, please don't interfere with what you don't
understand."

In this production Franchot Tone's reputation as "the finest
young actor of recent arrival" was acknowledged. Many small
parts or bits were played by such people as Bromberg, Carnovsky, and Stella Adler.

It was not easy for our actors to take second place in this and
later productions. People like Stella Adler had worked a long time
in the theatre to achieve a position their talents warranted. To be
thrust into a bit for the sake of an ideal was a form of torture.
I did not appreciate at that time how much of a torture it was.
But I could see in Stella's eyes a pain and puzzlement the depth
of which it took me years to comprehend fully.

It was sometimes thought that she alone in the Group had the
problem of adjusting herself to a discipline the value and need of
which were more than once questioned. But she merely gave
most poignant and dramatic expression to a crisis that was sooner
or later to grip almost every member of the Group.

With the actor, who lives through exhibition, the element of
vanity is necessarily strong (and, to a large degree, justified), but
the problem goes beyond that. For even when the actor is willing
to submit to the discipline that bids him submerge himself for
the general good, the outside world, not understanding his motives, shames him, gibes at him, and assures him that he is a
"sucker" to "fall for that stuff." It doesn't believe in the ideology
that inspires the group which has set itself up within (and, despite
itself, against) the current. The outside world talks in terms of its
own experience or indoctrination and instructs the actor to take
care of himself first, last, and all the time

Because such a group as ours senses itself threatened by external pressures, it becomes jealous of its unity. It has a horror

of losing its people to forces outside it. When Bill Challee, shortly after the opening of *Connelly*, was offered one of the leading roles in a Jed Harris production, there was a small to-do about it that was prophetic of future developments.

Harris offered Bill, who was an extra in *Connelly*, his first big chance on Broadway. No contract bound him to the Group; Bill came to the directors and confessed that he wanted to play the part in the Harris production (at a salary of $150 a week as compared with the $40 the Group was paying him). Nevertheless, Bill was ready to abide by our decision. According to Lee Strasberg, there would have been no choice but for us to refuse, except that Harris had a contract at the time with Bromberg — made before the Group had formed — and that if we yielded Bill Challee to him, Harris would be inclined to look more kindly on our holding Bromberg.

We would have to present the problem to the whole body of the actors, for an offhand granting of permission to leave a Group production for a more advantageous position on the outside would set a precedent whereby anyone who had a similar opportunity might avail himself of it. This was the first time a conference on such a subject took place in the Group between actors and directors. It arose from no legal obligation, but from the intrinsic demands of our situation.

The actors deliberated the matter at some length and voted to allow Bill Challee to appear in the Harris show. After the vote Phoebe Brand said that though she had voted with the rest, she was a little hurt that anyone should have the desire to play elsewhere. Bill Challee was thankful for our decision and, as the Harris show was a failure, most gratified to be able to return to us in time for our second production.

On the closing of *1931* — we decided to revive *The House of Connelly* for the Christmas and New Year holiday season. The revival was merely a stopgap. We were preparing to take *Connelly* on a short road tour — to Philadelphia, Baltimore, Washington, and Boston — during which we might have time to prepare a third play.

Connelly was liked in these cities, but, as in New York, it did only moderately good business in the first three. In Boston the reviewers were most enthusiastic, particularly the excellent H. T. Parker of the *Transcript*. His review, one of the longest on record, praised us more lavishly for the spirit and intention of our theatre as well as for the production than I should have done myself. Parker and the others nevertheless predicted we would do very little business.

Unfortunately they were only too right. We hadn't enough money to pay the actors. Here one of the first and finest expressions of Group feeling manifested itself. The better-paid actors volunteered to cut their salaries so that those poorly paid might get their whole salary, such as it was. In this way we were able to maintain the company during the two weeks of our Boston run.

I have already mentioned our friendship with Maxwell Anderson. He lived in New City, New York, and invited Stella Adler and me to visit him for week-ends.

He divulged his ideas and plans. He wanted to write drama free of petty naturalism, journalese, concern with ephemeral manners. He sought characters whose emotions had scope, whose spirits soared, whose acts were worthy of celebration. He was ambitious to write drama of an epic stamp. I recognized in what he said the author of *What Price Glory?*, *Outside Looking In*, *Gods of the Lightning*.

But Anderson had gone on from there. He wanted to give his characters a heightened speech, not such as they had spoken in his early plays, but as they had begun to speak in his *Elizabeth the Queen*. He wanted them to speak verse — the language of heroes. It was in verse that most of the great plays of the past had been written; therefore verse was the proper medium for the most exalted drama.

Though I could not follow him completely in this reasoning, I believed his argument stemmed from healthy impulses. What worried me, however, was that he brooded over a suspicion that

American life had produced and was producing very few men he could admire, the kind of men who aroused him creatively. He was seeking his heroes elsewhere, and they would speak a language not of our time and place. I urged, with perhaps more subjective feeling than logic, that heroes must be discovered in the present, or at least in America, and that their language, whether in verse or prose, bear an American stamp.

Anderson announced one day that he had read a play by Racine that had an intriguing plot line. A little later he came on an article in the *American Mercury* about the semi-feudal civilization of New Mexico just before the Yankees put in their appearance in that state. The classic French plot fitted the kind of world that was pictured in the *Mercury* article. He decided to do a play for us on this material.

In a short time his play, *Night over Taos,* was completed. He sent it to me at once. My first impression was not a happy one. The play seemed bookish, contrived, uninspired. I was reluctant to have the Group do it.

Our decision hung fire for a week or more, and Max, understandably irritated, suggested that he might submit the play elsewhere. I reread the play, and though I thought it no better than the first time, I could see that it was, at any rate, a playable stage piece. The Group hadn't been deluged with scripts even after the praise accorded our first two productions; there was no other script on hand. I decided to do the Anderson play despite my opinion of it. When I told this to Lee Strasberg, he asked: "Suppose it fails?" which indicated he believed its chances were slim. "Then it will fail," was my reply. "The important thing is for us to continue our activity." We put the play into rehearsal in Washington.

We had decided after 1931 — to organize a campaign for an audience. A few people were engaged to work on this campaign, under Cheryl Crawford's supervision. We were going to create a membership in a Group Theatre Audience — not precisely a subscription idea. We thought regular subscribers were something of an artistic handicap. They implied a commitment to produce a fixed number of plays regardless of whether or not you had plays you wanted to do. The Guild found it easier to manage on the subscription plan than we should have, because it employed a different company for each play, whereas we used virtually the same company in all our plays. At that time, too, we rehearsed our productions longer than the customary four-week period of the commercial theatre.

To our prospective audience we offered "for the sum of $2 a twenty per cent reduction in box office prices," and we would also give them one special production free. There would also be meetings for the Group Audience at which we would discuss our current productions with them.

A little pamphlet was issued describing our aims and our financial setup. It included, besides quotations from the press on our first two productions, a statement by Waldo Frank, and a list of plays from which we hoped to choose our future productions. On March 14, 1932 the campaign was officially launched by a meeting at the Forty-eighth Street Theatre, at which the three directors spoke. There were more meetings at which prominent writers and theatre folk appeared.

As with most campaign talks, very little of import was said at these meetings. Nevertheless, at a gathering of the librarians of New York, addressed by Gilbert Seldes and Waldo Frank in April 1932, the latter introduced a note, rare and probably impractical for the occasion, that foreshadowed something of the days to come. "I suppose," Frank said, "the reason why I believe in the Group is because I am primarily interested in what I might call the creating of a new world. I am not alone — I am sure — in a belief that there must be a new society, a new humanity in the moral and spiritual as well as in the economic sense. A new humanity must be created — literally made up of human beings who have different values, who have a different vision and a different sense of the dignity of life, who have a different loyalty to the truth, and a different technique in expressing this truth than most of us have today. . . . There must be groups of conscious people patiently devoted, because of these positive impulses, to the ideal.

They must be organized to work toward the creating of a new world. . . .

"The one method whereby the new society may slowly and laboriously be created is a new alliance in place of the alliance of the intellectuals with the money class, an alliance of the men of mind, of vision, the artists, with the People, consciously working toward this creative end."

On the whole, our campaign was a failure, partly because we had little time and insufficient funds for such a campaign, but mostly because we were extremely amateurish in the handling of our public relations.

The Guild was not interested in financing the Anderson play, *Night over Taos*. Cheryl Crawford and I had resigned our posts at the Guild early in 1932. On February 19, 1932, the *New York Times* announced that the Group Theatre was now an independent organization. This did not make me very happy. I realized with a shock that we were now financially on the same competitive status as any commercial management. This was precisely what I had not wanted. We were not a commercial theatre.

Our situation now was basically untenable. Logically it would have been proper to quit at this point, but logic had nothing to do with our position. There was nothing for us to do but continue, and make the best of it.

In a speech in Town Hall, published February 21, 1932, Miss Helburn of the Theatre Guild summed up our situation: "The Group Theatre is attempting an important experiment in maintaining a permanent company with a single production method back of it, and attempting to integrate its authors and designers with the fabric of a theatre as a whole. But it is up against tremendous odds in a city like New York where costs are so high and competition so keen. . . . The American Theatre is an uncertain gamble from start to finish." She went on to say very significantly: "Should any good-sized city in America offer the capital to finance a strictly professional theatre for the production of new as well as old material over two years I would be tempted to leave home, husband and Guild, to prove to them that a vital theatre could not only be created beyond New York but that the third year could even show a profit to the organization. . . . But I am safe. *No one in the theatre ever looks three years ahead.*"

I looked three years ahead; and I am glad I did not see too clearly what the future held in store for me. "A certain blindness," a cynical Frenchman once said, "is necessary to carry out any important action with some degree of confidence."

Night over Taos was financed by Franchot Tone ($1,000), Maxwell Anderson ($2,500), and Dorothy Patten's father ($1,000). Robert Edmond Jones was asked to design it.

He did a fine job. His set and costumes were lovely, and were probably the most highly praised element of the production. They were, however — particularly the setting — a little passive in quality. They added to a contemplative, cloistral tone with which Strasberg invested the production. Like all of Strasberg's early work, it was distinguished by moments of sensitivity and beauty, but, as Strasberg later admitted, this approach was not what the play demanded.

In an article I wrote about *Night over Taos* the following passage occurs:

The Group Theatre insists that its plays should not be judged on their separate merits alone, but should be seen in relation to the plays that preceded them, should be regarded, in other words, as parts of a message which the Group Theatre as a whole hopes to communicate through its work with ever increasing scope and clarity. . . . *Night over Taos* is, in essence, a poem in praise of heroes and the heroic life. Nearly all of Maxwell Anderson's work sounds this note of wonder and worship for the man who fights against the odds of difficult circumstances. . . . To recapture this sense of grandeur is something the Group Theatre feels is needed in times such as the present when the pressure of events makes it clear that to survive and to grow, man will have to develop a muscular, dynamic attitude toward life, or perish. Such an attitude toward life in relation to the contemporary scene will inform many of the future Group Theatre plays.

I quote this article because it mingles, in a curious form, elements of sincere feeling with the humbug of publicity. Privately I was rather apologetic about this play.

The reviews evinced respect and boredom. It looked as if *Taos* would have to close the first Saturday night of its run. The directors and author acquiesced in this fatality. This was announced to the cast. Then a strange thing occurred. Stella Adler maintained with unexpected force that we had no right to close a play so quickly, after so much hard and good work had been done on it. Stella had never thought highly of the play, she had disliked her part, and here she was saying: "Actors never close a play when there is the slightest possibility of keeping it running."

The actors voted to keep the play running and to accept any salary for the next week that the management could afford to pay. The company on closing night received ten dollars apiece, and the few who could afford to refused even this.

The closing of *Night over Taos* meant the closing of our first season. To the ordinary theatre manager the end of a season is in some respects a relief. He dismisses most of his employees while he seeks a new property. "Group life" was a continuous activity. We were concerned with each of our people fifty-two weeks a year.

Our last attempt to secure a patron was a visit to Otto Kahn made by Cheryl Crawford and me. He had seen our first two productions and was impressed by them. We had ideals, he said, and the ability to realize them. What did we want? Not money, I said, and went on to explain the Group's problems generally. He interrupted me: "But you are talking of nothing but money!" No matter how it was put, the economic problem was closely related to all the others.

Cheryl Crawford apparently knew how to state our needs more acceptably to him. Yet his response was dejected, vague, uncertain. We did not know how hard hit he had been by the crash. We could not conceive of his millionaire's worries. We wondered when he spoke of "those damn-fool congressmen," when he murmured something about the capitalist system not working very well, "but what else is there?" Finally we were puzzled when he spoke, as if in soliloquy, of a total abandonment of effort. "Perhaps Mahatma Gandhi is right," he said. Kahn spoke gently: he was tired, at a loss, unable to interest himself in many things — such as the Group — that a few years before would readily have won his support. We were witnessing a breakdown from the top.

Our personal situation was very bad. In Boston I had begun to borrow. The apartment I lived in was hardly furnished except for a few beds, chairs, and a long table salvaged from *Taos*. Some of the actors could not manage to pay their rent. What resources they had were pooled so that a few of them could live together. Several were given shelter by the few who had money.

At first we were able to use the offices above the Forty-eighth Street Theatre in which to conduct our business. A little later we had to move, and my bare but large apartment on West Fifty-eighth Street became our center. Our landlady protested that I was using the apartment for business, that we were exhausting the electric supply of the building, and that, to add insult to injury, we were not prompt with the rent.

Despite all this, an intense spiritual as well as professional activity was going on all the time. I gave a series of talks on the lessons of the first season. I pointed out, in one, that playwrights were still "behind" us in our thought, by which I meant that none of the plays I read seemed representative of us; they were not our drama. What was "our thought" and "our drama"? My definitions may have been nebulous, but I had a sense that we were still to reach something — a combination of rhapsodic statement in an essentially American vein, expressed through realistically conceived characters — and that the continuance of our effort, despite all hazards, would help produce such a drama.

We did not just talk. Cheryl, for her part, raised money. Joseph Verner Reed contributed a check of $1,000. There were a few other contributions of a similar nature though of smaller amounts. Together with the two-dollar checks that had been sent in we were able to finance the second summer of country rehearsal.

New actors came to us: Roman Bohnen from the Goodman Theatre in Chicago, Russell Collins from the Cleveland Playhouse. New apprentices applied, like Elia Kazan and Alan Baxter from the Yale School of the Drama.

But the big problem, we knew, was the play problem. We planned to invite young playwrights to accompany us to our summer camp. We hoped that a live theatrical environment might stimulate them to write plays for us. Lynn Riggs and Paul Green were on our list of guests. I had read two or three of Albert Bein's unproduced scripts, which, despite crudity, showed promise. Bein was asked to join us. So too were Albert Maltz and George Sklar, whose play *Merry-Go-Round* had created something of a stir during the spring. We made overtures to the poet George O'Neil, who was going to write a play. He was rather timid about us, and asked: "Is it true that from now on you are going to do only labor plays?" This was the first we had heard of this, and we laughed at the notion.

A writer recommended by Edmund Wilson brought in a script entitled *Crazy American*. It was the story of a mercurial, imaginative youth with a genius for inventing. What was he going to do with his talent? The play was a kind of realistic parable of America's quandary in the early thirties. It wasn't an altogether clear play; the writing had an elusive nervous quality as if in constant flight from a fixed point, but its theme and manner interested us.

We told the author, Charles R. Walker, that it would be our first production the following season. It needed more work, which we would do together when he returned from a motor trip he was taking around the country. (From 1931 through 1935 all America's younger writers were going on bus and motor trips through the country.)

On his return Walker announced rather curtly that he had decided to give his play to a new producer who would try it out in a summer theatre. What had prompted this change? We were not a commercial theatre, he said, so we offered none of the advantages of such a setup; on the other hand, we were not "a real revolutionary theatre," for which alone it might be worth making sacrifices.

Practically speaking, all this was, of course, utter rot, but it

introduced me to a vein of discussion with which I was to become much more familiar in another two years.

Bitterly disappointed by this experience, I raked my memory
for suitable scripts that I had read at the Guild. One was by the
novelist Dawn Powell. It had been called *The Party* and had
struck me as tough, but none the less talented and witty. In this
play a salesman for an advertising house practically forces his
pretty wife into the arms of a big buyer from out of town in order
to get his business. In my original reader's report I had written
that I was skeptical of the play's success because audiences might
find it unpleasant. I forgot this now and decided to buy it. Plays
of an original character were rare, and though this play was not
particularly in our line, it did have an unusual sting to it. It
gave us, moreover, an opportunity to introduce a new writer.

At the same time a revised version of another play I had read
at the Guild was submitted to us. It was John Howard Lawson's
Success Story. On rereading it I found myself most enthusiastic.
When I had finished the first two acts, I rushed a wire of acceptance to Lawson.

Some actors were dropped at the end of the first season; one
resigned. With others we confessed frank misgivings as to their
future possibilities, but we agreed that as long as an actor knew
of our doubts and was willing to pursue his career with us, we
were glad to give him the opportunity to prove us wrong.

Stella Adler hinted of a certain vague dissatisfaction she felt
with Lee Strasberg's technique in regard to the actor. That is,
while she hinted it to Strasberg, she hurled it at me. Strasberg
was aware of Stella's uneasiness, but ascribed it mostly to tempera-
mental difficulties and to the fact that she had to adjust to an
organization in which she was one of many, who were given, so
to speak, equal treatment, whereas she was accustomed to being
treated as a special and favored personality. Strasberg told Stella
frankly that perhaps their difficulties might "work out in time,"
and that, after all, he would not direct all the Group plays.

It was true that the Group environment, as well as some of its
methods, were a real trial to Stella. She was both attracted and

repelled by the Group. I did not quite understand this divided re-action in Stella, though I was aghast at its sharpness. Sometimes I thought the whole question reduced itself to the matter of parts: her first season had been very disappointing to her from this stand-point. But there was more to it than that. She seemed cut off from her old environment and could not accept the new. The old was flattering, pleasant, homelike, but without very much crea-tive future. The new struck her as raw, cold, indifferent to her as an individual.

My attitude was that even if the Group hurt her (as I could not help seeing it did), it was still good for her. After all, I rea-soned, the Group would hurt all of us in different respects. New movements have a way of being just as harsh as they are helpful; but if we allowed the difficulties to deter us from going ahead, none of us would make any progress. Avoidance of difficulty (or pain) is often the plausible first step in a person's degeneration.

I remembered Stella saying to me just before she joined the Group that she hoped I would not have her playing small parts. I answered: "In our first production you will play a maid who bobs on and off the stage." She grimaced and grinned, knowing I was joking, and yet she sensed something like a warning in the joke. But I was in love with her, so surely she was protected. I would want her to realize her great potentialities and to shine. I did.

I felt the Group was a place where we would ultimately all shine according to our talents, and hers were real and consid-erable. But we did not need to think of shining; we simply had to do our work. The rest would take care of itself.

I did not want to force Stella to be part of our theatre. I did not believe anyone should be forced to violate his own nature, no matter how right the cause, but I could discern in Stella an ideal-ism that craved such a theatre as we promised. For this reason I struggled with her doubts, bore her personal blame. I did not relent before her very real grief — I even defended Strasberg, the Group, and myself against many just criticisms — because I be-lieved that to accept defeat now was to yield to a weakness that in the end would prove destructive.

No doubt this drama between Stella and me was a personal one.

Perhaps I should have been less patient (demoniacally patient, someone said) if I had loved her less. But it was a personal drama in which was mirrored my whole attitude toward the Group. Stella's love and hatred of it, her self-torment over it, her objective battle against it, symbolized for me all that the Group had to overcome within itself, within the world, and each member within his own nature. To Stella, my ability to treat a personal matter like this — a matter in which the girl I presumably loved was involved in a life and death agony — was a sign of an impersonality that was inhuman. And she did not like me any better for it.

Very late one night, shortly after the closing of *Taos*, I was awakened by Luther Adler. He had recently joined us (having given up a good part in a Broadway success to play a bit for us at practically no salary) and he was now living with me, for he had even less money than I, and no apartment at all. He awakened me like a man who has an unendurable torment racking his soul. "Harold," he said when he succeeded in arousing me to some semblance of consciousness, "it's March and we are not going away till June. That's over two months. How are we going to live until then?" "I don't know," I mumbled, heavy with sleep. "We'll live." "But, Harold," he persisted, "*how* are we going to live?" "We'll live," I insisted. "We'll just live." That is how I solved many of our problems!

When we arrived at Dover Furnace, New York, for our second summer, we were all very much alive.

CHAPTER SEVEN

Ferment

ABOUT fifty people spent the second summer of the Group's life under its auspices. We read the two plays we had chosen for fall production. The actors thought Dawn Powell's *The Party* (soon renamed *Big Night*) very funny; they were impressed with Lawson's *Success Story*. I had planned for Strasberg to direct both plays, not being sure of Cheryl Crawford's ability as a director and still lacking confidence in my own. Strasberg assured me *Big Night* wasn't for him; and both Cheryl and he tried to persuade me to direct *Success Story*, the content and manner of which they thought suited my temperament. But I held to my belief that Strasberg was the man to continue the Group actors' training. It was decided that Cheryl should direct *Big Night* and Strasberg *Success Story*.

As *Success Story* was still being revised, rehearsal of *Big Night* began first. Strasberg initiated classes designed to stimulate the actors' imagination and resourcefulness. During the first summer truth of emotion had been emphasized; now it was theatricality and clarity of interpretation. One of the exercises the actors had to do was improvisation of a new sort. Three unrelated words were announced — "soup," "kill," "store," let us say — and two actors were to compose a scene forthwith in which these three words were to serve as a springboard for a coherent dramatic text. Another exercise consisted in taking words like "liberty," "America," "success," for which each actor was to find a concise pantomimic equivalent.

Later in the summer, while Strasberg was busy directing *Success Story*, I continued these classes. I had actors take poems and create acting scenes with them not necessarily related to the original meaning of the poem. Bobby Lewis revealed a special talent in these exercises. He converted Whitman's "I Sing the Body Electric" into a farcical scene in which a peculiarly unheroic character prepared for the day, brushing his teeth, taking a shower, and so on. The "To be or not to be" speech from *Hamlet* became a soap-box orator's harangue, calling for action!

Strasberg had asked the actors to prepare dramatic scenes based on well-known paintings. I had records of classical music played, and the actors improvised scenes suggested to them by the music. One of the most interesting, inspired by a Brahms quintet, was that of a child's death during an operation. Later it became quite a well-known piece at special Group occasions, benefits, and the

like. Morris Carnovsky and Joe Bromberg grew especially proficient in comic improvisations in gibberish, the idea of which was
to make the actor dramatically expressive without the use of real
words.

The most ambitious achievement of this phase of the Group's
experimental practice was an odd pantomime, conceived by Art
Smith, in which George Grosz's postwar drawings were combined
with words from the Book of Psalms, accompanied by a song in
which Marlene Dietrich invites her boy friends to try her pianola.
Almost half the Group company played individual characters in
this pantomime, which had its first performance on our tennis
court. It had a mordant quality of weird satire, reflecting the
decadence of postwar society, but it seemed somehow to fit the
atmosphere of 1932-3. It was done at workers' clubs that year,
and the following year Ralph Steiner made a film of it.

Tamiris came up with us that summer and gave "body classes"
to all who were strong enough to take them. They virtually crip-
pled Franchot Tone and Clifford Odets. Strasberg gave a few
talks on the history of the theatre, while I worked with Lawson
on his script, and held classes for the new apprentices — young
actors not officially part of the Group company.

The central role in *Success Story* was assigned to Luther Adler,
which was something of a shock to several of our actors. Though
he had joined us in our third production, he had already encountered some resistance to his entry into our midst, which was significant not of any animus against him but of the resistance that
confronts any new person upon entering a tightly knit unit. Such
a unit, contrary to logic or its own will, quickly develops the psychology of a protective society. It forgets that it was organized
for an objective task, and begins to consider its function one of
guarding the interests of the individuals who compose it.

Every new face around the Group began to constitute something of a challenge to every old member. This condition was
probably made more acute now because while our first three plays
offered some sort of activity for all our actors, the two plays we

were now doing called for small casts, and a few actors had no part in either play.

Among the people who accompanied us that summer were friends of certain Group members. They paid their way, thus adding to the small profit that our summer supervisor (another friend) was to make for his time and trouble. These visitors and others who drove up over week-ends began to remark a certain coldness toward them among the Group.

People who were unfamiliar to the Group or not supplied, so to speak, with a moral or professional passport of some kind were practically shunned. They began to resent this and complained to me about it. I did not understand it then, nor did I know how to cope with it. Without realizing or wishing it, the Group was turning in on itself.

Visitors, I say, were shocked by this, but the more socially easy Group people were equally annoyed. Stella Adler, for example; Franchot Tone, too. In Franchot's case the matter was special. The girl Franchot was attached to at the time, the one who worked with us in the old Riverside Drive days, visited him one week-end. Somehow we didn't think she was Group material. Franchot's life with the Group would have been much easier if she had spent more time with us, but Franchot was too proud to say so, and we were too one-tracked in our thinking to notice it. The girl felt separated from Franchot by us and would have been pleased if we had asked her to remain and work with us, even as an apprentice. We disregarded her very existence, and Franchot was irritated by our tactlessness.

Franchot's problem, however, was deeper than this. In Boston, when I finally got around to talking to him about his refractoriness, he asked me questions relating to my estimate of him as an actor. By my lights, how good would he become? In answering him I dwelt on his need to stick by what was strongest and most alive in himself. Tears came to his eyes. He confessed later that when I left he had actually sobbed, but he added with a sly grin: "It didn't do much good: the feeling didn't last."

Franchot loved us out of a great need, a feeling that we were good people who were bringing him just that supply of sound work and clear faith that, despite the advantages of his background, he had missed all his life. But he was very much part of the world that had provided him with these advantages, and he could not, would not, turn his back on it; it was the *big* world, the substantial world, in which all of us, willy-nilly, were living.

Of course, even in his attachment to the big world there was a contradiction. Franchot's father, though associated with business, was basically a scientist; and Franchot's mother was as much of an aristocrat as we ever get in America. Both of them were glad that Franchot preferred the Group to the ordinary commercial theatre. But the entertainment channels of the big world lie in the commercial theatre. We have no national theatre for our "best people." We have Broadway, and Broadway has Hollywood. The cradle of opinion with theatre folk was not some Mermaid Tavern of intellectuals or artists, but the speakeasies of Fifty-second Street.

There they laughed at Franchot's devotion to the Group. Franchot probably thought Lilyan Tashman and her crowd who came to see him in *Taos* lacked taste, but he did not, for all that, feel particularly comfortable at their seeing him in a flop that had been preceded by another, whose most enthusiastic audience sat in the balcony uttering strange cries of approval. Franchot was torn between this Group of tactless people, led chiefly by two exasperated hotheads who offered a way of life that was personally real and perhaps part of the mainstream of the time, and a Broadway plus Hollywood which, though he knew it to be shoddy, actually possessed the only power and glory the world could offer today.

Franchot behaved more peculiarly this summer than the last. He was remarkably fine at rehearsals of *Success Story*, but he was rather antisocial in other ways. He drank stiffly, and carried off some other pretty good bottlemen to drink with him almost every night after rehearsals. When he came back he sometimes took delight in driving his car over the main lawn and crashing all the garden furniture left there during the day. He grew a beard, walked about in a loincloth, went shooting fairly close to the rehearsal grounds. He shied away from most of us, alternating between a distant courtesy that implied an insult, and the manner of a cagey maniac.

With all this, Franchot was always shrewd and observant. He saw what was going on. What was going on was a subtle transformation within the Group as a whole. The very air was fermenting with something new that blew from we know not where, but which roused everyone to doubts, questions, wonder, eagerness, dispute.

When I spoke of *Success Story* to the actors I said something about the problems of "sensitive people" in our civilization. An actress who had tried to provoke me to debate during the first summer said to me after this talk: "You seem to divide people into the sensitive and the crass. That is a very sentimental distinction. People are divided by economic classes. There is the capitalist class and the working class." In relation to the play we were doing, I replied, her distinction was less useful than mine, and I was interested in the interpretation of our play for actors, not for classroom analysis.

Immediately I found visitors, friends, and friends of friends crowding me with questions, such as: "Why is a specific political education harmful to actors or artists?" "Why do you stop short of the logical consequences of your theories?" I was more surprised than I admitted.

This sudden preoccupation with social, economic, and political matters was like a fever running through our camp. Where had it come from — from the inside or the outside? None of the people around us were connected directly with business, industry, labor, or politics. It didn't matter either what sides were taken. In truth, there were as yet no sides.

Some evenings Lee Strasberg, who had received copies of newly arrived publications about the recent Soviet theatre, had a Russian acquaintance, who worked in our kitchen, translate these volumes for those who were interested. A good many gathered around and listened to the extemporaneous translation as if some tale from a new *Arabian Nights* were being told.

The books were mostly æsthetic and technical, but the quality of the listening was, for the most part, one of romantic awe. Russian theatre people had done great work under the most crucially difficult circumstances. They had been devoted, courageous, and boldly creative in times that might prove either the crack of doom or the dawn of a great age. Weren't we people of the same stripe?

"A theatre," said Vachtangov, "is an ideologically cemented collective." In essence that is what I had said before I had heard of these post-Stanislavsky Russians, but they had added the glamour of a new phraseology that smacked of science, of something new. More than that, behind the Russian's words was the authority of a great historical event — a Revolution — the brilliant example of a theatre carried on in days of upheaval and starvation, and, above all, something that seemed very strong and definite compared with our verbose incantations. What ideology cemented our collective? Nothing that could be put in a single phrase, only things that could be set down as "mysticism," whereas the Russians, no matter how vague or foreign their terms, had the prestige of a whole world behind them.

There was a buzz, a hum, a spirit of inquiry and controversy all around us. The translator of the Russian books was himself a philosophical anarchist who disliked any system, but the Soviet system particularly. Among our guests was a schoolteacher whom somebody labeled a "Right deviationist" (whatever that meant); there was still another person who suspected every statement he disagreed with as "Trotskyism," while most of the actual members of the Group listened, amazed.

Just as new topics for discussion had developed, so all kinds of people appeared among us, and the more remote from the world of the arts — the closer to real life at its realest — the more they held our attention. From out of the West came an Irishman who had heard about us from someone in New Mexico. This pilgrim had actually served as a high officer in the IRA back in 1920, and was still in bad odor at home for his irreconcilability. Later he published a book, *Army without Banners*, containing much of the material with which he held us spellbound. But at that time Ernest O'Malley was a symbol of the restless, adventurous, some-

what militant spirit that had descended upon us. Eminently proper
in background (his father was an M.D. of Tory opinion), he had
broken from his family, become a dispossessed rebel, risen
through youthful daring and pain to a new kind of eminence. Far
from the scene of his original revolt, he remained a seasoned,
ribald, rather gentle, lonely figure of a man, seeking some new
cause to fight for — though it was only in Ireland, he confessed,
that he could ever feel rooted and true. His appearance and presence among us that summer, though they went unnoticed by
some, were altogether in tune with the spirit of our environment.

John Howard Lawson, whom I considered at the time the hope
of our theatre, also fitted into our scene not only by his contribution as a playwright, but by his love of discussion, even of dispute.
From time to time he vented opinions that led us to believe that
though he was definitely of progressive, even radical opinion, he
was violently opposed to official Communist doctrine. He was
mulling over a play that bore the tentative title *Red Square*
which would deal with the revolutionary movement all over the
world.

Some people were troubled because Strasberg and I, despite our
interest in all the subjects studied, debated, or jabbered about,
refused to commit ourselves very definitely. No one could tell
where we stood. I particularly seemed to resist being swept into
any final conclusions. Despite my propensity for critical generali-
zation, I listened with a certain skepticism to the big terms that
were bandied about, since I am a little suspicious of ideas that
the mind borrows before blood or experience have made them
part of us. When Joe Bromberg asked me one day: "What do you
think of all the talk and reading that have been going on this
summer?" I replied that it was a sign of growth, a healthy response to the currents of the day, but that it would be valuable
only if it became particularized with each individual. Whatever
information could not really be used by us was false knowledge,
a detriment rather than an advantage.

The atmosphere of our camp was much more unsettled than it
had been the first summer. Albert Bein was bitterly unhappy be-

cause his *Heavenly Express* seemed more of a good notion to me
than a producible play. George O'Neil was disturbed in these
overemotional, overloud surroundings. He needed greater soli-
tude for his work than our camp could allow, and he felt spiritually and physically jostled, surrounded as he was by so much
brawling youth. During the summer he managed to finish a play
called *American Dream*, which the Guild produced next season.

Clifford Odets also wrote a play — a very bad play — about a
genius of the Beethoven kind. It showed no trace of talent, which
was rather surprising after the interesting if confused start of his
previous (Philadelphia) play. I hardly said a word to him about
his new play, but I suggested instead that he write about the
people he had met and observed the past few years.

The day came when Strasberg was no longer able to tolerate
the disruptive ambiguity of Franchot's behavior. He decided to
have the showdown I had recommended the year before, and
both of us now confronted Franchot with ultimatum written on
our faces. Franchot admitted at once that he had decided to quit
the Group, that he was going into pictures. I do not know whether
he had already made arrangements or whether our severity at
this meeting finally decided him. I am inclined to believe that
some of his mischievous conduct arose from an anger with himself,
and some was designed to provoke us to such a discussion as we
were having. Perhaps, however, he expected a gentler approach,
for people like Franchot always want evidence that they are
loved. Strasberg, hurt himself, lashed forth a white-hot "We don't
care" when Franchot disclosed his intentions. "I know you don't
care," Franchot answered quietly but painfully, as if to say: "That
is exactly why I wish to go."

That day the bad news of Franchot's resignation was announced to the Group at a special meeting addressed by Strasberg. It was the first resignation of any importance from our
organization. The actors were shocked, for they appreciated Franchot's value. Strasberg's talk was calculated to affirm the strength
and integrity of the Group, which could ill afford to keep a member whose spirit had turned against it. When the day came for

Franchot to leave, he told me he was going to try Hollywood. At
Tony's, on West Fifty-second Street, he wept over his drink.

The last days of our summer in Dover Furnace were nervous
and gay. There was the renewed vigor that always preceded the
return to New York and the season's challenge. There was a kind
of boiling up of all the conflicting currents that had been rife
throughout the past two months.

On the serious side I had suggested the creation of a Group
restaurant. This idea indicates how I had begun to regard the
Group. It was to be a center, not alone for theatre folk, but for
everyone interested in our work and ideas. The presence among
us of so many different creative people proved that the significance of the Group extended beyond the limits of the theatre.
What I wanted for the Group, what all these people wanted, was
the chance to tie sporadic individual work into units of collective
endeavor. This would not only strengthen them individually but
would serve to make their values objectively effective, forceful,
permanent.

All the next fall I made various attempts to get someone to set
up this Group restaurant for us, since naturally I knew very little
about how such a thing would actually function. I hoped it would
be the first and, in a sense, the humblest expression of a way of
life that would later produce its own new magazine, school, concerts, art gallery, picture house, lecture platform, publishing establishment, and what not. But we were so financially infirm in
our own chosen field that nothing could be done even with this
modest proposal.

The restaurant came to be something of a Group joke. A Group
magazine? A Group school? A Group film project? Small gestures
in these directions were made later, but with no support except
for single stage productions, all these projects remained merely
inspirational, expressions of hope and intent rather than major
activities.

Was all this, then, just futile? No. When I described these
dreams, I pointed out that the Group could not realize them alone,

that it could only serve as a focus or clearing house for such activities. To a certain extent this actually happened. Four years later, for example, Paul Strand and Ralph Steiner derived much from us in the formation of their Frontier Films, which produced two or three notable documentaries.

It matters little that some of these people came to disagree with us, even to attack us. It is even of little moment that magazines, theatre groups, and schools which drew much of their first impetus directly from us often appeared to us narrower, more sectarian, than we thought desirable. It is hardly important today that certain organizations, which I shall have occasion to describe, never acknowledged their kinship, but rather attempted to prove their innocence of any relationship with us, by ignoring or denouncing us. What is important was that the Group as a whole and many of its individual members began to contribute direct support and influence to various constructive activities inside and outside the theatre.

While I was expatiating on the larger purpose of the Group, a very concrete situation had to be faced. Lee Shubert, after seeing a rehearsal of *Success Story*, had agreed to back it, but the amount of money he was ready to provide as the weekly salary budget for the cast, while it was greater than the sum actually needed to pay the actors who composed it, was not sufficient to maintain all the members of our Group. Indeed, in order to render the sum laid out by Shubert adequate to the commitments made to the actors, the directors agreed to forgo their own salary for a period of at least five weeks.

Cheryl Crawford proposed therefore that we explain the situation to our actors and frankly admit that a certain number of our people could not be taken care of while they were not engaged in either of the two productions then in rehearsal. We would grant these people the right to seek parts elsewhere during this period, though we would continue to regard them as Group members. This was an eminently practical suggestion. Lee Strasberg, however, objected. He pointed out that while this plan represented sound business practice under the circumstances, it meant

that our actors merely constituted a stock company, not members
of a Theatre. I sided with Cheryl in this matter, partly because
her plan seemed the only reasonable one and partly (though I
would not confess it then) because I suspected that we had un-
dertaken to support too many actors whose abilities and useful-
ness by no means merited such support. Thus only about eighteen
of our thirty people were to be paid during the season of 1932–3.

On the lighter side the last days of the summer were marked
by a kind of Rabelaisian playfulness. There were a series of house
entertainments — shows the actors put on for themselves and their
visitors. A sketch in doggerel represented the three directors in
outlandish caricature. Margaret Barker as Cheryl Crawford was
a kind of female cowboy, addressing herself with laconic shrewd-
ness to her two quixotic partners. Art Smith as Lee Strasberg was
bowed over with books, stuffed in every imaginable place in his
clothing. Morris Carnovsky did me as a heavy bearded angel, an
electric light and a symbol of lightning on his brow, while in his
arm he cradled a stuffed silk stocking to represent a lady's leg.
In addition he prefaced every remark, high-sounding and unintelligible, with an explosive "Goddammit." In another sketch
the spectral Grover Burgess, for some obscure reason assuming a
thick German accent, thundered: "The Group does not produce
plays — only Works!"

This was the summer a visitor unknown to me, but reputed
to be a poet, asked his friend in New York to wire him if the
"revolution" broke out; it was the summer that one of our week-
end guests was the seventy-year-old president of the Detroit Edi-
son Company; it was the summer Stella Adler, early one morning, shoved me as I tossed restlessly in bed and said: "Don't sleep
like a great man, just sleep"; it was the summer that provoked
the rumor on Broadway that the Group was a free-love farm and
that we had all been converted to Communism. For myself, I
remember it as the time my friend Sykes said to me: "The Group
is really a training-ground for citizenship."

CHAPTER EIGHT

Hard Going

THOUGH I hardly ever thought in terms of box office, I had a feeling that *Success Story* would live up to its title. Not only was there something provocative in its theme and main characters, but it was written with a new kind of vividness, in which a hectic poetry was compounded from the slogans of advertisements, the slang of gangsterdom, and echoes of Old Testament music.

It was not a success. The press was divided, and even the favorable notices had a forbidding quality. "For the first time this season Broadway has seen a play about which audiences may disagree with some point and passion," said Joseph Wood Krutch in the *Nation*. Heywood Broun thought it "one of the most moving and interesting of current dramatic attractions," but, as another reviewer noted, "When John Howard Lawson writes a play he runs a temperature." Though you would think otherwise, the big audience does not enjoy getting that hot.

The reviews of this play were the first to rouse my indignation against the dramatic columns of the New York press. As I reread these and other notices of our productions, I realize that much of what was said gave a fair and accurate picture of the average intelligent reaction. I shared many of the reviewers' opinions myself; often, indeed, they were extremely generous — in a number of instances more generous than I should have been. Yet they made me angry. I do not speak of a producer's anger that springs from the disappointment and frustration of his hopes, I refer to an impersonal protest that cannot be directed against any individual expression of taste.

By virtue of his independence the reviewer's position is at once too modest and too powerful. His position signifies, in effect, that he writes only as a representative member of the audience; he states his reaction without ties, prejudice, or special authority beyond whatever competence the reader may find in him. The reviewer always implies that he stands for nothing, that he is not responsible to anyone, that he writes as he pleases. Thus he is an honest, even unpretentious man.

It is precisely in his independence, humility, and freedom that the reviewer's evil lurks. For he cannot be held to anything, he represents nothing definite, he has no intellectual identity; his mind is a private affair, and his change of mind may be an accident.

When Bernard Shaw wrote about a play, we cannot be sure he was fair or right, but what he demanded of the theatre and its artists and why he wanted these things was always made entirely clear. He was committed, not "independent." He preferred a bad play of Ibsen to the best of Pinero, and the substance of his review was not to assert this, but to make his readers understand the reason. He spoke more kindly of the immature efforts of some insurgent group attempting the "new drama" than of the most solid achievements of Henry Irving's Lyceum productions. This was perhaps improper and certainly unfair, but it was constructive — if you were of a like mind; and, though exasperating if you weren't, it was something that could be fought as a clear issue.

The reviews of *Success Story* were not bad. If they said the play was "confused," had I not thought and written the same when I reported on it for the Theatre Guild? What made me angry — as I was to be many times again until I began to understand the root of the mischief, which did not begin or end with the press — what made me angry was that so few reviewers ever came to grips with the play itself. If one of them had written: "We know what the author wishes to say, and despite the fact that his play vaguely resembles such harmless entertainment as *Counsellor-at-Law*, we think it a dangerously false play," I would have fought the man, but I could not have been angry with him. For a critic such as this would prove himself a man of standards, and, having standards, he would be constrained to defend them; he would himself have to be a fighter. But how combat a force without definition, how carry on a debate with a man who disarms you by admitting his opinions are only a "smattering of ignorance"? Unlike other people, our reviewers are powerful because they believe in nothing.

In this instance, for example, the reviewers pointed out that *Success Story* was the old story of the boy who makes good, only to find that his victories are vain and bitter. Actually this was merely the visible framework or schoolbook aspect of the play. Its essence was an account of what happens to an idealistic force when it finds no effective social form to contain it. The protagonist of *Success Story* becomes a desperately destructive man because he sees no way his unusual energy, imagination, and sense of truth can operate in harmony with the society that confronts him. It is only by becoming society's enemy and the betrayer of his own deepest values that he can succeed in it.

It does not matter whether my interpretation is the correct one. It is significant only in so far as it *is* an interpretation, while most reviewers offered none of their own. More serious than this, however, were the comparisons made in reviewing the play — comparisons I cite only because they are typical of a permanent disease in our theatre and its critical world. "Altho *Clear All Wires* is the most nearly expert of the new plays, *Success Story* is the most stimulating." *Clear All Wires* was a farce comedy about a loud-mouthed reporter in Moscow. Why was it brought up at all? Because it opened about the same time as *Success Story*. It was another piece of theatre ware for sale. Lawson, whose main theme at the time was the anguish of choice between the acceptance of or resistance to society was set beside writers who desired no more than to offer a "good show."

One major part in *Success Story* was disastrously miscast. (We believed in those days that proper direction could make any competent actor give a satisfactory interpretation of a role.) We were severely criticized for this miscasting — and justly. But one reviewer went further by asserting that we did not cast our plays as well as Mr. Shumlin had cast *Clear All Wires*. "The warmest friends art has in this city could wish that the Group Theatre had considerably more expertness in the casting and direction of its plays." The season before, the same reviewer had pointed out that we could not cast strictly to type as we were working on the basis of a permanent company; he had had nothing but praise for the direction of our first three plays, but now he chose to imply a certain amateurishness in Lee Strasberg, who had directed all those plays as well as the present one.

The same reviewer proved the pretentiousness and emptiness of our claims every time he disliked one of our productions, while asserting these same claims were vindicated whenever he liked one. For nine years he flattered or traduced us in turn, till he ceased to have any individual personality for us at all and became simply one of the press whose kiss or bite was almost equally impersonal, unpredictable, savorless, and incomprehensible. The press was finally nothing you could argue about; it was a kind of natural phenomenon as pleasant as a zephyr or as disastrous as a hailstorm — a perhaps necessary evil which sometimes brought benefits, but at all times remained outside the theatre, parasitic and dangerous.

In my own view, the production of *Success Story* was uneven and remarkable. Luther Adler gave what most people agreed was "one of the finest performances the present day theatre has housed." Not only was his theatrical flair striking, but there was a detailed observation in his portrait of the progress of the play's protagonist from the impetuous uncoordinated boy in the beginning to the mordant and precociously leonine captain of industry at the end that had meaning as well as color. No less creative was Stella Adler, both poignantly sensitive and powerful, with something of the grand line of the heroic tradition. Franchot Tone, who had agreed to open in the play and appear in it during the first five weeks of its run, achieved a wistfulness, a humor, and a sense of dignified though bewildered defeat that was a truly profound marriage of the actor and the part. These performances, the heart of the production, except for the fourth part that was wretchedly costumed and wigged as well as miscast, were the fruit not only of the actors' fine gifts but of a directorial understanding of a high order.

For the rest, there were flaws in the handling of a few minor characters that were partly due to Strasberg's desire to direct according to certain new ideas he had about social interpretation and theatricality. The characteristic feeling of the salesman type, he thought, could be embodied in a jazzlike rhythm. At one time he suggested that he would make the play's heroine a little unsympathetic because she represented a retrogressive social type. This, fortunately, he did not succeed in doing because of the part itself, the actress who played it, and his own talent. But it was significant that he was sufficiently influenced — disturbed would perhaps be a more accurate term — by his reading and the prevalent discussions of the day to attempt artificial manipulation of his actors.

When we recovered a bit from the shock of the mediocre notices, which had a disastrous effect on the box office, we were full of fight. We wrote letters to the press, caused others to be written, and tried to counteract the reviewers' reservations by publishing the more enthusiastic statements of prominent artists and publicists. We held a symposium on the play; and, urged by Luther Adler, who protested that we were not exploiting the play's full possibilities, we began a special campaign to reach the audiences that might appreciate the play and the performances. All this was not without effect; for some weeks business improved and the production won a great many admirers.

I said we fought for the play, but this must be qualified by a further statement. We suffered from a peculiar kind of sensibility. Failure to the ordinary producer is a business setback, which he remedies by the hope of a subsequent success. To us failure when we believed in a play, as we did in *Success Story*, was a blow to the solar plexus, a kind of moral defeat in which we sorrowed for the world as much as we did for ourselves. The effect was frequently a loss of strength, and though we remained dogged, we were also somewhat lamed.

Lee Strasberg was in this condition after *Success Story*. I was frequently in the same condition, but often my fellow directors and many of the actors suspected that this was due as much to the personal difficulties of my "love life" as to professional worries.

Sometimes they were right. When her two men were under the spell of the "sleep-walking" trauma, Cheryl Crawford succumbed to a sense of despair, for in the Group she needed at least one or the other to sustain her.

At this time, however, it was not simply financial difficulties that were affecting us. *Success Story* after all managed to stay on the boards for sixteen weeks. The honeymoon period for the Group was over; growing-pains were beginning. The determination to carry on, the unquenchable need, were present as much as ever, but there was something shadowy now that spread over us in a gloomy haze.

That our will was not actually impaired was demonstrated by the fact that poverty did not deter us from going on together without wavering. After the first three weeks of our play's run Lee Shubert informed us he would have to withdraw his support, which meant the use of his theatre as well as his funds, unless we would permit him to take "first money" at the box office. Our actors would have to risk not receiving their full salary.

Some weeks the actors received half pay, more often less than half, and for New Year's Eve 1932 there was no pay at all. It would be hard, I thought, to go backstage and face the actors with such news. When I arrived at the theatre they had already been apprised of the state of affairs. Morris Carnovsky greeted me with "Harold, you are the father of all our woe!" But he spoke affectionately, and laughed; and throughout the company there was no murmur of complaint.

We were all living in remarkable fashion. At least half the Group had moved into a ten-room flat on West Fifty-seventh Street near the railroad tracks. The rent was fifty dollars a month, for besides its unfavorable location, the house was a neglected old brownstone with insufficient heat and a generally damp atmosphere.

Meals were provided for through a common fund, marketing was done by the two girls, and the cooking was attended to in turn by four or five of the men who had a knack for it. Clifford Odets's virtuosity in this field was confined to potato pancakes and hot chocolate, but the others were more versatile. Each of the occupants took care of his own room. On special occasions a friend or a more fortunate Group member sent a chicken or meat for a pot roast. Almost every night there was a guest for dinner, and, all things considered, the atmosphere was jollier than one would expect.

One of the actors who lived here was seized with a mania about "saving" the Group; he did all sorts of odd things to carry out his self-appointed mission — ranted like a revivalist, and borrowed money right and left. Shortly after, he disappeared, discouraged by the unconcern of his fellow actors. Alan Baxter afforded amusement by his trick of buying himself a special little dessert for each meal — a fact that he endeavored to conceal. Sometimes, too, he would drink enough to let Odets egg him into calling up various prominent stage directors during the small hours of the morning, under the pretext that it was a matter of life and death, only to berate them mercilessly for having done bad jobs on this or that production. Morris Carnovsky, prim, professor-like, witty, sat apart, ruminated, and made catty remarks about everything that discontented him, particularly the Adlers, whom he described with some asperity as an "island in the theatre."

For part of the winter I lived at the Barbizon-Plaza, but the time came when I, too, was forced into the Group's poorhouse. I stayed only a short while, but long enough to learn that Odets was writing a play, bits of which he read to his companions, who were highly entertained by them. There would be parts, he assured, for all who listened. Odets's room was the smallest in the house, also the coldest. There was not enough space in it for a desk, so he sat on his camp bed and typed with the machine on his lap. His play was called *I Got the Blues* before it acquired its title, *Awake and Sing*.

Lee Strasberg lived there with his newly-wed wife, Paula Miller, like a man in exile. He sat intently, making keen observations on everything. He retired to his room to read in terrible isolation, and slept like a man burying himself in oblivion.

It is related that during this period a Mrs. Eitingon, attracted to the Group and its works, was trying to reach Lee Strasberg, as

he, the director of all its productions up to this moment, was its
most notable member. Mrs. Eitingon, who knew Sandy Meisner,
told him she had a sum of $50,000 her husband had provided for
investment in the theatre. Meisner imparted this information to
Strasberg, who acted as if he were but mildly interested. Strasberg
no longer believed stories about people who wanted to give us
money. He never called Mrs. Eitingon. Finally the poor lady
called Strasberg herself. The reception she met with led her to
conclude either that we had all the money we needed or that
Strasberg was so contemptuous of moneyed people that he could
hardly bear to talk to her. Mrs. Eitingon consequently took her
money to Frank Merlin, who produced one play with it and
bought another.

In the theatre itself — we were then located at the Maxine El-
liott — the atmosphere resembled that of the actors' quarters. Its
old star dressing-room, right off the stage, had become the Group
office. There was hardly any privacy at all. Everyone wandered
in at will. There we conducted a little business, interviewed actors,
chatted, carried on controversies, prepared publicity, discussed
policy.

Performances were kept at a high level, however, except when
Luther Adler was overcome by lassitude. On such occasions we
pepped him up by inventing distinguished guests in the audience.
Stella Adler was almost always at top form, owing to her craft integrity and to her unusual energy. This energy, with which she
jolted her brother, often shocked him into fierce resistance. They
quarreled at least four times a week, and the curtain calls amused,
amazed, and terrified the company because between bows they
turned on each other to resume their cat-and-dog fight.

Carnovsky regarded the Adlers' conduct as undisciplined. Besides their quarrels they sometimes delayed the curtains by their
tardiness in coming from their dressing-rooms. But one night Carnovsky himself failed to appear for his entrance. Luther and Stella
had to ad lib. for an unconscionable time. Finally Carnovsky appeared and instead of speaking his usual line: "I am five minutes
too early," he confessed: "I am five minutes late." Hilarity fol-

lowed the tension backstage. When I inquired into the cause of
this late entrance, something almost without precedent in Carnovsky's career, someone misinformed me, with a touch of malice,
that he had been reading the *Communist Manifesto* of Marx and
Engels in his dressing-room and had thus forgotten his entrance
cue.

For the rest, the actors, insufficiently occupied, demanded more
opportunity to work at whatever duties we could find for them.
Walter Coy alternated with Bill Challee in a small part in the
play, as did Grover Burgess with Russell Collins. The graduate
apprentice Elia Kazan, or "Gadget," as he was called for unspeci-
fied reasons, served as an example of enterprise by painting display signs, typing and aiding our harassed, underpaid press agent,
whose office was a dressing-room with a privy, around which a
screen had been placed, a screen that perversely fell whenever
visitors appeared.

Some of the actors began to seek an outlet for their energies
outside our circle. There were, as noted, occasional performances
of our experimental work at workers' clubs. But more than that,
certain new groups were forming, and they asked some of our
actors to help them, perhaps to give talks or classes. Besides Gorelik's new Theatre Collective — which, according to him, was to be
a "realistic" organization in contrast to our "romantic" Group —
Charles and Adelaide Walker had spoken to me of a project on a
larger, more professional basis than the modest Collective, a "proletarian theatre," which was to develop into the Theatre Union,
which opened on West Fourteenth Street in the spring of 1933.

At this time the Theatre Collective and the Theatre Union were
holding formative meetings for discussion, some of which I attended. I noticed the presence of a few Group Theatre actors,
notably Joe Bromberg. When word about these meetings was reported back to our people, a certain suspicion, even resentment,
manifested themselves among some of them, because they feared
that people like Bromberg would be estranged from us. Actors like
Carnovsky spoke for a moment, without meaning to, as if these
new organizations were upstarts, with no right to divert serious
actors from their legitimate work in the still struggling Group.

Bromberg pointed out, quite properly, that there was not enough for him to do around the Group then. He drew himself up to his full height (unfortunately insufficient for the occasion) and announced in an almost defiant voice: "Besides, I like workers," a statement that struck everyone as a bewildering *non sequitur*.

Though no official policy had been announced by the Group directorate, it was now established that our actors were free to use their extra time as they would; and if some were interested in contributing to the development of new groups, amateur or professional, no one would gainsay them in any way.

When Franchot Tone left during the run of *Success Story,* he was replaced by Roman (Bud) Bohnen. But we had difficulty in replacing Tone in *Big Night.* Several weeks after we cast one actor in his part we discovered we had made a mistake and were obliged to replace him with another — a very rare occurrence in our productions. The actors were rather critical of Cheryl Crawford as a director, and she had grown weary of both the play and the captious company. I took over for the final weeks of rehearsal.

The change gave the production a little spurt of life, but basically everyone was working through the doldrums. The play was one that should have been done in four swift weeks — or not at all. We had worried it and harried our actors with it for months. It dealt with a group of what today we would call heels, and our tendency to explain and justify — that is, to "humanize" — the callousness of this environment made for some confusion of style and values. The result was naturally a failure.

The press as a whole loathed the play. Yet even here, where we were ourselves dissatisfied with our work, we felt there was something too cavalier and uncritical about the play's reception. The reviewers were able to discern nothing in the play but its unpleasantness. They ran from it, screaming like so many maiden aunts.

There were, however, some compensating elements. In the playing, for example, Joe Bromberg was capital; his characterization (as a big buyer on a binge) was a comedy portrait of impressive contour and quality. A number of scenes had a kind of Hogarthian mordancy. Robert Benchley in *The New Yorker* put the matter this way: "The party of advertising men and their wives which Miss Dawn Powell has seen fit to throw into the midst of a rather drab bacchanalia did not offend me more than any group of white-tied drinkers would have done. . . . Are we to have only high class cads on the stage?"

Big Night closed after nine performances. In later years it was quite a joke around the Group to repeat a crack made one day by Stella Adler on finding me in an enthusiastic state of mind. "Harold has a great idea. He's going to revive *Big Night!*" The real point of this was not simply that the play had failed, but that its failure was attended by disaster so complete as to be almost comic.

We had had great difficulty in raising the small sum needed to produce *Big Night*. I can no longer remember who provided what little it did cost. I know I borrowed $500 from my brother to raise the first-night curtain. None of the directors was paid his fee for the production. The actors' bond, guaranteeing two weeks' salary, was to be put up by a Broadway manager who had seen a rehearsal and laughed his head off over it. But our secretary, who was to have mailed the promissory statement for the manager's signature, forgot to do so for a day. By the time the manager received the papers for signature, the notices had appeared. He knew the play was a flop. He refused to live up to his commitment. After working on the play for months, the actors received no pay at all. In fact, none of us save the scene-designer, the builder, and the stagehands ever received a penny from this production.

Despite the truly difficult situation that almost every member of the Group faced at this time, all of us, without exception, wanted to put a new play into rehearsal, though this involved many more weeks of uncertainty. But money did not mean certainty to us; only work did. We were depending for our third play on Sidney Howard's *Yellowjack*.

I had been corresponding with Howard for almost a year. From time to time he would drop me a note telling me he was making progress with his new play. It was finally sent to us and, wonder of wonders, we liked it and wanted to put it on immediately.

But Howard was no longer sure he wanted to let us have it. He was undoubtedly affected by the poor notices of *Taos*, *Success Story*, and *Big Night* and the chill atmosphere that had begun to surround our names with the failure of these plays. Also he had counted on the presence of Franchot Tone in our company, and Tone had abandoned us for pictures. He was not sure whether our youngish company would be convincing in a play which called for older people in vital roles. When we met with Howard, we could feel as we spoke to him that he was now turning his practical ear to our argument, as a year before he had lent us his idealistic one.

A year before he had declared publicly that the theatre needed such groups as ours, and that was why he would give us his next play for production — a play requiring a true ensemble performance. At our first meeting Howard had struck me as a very interesting person, because he seemed to be debating out loud two courses of action — courses that had no specific names, only vague emotional meanings. The Group apparently was connected with one course. He made strange statements I barely understood such as "I am a man who knows better than the Communists do what they want. But — " Here either his conclusion or my memory wanders into blank space.

Yellowjack, as I read it, was a play about civil heroism and about the mixed motives that went into the making of a hero. The boys who offered themselves as human guinea pigs did so for reasons hardly connected with either science or a concern for the welfare of humankind. Yet to me they were none the less heroic. As I was considering this problem in relation to the play, I realized that a good part of Sidney Howard's work revealed the recurrent theme of compromise, a theme that in various guises appeared in the work of Lawson, S. N. Behrman, and (later) Odets. It was connected in some way with the breached consciousness of sensitive middle-class Americans in the two decades between the wars. In Howard the emphasis seemed to lean toward a resolution that might be read as "Man lives through compromise."

Before Howard definitely refused us his play, I received a note in which he referred in somewhat unintelligible manner to the paradox of the Soviet director Eisenstein's presence in Hollywood. All this began to shape itself into a kind of pattern when the bad news became final.

When Luther Adler, shortly after this incident, joined the Katharine Cornell company that was doing Howard's *Alien Corn*, he told Howard how he had hurt the Group by denying us the right to produce *Yellowjack*. Howard, after listening in silence for some time, said: "You make me feel like a sonofabitch."

With the closing of *Big Night* and our failure to acquire the Howard play, it seemed futile for us to continue our season's work. Closing night — January 16, 1933 — we held a meeting at which we communicated the disappointing decision to our company.

Lee Strasberg did not like my putting it that way. He was impatient with me because he read a note of apology in my declared reluctance to arrive at this decision. To him this was sentimentality. When retreat is necessary it is weakness to regret it.

Several friends rose to hint that we wouldn't be in such a fix if we had not held so grimly to our uncompromising attitude. Strasberg contested this hotly: he felt that people who begin with compromise usually end there. One or two actors brought up the possibility of the Group's establishing itself in a smaller city, but Strasberg retorted that, for better or worse, we were a New York group.

The meeting ended in bleak irresolution. Luther Adler had been engaged to play in *Alien Corn;* Carnovsky, Bromberg, and Collins were to go into Maxwell Anderson's *Both Your Houses*. Stella Adler first went into a nondescript production and then left for the road. But none of them was happy. Despite every hazard or distress they believed in the Group and wanted it to go on.

The *New York Times* next morning announced that the Group was out of business for the season — and perhaps forever. For most columnists the reported demise of the Group was no news,

since rises and falls on Broadway are something like the ebb and
flow of the seasons.

I addressed the following statement to the *New York Times*
(January 25, 1933):

> The actors and directors of the Group Theatre have never
> produced a play in anticipation of a "wow." The need for such
> anticipation is one of the good reasons why the establish-
> ment of any permanent theatrical organization with a coher-
> ent policy is rendered particularly difficult in our New York
> theatre. . . .
>
> The Group began its career during a period of severe eco-
> nomic depression, and therefore had to go about its work
> without the benefit of a subsidy or patronage of any kind.
> This meant it had to present its plays on practically the same
> basis as any other producer. But what the Group Theatre
> aimed to do was fundamentally different from Broadway,
> and its position as a competing organization was entirely ir-
> relevant and was even injurious to its aims.
>
> . . . When you choose your scripts not as commercial bait,
> but for the pertinence of what they have to say, when you
> know beforehand that some of the scripts chosen are by no
> means perfect . . . when you do not cast strictly according
> to the "type" system, which not only managers but many
> playwrights and even reviewers insist upon; when you have
> undertaken to sustain a permanent acting company which
> does not limit itself to the customary four-week rehearsal pe-
> riod; when, finally the number of so-called good plays is alarm-
> ingly small in any event, *persistence in pursuing the ordinary
> course of theatrical production becomes folly. In other words,
> the Group Theatre might continue as it has for the past two
> years. But it refuses to strain along lines that do not advance
> or clarify its aims, but that, on the contrary, impede and fal-
> sify them.* Thus it has decided not to resume production un-
> less it can create conditions for itself that will permit it to
> carry on freely to do what it really wants to do, of which its
> first two years of activity give only the first bare indications.

PART III

SECOND WIND

CHAPTER NINE

The Winter of Our Discontent

THE PERIOD between the closing of *Big Night* in January 1933 and the opening of *Men in White* on September 26, 1933 was both one of the most painful and one of the most pregnant periods of our Group life. It was a time when I myself was utterly wretched and, in some strange way, profoundly happy.

Despite the bold front I showed the press, we were in a state of rout. The actors who did not immediately find work were helped for a while by the generous personal assistance of Margaret Barker and Dorothy Patten, who made contributions to the Group to be turned over to the individuals most in need. In an effort to maintain the link of common work, the Group people begged Strasberg to conduct classes for them. But the actors, though they were unaware of it, did not need classes so much as relief. When Strasberg acceded to the actors' pressure and met with some of them, he was wan and they were listless.

Cheryl, Lee, and I met frequently and mulled over our prob-

lems, always finding ourselves at the end in some no man's land
of empty cogitation. Once Cheryl came forward with the idea
that the Group solve its problem by becoming a motion-picture
unit. But we were trained and conditioned as a theatre group.
No matter what our opinion of pictures, they were a separate
medium, requiring artists specially equipped for them. Cheryl
dropped her suggestion at once.

For the rest of the winter Strasberg lived by borrowing and by
directing one of those productions that crop up on Broadway
every spring. What little I earned came from a lecture course
given at the New School for Social Research. It was poorly attended, and my takings were lean.

About this time I began to notice with sharp clarity the transformation that had come over New York during the past two
years. It seemed as if the very color of the city had changed.
From an elegant bright gray by day and a sparkling gold by
night the afternoons had grown haggard, the nights mournful.
The neon glow that had come to replace the brilliance of the
twenties was like a whistling in the dark.

The town was visibly down at the heel; it seemed to shuffle
feebly as if on chilblained feet. The comfortable middle class began to show faces pitted with worry, and the intellectuals I knew
no longer seemed so concerned about the validity of Joyce's experiments in prose or the spiritual hollowness in Eliot's wasteland,
where everyone was sick from having read too many books. They
were beginning to worry over rent and the bills at the A. & P.

Official reports told us there were 10,908,000 unemployed in
October 1932, and in the first two months of 1933 the number
rose to 12,000,000. There were brutally shameless breadlines on
Times Square and Columbus Circle. When I held the first Group
meetings in 1931, I had made constant reference to the boom
days of the past, and Clifford Odets wondered what I meant,
since in the so-called good times he had virtually been starving,
while with the depression the Group had come along and given
him hope, enthusiasm, and little but comparatively steady money.
"What boom days?" he would ask repeatedly.

It is true that a period has, first of all, the tone of our personal relation to it. At the end of his novel *The Big Money* Dos Passos contrasts the prosperous young man of the Harding-Coolidge era winging his way westward on a luxury airliner with a vagrant who stands on the concrete road trying to thumb a ride in one of the cars that whizz by oblivious of his plight. There were the homeless and broken in the good old days, as there were rich people after the crash. However, just as the sleek young man in his mechanical splendor seemed typical of the twenties, so the candidate for the poorhouse struck the tone for the thirties.

My own experiences, however, offered not so many examples of the starved and battered worker or the suicidal business man, but rather of the in-between professional man. I could see it in my parents' home. Outwardly very little had altered since the better days, and I could not quite understand why they were unable fully to enjoy their good table, their comparative peace. Against all reason, it seemed to me, they and their friends were increasingly terrified, as if soon the walls would disappear, and they would remain naked and alone on the cold empty street of a night without a morrow.

Yes, we could smell the depression in the air. It was like a raw wind; the very houses we lived in seemed to be shrinking, hopeless of real comfort. In these days of gloom and fear outside me and personal frustration in my work, I roamed the streets, where my own bleak state seemed to be reflected in thousands of faces, signs, and portents.

In my disconsolate meanderings from place to place I found Clifford Odets constantly by my side. I cannot remember how this came about, for, as I have said, his personality, though peculiar enough, had not strongly impressed itself on my consciousness. We began to see each other nightly, and with hungry hearts wandered aimlessly through sad centers of impoverished night life. We would drop in at some cheap restaurant and over a meager meal make dreams of both our past and future. We would see a movie on a side street, pick up more friends, who, whether working or not, seemed equally at odds with the now consumptive city. We listened to queer conversations on street corners, visited

byways we had never suspected before. There grew between us a
feeling akin to that which is supposed to exist between hoboes in
their jungles, and we were strangely attracted to people and
places that might be described as hangdog, ratty, and low.

At no other time before or since did either of us visit so many
burlesque houses. The shows had no sex lure for us; they had
the appeal of a lurid dejection. Somehow we felt close to the
down-in-the-mouth comedians and oddly tender about the bruised
beauties of the chorus. (One night we saw a girl we knew in a
naked tableau of indescribable drabness. The night we happened
into the middle of the show was the first night of her new work.
She had never had such a job before, but now it seemed the
only thing available to her.) Most of the jokes, aside from the
usual rancid ones, concerned the low estate into which the world
had fallen. An empty pocket, for instance, was called a Hoover
dollar. There was more social significance buried in this grime than
in all of Burns Mantle's collection.

We heard that a special showing of a picture based on Hauptmann's *Weavers* was being given at the old Proctor's on Broadway and Twenty-eighth Street. When we arrived at the theatre,
we were overcome by an atmosphere of neglect, of damp, of cav-
ernous emptiness. Only a few hollow-eyed people composed the
audience.

When we had seen the film and were ready to leave, a man, in
a navy-blue flannel shirt with a suit and face that matched it,
came out and addressed the audience with a simple conviction
that must have been hard to maintain under the circumstances.
He was a radical of some kind — the real article, not its phony
counterpart — and he urged strong political action against the terror of the crisis, the unemployment, hunger, destitution of the
day. Odets applauded with sudden spontaneity, — as if unprepared to do so and himself surprised that he had. I was no less
surprised, but did not question him. I understood that his applause
was not so much a matter of intellectual approval as almost a
physical movement of union with the speaker who had uttered
words that needed to be spoken one way or another.

On this same platform, where I had once seen Stella Adler in a dramatization of Feuchtwanger's *Power*, in another two years *Waiting for Lefty* would be presented at a benefit for the taxi-drivers' union.

After these excursions into dubious places of amusement Odets and I penetrated the mysterious night that separates Times Square from Greenwich Village. There was a very popular meeting-place in that year of the hunger and bonus marches: Stewart's Cafeteria on Sheridan Square, where the Greenwich Village The-atre, in which I had made my stage debut, had once stood. At midnight it had the festive air of Madison Square Garden on the occasion of a big fight. Here the poor and jolly have-beens, ne'er-do-wells, names-to-be, the intellectual, the bohemian, the lazy, neurotic, confused and unfortunate, the radicals, mystics, thugs, drabs, and sweet young people without a base, collected noisily to make a very stirring music of their discord and hope.

Though this cafeteria must have represented a high degree of affluence to the really hungry, it struck me as a sort of singing Hooverville. For, strangely enough, this incubator of the depres-sion, with many marks of waste and decay upon it, was in point of fact a place rank with promise. Some of the old Village (1915–25) was going to pot here, but also something new, not wholly aware of itself, and to this day still immature, was in an early state of gestation.

At one table we met a phenomenal young man who, under the influence of a duly proportioned diet of spirits, could speak su-perb Gertrude Stein by the hour, making insidious sense in a curiously fascinating way that held Odets spellbound, while it discomfited me. At other tables youngsters who had left homes in other towns only to find New York more hybrid but no less stricken were carrying on conversations that mingled despair, yearning, and eagerness in a compound that is nearly always tonic and of good augury. Most of these kids did not lead good lives, but much that was useful and healthy was eventually to come from them. The evil that they witnessed, and of which they were often products and victims, was in full bloom; the good that they sought and would do was still embryonic and would perhaps

remain so for years. Yet only the dull or the priggish could fail
to notice the seeds of some future growth.

Odets knew many of the people here. In some respects he was
like them. Before the formation of the Group and during its first
winter he had lived in a dismal hotel west of Columbus Circle,
and here he had cultivated a little horror and more love for the
atmosphere of dejection and defeat. It was as if he wanted to be
one with the semi-derelicts who were moldering in this pesthouse.
Now that he was moving from the Fifty-seventh Street Group
apartment down to the Village, he came upon an environment
that corresponded in poverty with that which he had already
known, but the difference was that in the first instance there was
a feeling of permanent breakdown, while here, despite much
looseness, there was a seeking for the future and some hope for it.
Odets seemed to share a peculiar sense of gloomy fatality, one
might almost say an appetite for the broken and rundown, together with a bursting love for the beauty immanent in people,
a burning belief in the day when this beauty would actually shape
the external world. These two apparently contradictory impulses
kept him in a perpetual boil that to the indifferent eye might look
like either a stiff passivity or a hectic fever.

Odets introduced me to many of these people at Stewart's,
where, despite myself, my first reaction was a middle-class shrinking. (My home had always been enlightened, liberal, and inalter-
ably proper.) One girl especially — tiny, blonde, miserably poor,
and equivocally attractive — stands out in my mind because she
was typical. Some years later, influenced by the Group Theatre
and the Odets literary manner, she was to write a play produced
experimentally by the Federal Theatre Project, in which the young
girl's life of this period was dramatized. (It was the kind of young
person's play that was both imitative and authentic; it described
seediness and youthful corruption with a mixture of indulgence
and honesty that made it a lyric document of more value than
might be supposed, for which our straitlaced theatre has absolutely no place.)

This girl, without sufficient funds to fix her teeth, too pretty and
pushing to remain in her proletarian home somewhere in the

hinterland, too unprotected to receive proper guidance for her incipient talent, too ignorant to amount to much without such guidance, too alive and clean-souled to make any convenient adjustment, and finally too unconcentrated because of all this to cut through to a sane consummation of herself, was living somehow, nohow, like a fresh plant in the center of chaos. She met a handsome boy in flight from an important Oklahoma family. What must have seemed to him at first an adventuresome life and background attracted him to her; and he must have seemed to her a Western Galahad, strong, educated, and thoroughly at home in the big American scene. They were married. In the middle thirties she was "radicalized" along with others of her age and experience, hung on the fringes of the Group, acted in the Federal Theatre, where, as noted, her play was given a trial performance — and drifted. Her husband began to get parts on Broadway, disapproved of her friends (his uncle was a notorious reactionary in Congress), grew successful, divorced her. With time he developed into a Hollywood picture star till he received a commission in the army. Today she lives in Hollywood, married to a labor lawyer who is also in the army.

Odets, I repeat, was very sympathetic to such characters, as he was to many failures — those failures in whom he could discern former power, and those whose potentiality he felt threatened by unfavorable circumstances. Later he would say that he had written his first plays because he had seen his schoolmates, whom he had always thought cheerful good fellows, turn into either tasteless messes of nameless beef, or become thin, wan, sick ciphers. He wanted to explain what had happened to them, and, through them, to express his love, his fears, his hope for the world. In this way, instead of wallowing in his unhappiness, he would make it a positive force.

Here at the Stewart's Cafeteria, Odets began to tell me a little about the play he was writing; he sought my opinion of such new projects as the Theatre Collective and the Theatre Union, and probed the content of my mind and the secrets of my soul. Neither of these was very secret. And apropos of one of my problems he ventured the opinion that "no Adler could ever be made a Group person"! He knew that I was disconsolate, frustrated, stewing in creative juices. This and funny habits I had, idiosyncrasies and gestures of helplessness or naïveté, seemed to endear me to him.

One absurdity we developed together: the poorer we both got, the more solace we seemed to take in smoking cigars. Together with a sandwich, coffee, and pie at the cafeteria, we rarely failed to order two small Coronas. I like chewing the thick weed, and the cigar's red band under the electric light in the tobacco rack seemed to beckon me with an undercover hint of well-being. I puffed like a kid, not a capitalist, and it made Odets laugh. He was younger than I, but he treated me as if he were an affectionate older brother. I liked him too perhaps because he listened to me so understandingly and responded warmly to my moods, but if I had been asked about him, I believe I should have confessed that I liked him for being so physical a person. He reacted to everything, not with words or articulate knowledge, but with his body. His senses were extraordinarily alive, though he was not professionally "sensitive." To be near him was like being near a stove on which a whole range of savory foods was standing ready to be served.

The strength I drew from this period of apparently aimless ambling through the dark of depressed areas in place and spirit was crystallized for me one day when I was struck as if by the miracle of conversion with the feeling that no matter how bitter things became for me, personally, professionally, economically, I would never allow myself to be destroyed from within; it would never get me down; I would sustain all kinds of disappointment and distress without ceasing to believe, to hope, to love. I would never yield to the temptation of pessimism, to the ease of despair or withdrawal. It was as if I took an inner vow

> *never to allow gradually the traffic to smother*
> *With noise and fog the flowing of the spirit.*

I believed, as some ancient had said: "It is not within thy power to finish the task, nor is it thy liberty to abandon it." From this

inexorable maxim I drew an abiding joy. In this sense I swore
fealty to myself.

Thus that historically cruel winter of 1932–3, which chilled so
many of us like a world's end, became for me a time of renewed
faith, because I appeared to be withstanding a sort of test. In
our exchange Clifford Odets and I contributed much to each
other, but we both received most of our nurture at this time from
the world around us, even as it was reflected in such humble, none
too glamorous haunts as I have described.

What was happening to us, unknown figures in a backward art
practiced in a tiny corner of our land, was part of a universal
convulsion that was affecting every class, profession, and trade.
And just as the party I described in the opening pages of this
book seemed to me typical of the twenties, a party I was invited
to by Edmund Wilson during the present period became symbolic
to me of the transformation wrought by the thirties.

William Z. Foster, the Communist candidate for the Presi-
dency in 1932, had just written a new book that the conservative
house of Harcourt, Brace and Company was publishing. To launch
it among the intelligentsia, the publishers asked people like Wilson to arrange small gatherings at which writers and artists might
meet Foster. Among those present at this particular occasion were
Gilbert Seldes, John Chamberlain, John Dos Passos, Charles
Walker, Kenneth Burke, George S. Counts, Lawrence Dennis.

Drinks were served throughout the evening, while two or three
of the guests plied Foster with questions. As I recall, the one
most intent in this questioning was Lawrence Dennis. Many
questions related to the economy of the Soviet Union. Others were
concerned with the attitude in Soviet society toward the intellectual and the artist. The majority of the guests simply hung on
the sidelines, so to speak, and listened. When Foster had left, one
of the guests, rather potted, began to show concern over the fact
that here were American intellectuals looking with interest toward a country and a regime where machinery and the achievements of Henry Ford were idealized. What was going to happen
in the society of the future, he wanted to know, to the values

represented by a William Butler Yeats? Another guest reassured
this troubled soul by vowing that the Yeats of the future would
hold an honored place in a socialist world. "In that case," the
perturbed one, now appeased, said, "it's all right" — and fell on
his face.

The characteristic feature of this gathering was that while some
of the guests were incipiently sympathetic, and others either
skeptical or hostile, all were attentive. More than that, of those
ready to go along with Foster's viewpoint, some became violently
anti-Soviet within five years in different modes and manners, including the fascistic. The point is that so deep was the crisis at
this time, that virtually every conscious person was attempting
to find some basic answer to society's jitters, and for the moment
they were willing to consider any idea that promised a solution,
no matter how extreme or unpopular. In the theatre, for example,
Sidney Howard, eminently respectable, had caused something of
a sensation by announcing that in the next election he would
campaign on behalf of the Intellectuals Committee for Foster,
because he was fed up with the impotence and bungling of the
two old parties.

Another sign of the times was the urge among our people toward greater participation in the running of our organization. I
call it a sign of the times even though, like the others, it was actually a natural outgrowth of the Group's history, aims, and tendencies. In cold logic, nothing the directors had said when we
got together necessitated giving the actors an official voice in the
making of decisions. But reality is subtler than logic, and the
ideals implied not only in the directors' talks but in their actual
conduct of affairs slowly but surely brought about a conscious
demand for an open recognition not only that the actors were an
integral part of the organization but that they had every right
to function systematically as such.

In a dispute that arose during the run of *Connelly* over the
impertinence of our stage-manager, whom I declined to fire, I
told the company that my forbearance did not signify that the
directors considered the actors' position in the Group inviolable.

The Group, I pointed out, was organized by the three directors and was, in fact, their theatre. Only one person expressed any surprise or shock at this statement. Even now, when doubts began to arise over the wisdom of some of the directors' decisions, the actors had nothing more in view than a desire to be helpful, to contribute toward the execution of what they knew to be a very difficult task. There was no question of superseding the directors' authority, for the actors professed an undiminished belief in at least two of them.

I make this qualification because very late one night I was visited by an unofficial delegation of five actors who had worked themselves into a pother over the Group's problems. There were people in the Group who worried them very much. Of one there was nothing more to say, since he had just resigned. But the other, they confessed, was Cheryl Crawford. I listened patiently, but my silence ended by embarrassing my visitors. They did not like to incur my disapproval. I answered none of their arguments; I simply stated that the Group was a living organism and, I believed, a healthy one, so what was good for it — not always clear at first — would remain and prove its value, and what was injurious or useless would finally fall away as through a process of natural selection. One of the actors called this "mere rationalization."

My attitude on this occasion represented a deep-rooted conviction, and though it had certain defects, it proved itself sound in the long run. For had I yielded to such pressure from outside or even to subjective pressure of my own, I should very soon have dismembered the Group. Waves of dislike or distrust, not to speak of well-founded complaints, at one time or another fell upon almost every individual among us. The very actor who accused me of "rationalizing" was guilty of gross professional misconduct four years later, and his expulsion was demanded by many of his colleagues. I not only refused to take such action, but prevented his fellow actors from behaving in any way that might lead to his resignation. The actor not only stayed with us but, despite recurrent bad moments, became one of our most useful co-workers. My persistent refusal to fire anyone, even where there was cause, not only helped maintain the Group, but saved some of our most valuable people for us. And, in truth, when it was proper for people to resign they did, without any deliberate pressure upon them. But to hold to my policy, I myself had to bear the brunt of every criticism — of which the accusation of "merely rationalizing" was to prove the mildest.

Nevertheless, when the actors began to campaign for greater participation in Group government, I found myself at variance with my fellow directors. The difference between us was of a subtle kind. I felt that in the three directors' first impulse to comply with the actors' demand, there lurked a fear of responsibility. Strasberg and Crawford, I suspected, were made unhappy by the sense of guilt they sometimes felt when ill luck overtook us. It is true we had been unjustly criticized by the actors on more than one occasion. I thought this to be the fate of leadership, and I could not agree that the proper way to overcome the leaders' dilemma was to have the actors share their responsibility. This seemed to me to be a way of weakening leadership by a dissipation of its responsibility.

For this reason, I suggested that instead of increasing the number of those with the rights of decision to include the actors, they be narrowed down, and that one director take final responsibility, while the other two would serve as a kind of cabinet. I suggested further that I be the one to assume the authority, for while I too was distressed by the misunderstandings we had suffered, I believed I could bear them more readily than the others. My proposal had no success whatsoever. I dropped it at once.

Strasberg had explained to me that I failed to take into account what had happened in two years. The actors had grown up, and their growth had to be permitted objective expression. However, when he met with the actors and heard certain of their proposals, he looked so hurt and even outraged that he appeared to be more opposed to them than I. This contradiction derived, I suppose, from the fact while he accepted the situation intellectually, he was emotionally disturbed by the slightest suspicion of distrust that he might detect in any specific suggestion.

A kind of paternalism had arisen among the directors. Unwittingly we took pride and sustenance from it, even though at times it became an intolerable burden — particularly in later years — bad for both the actors and the directors, bad for the organization as a whole.

Experience has shown that theatres are best run by a highly centralized — in other words, a single or dual — leadership. This applies not only to commercial managements, where the problem hardly exists, but to such theatres as ours, where the profit motive for the individual leader has been reduced to a minimum, and where an ideal of co-operativeness is not only espoused but practiced.

In our case more than a theory was involved, more than an abstract ideal of democratic procedure, although it was at about this time that the word "democracy" began to be applied with fresh and widespread significance beyond the realm of politics and government. The fact was — I see it more clearly now than I was able to then — that since the directors were unable to assure even the small security that our program of continuity called for, it was inevitable that the actors should be deeply concerned with every decision made, and wish to take some part in making them.

Not all the actors felt this need. But the majority voted an Actors' Committee, which was supposed to advise with the directors on the Group's various problems. In the beginning this committee hardly functioned at all.

Though the actors tended to lump the three directors together, matters were not altogether peaceful among the directors either. One day when plans for the next season were being discussed, I suggested that I direct Lawson's *The Pure in Heart*, a play which I believed I could give an interesting production. Strasberg blurted out that he did not agree with this; that I had given no evidence of directorial capacity or enterprise, and that if he were a backer he would not trust me with the play. I was more shocked than I could say, particularly because Cheryl Crawford seconded him in what looked like a previously planned strategy. I remained silent, and Strasberg breathed relief at having unburdened himself of his secret thought. As I had previously refused to direct, though urged to do so not only by my colleagues but by my friends outside, the present contretemps struck me as a betrayal.

Lee Shubert had brought to Cheryl Crawford's attention a script by a new playwright, Sidney Kingsley. It was about internes in a hospital, and she believed it had great possibilities. Strasberg took her word for it, while I had a rather neutral reaction. The play had been sold to a new theatrical combination — Harmon and Ullman — and they had brought it to Shubert for backing. He had suggested that we produce it for the new managers, while he would act as silent partner. This arrangement was made.

We still had no money for a summer rehearsal period. A benefit for a Group Theatre fund was arranged by Bobby Lewis. Only enough money was raised to take care of our most needy cases.

The situation was saved by the existence of that peculiar institution, the adult camp. One of the largest of these places was called Green Mansions, some fifteen miles north of Lake George. The camp management offered to house and feed the entire Group, including wives and children, as well as a scene-designer, dance director, speech teacher, and all our assistants, in return for four nights of entertainment weekly, to be given in a small theatre on the camp's premises.

A greater windfall was the result of Franchot Tone's generosity. We needed money not only for Kingsley's play, but for other scripts. Though by this time I was reckoned an important producer, I had hardly enough money then to buy postage stamps for my various negotiations. Since his departure I had carried on a spotty correspondence with Franchot Tone. One day I received a letter in which he said that the Group had been the most important influence in his life, and that he had thought of returning to it, but that he had fallen in love with Joan Crawford, and he would therefore stay on in Hollywood. There was something refreshingly simple about his letter. His writing in this vein made me realize that the Group had meant more to him than I or anyone else could have suspected. I appealed to him for help so that we might have sufficient funds to pay advances on the scripts we wished to acquire. Now that he could not take part in our work himself, Franchot expressed his devotion by contributing this money toward our next productions.

On Decoration Day I accompanied a small contingent of our Group up to Green Mansions to provide holiday entertainment prior to the regular season that would begin for all of us in late June. We gave a one-act play by Galsworthy and an improvised revue. I remained at Green Mansions for several weeks in a kind of retreat from the city, which had become almost hateful to me.

When I got back to town from my preliminary excursion to Green Mansions to report on its merits and to make final arrangements for the Group's trip, I found that Cheryl and Lee had commissioned the young novelist Melvin Levy to write a play about a California steamship magnate from 1860 to the San Francisco fire of 1906. It looked as if Cheryl and Lee had about decided to act without me, as I must have seemed to them to be in a mood of hopeless dejection and inactivity. They were not altogether wrong, but the independent steps they had taken — perfectly proper in themselves — did not diminish a kind of icy bitterness that separated me from them at the time. There was no question in my mind of a break, only a sense of doleful withdrawal. In a way I did not even know with what precisely I was dissatisfied, what hurt me. But hurt I was. I retired into a kind of cataleptic state, awaiting the day of restored energy.

CHAPTER TEN

Success

THE GROUP that arrived at Green Mansions in Warrensburg, New York, was the largest we had assembled in our three years of life. Rehearsals of our play, first called *Crisis* and later renamed *Men in White*, began at once. The play was to be financed by Doris Warner (from Hollywood) in addition to those previously mentioned. The leading role was assigned to Alexander Kirkland, who had spent some time in pictures after his Theatre Guild success in *Wings over Europe.*

Cheryl Crawford felt Kirkland would prove an important addition to our company since we had done nothing to fill the gap in our ranks made by Tone's departure. Kirkland was eager to develop as an actor, and the Group's growing reputation as a training-ground for actors had attracted him to us. He was very fortunate, because Lee Strasberg worked even more carefully and confidently on the present production than he had three years before.

In a sense this was a triumph of concentration on Strasberg's part since the company as a whole was not entirely convinced of the play's merit. In fact, one of the actors came to plead with me to call off the production as it would surely ruin the Group. I was not very sanguine myself about the play's chances of success, but I had no intention of doing what the young actor asked. It was the most immediately practicable script in our possession and therefore had to be done. When it became a box-office success, many of my friends were bitter over my having agreed to its production just to make money.

While the rehearsals were in progress, the Group was at work preparing its entertainment program according to our agreement with the camp's management. This work, first regarded as a burdensome and perhaps undignified chore, proved very valuable to us. Beside doing the second act of *Big Night* and two acts of *Success Story,* we gave, among other things, an outdoor performance of *Emperor Jones, Ten Nights in a Barroom,* one act of *Marco Millions,* one of O'Neill's sea pieces, Chekhov's *The Bear,* revue sketches both original and borrowed, specialty numbers, such as Tony Kraber's cowboy songs, and evenings of experimental pieces, the fruit of our summer labors at Dover Furnace.

Most important in this line were the two evenings we devoted to giving the second act of Odets's play *I've Got the Blues.* When I read it first, I could not see the woods for the trees. The first act was cluttered with some rather gross Jewish humor and a kind of messy kitchen realism; the last act I thought almost masochistically pessimistic. I wasn't sure how it would play even though Odets told me categorically that it would go "like a house on fire." As my reaction on the whole was rather confused, I promised Odets to do the play's second act as a kind of try-out.

The first performance was a source of pleasure to everyone, save perhaps to Odets himself. For he could not understand why we did not leap at the opportunity of producing his play. He had certainly been proved right about the play's complete stage-worthiness. The audience loved it. If I did not recognize the play's value then, despite the enthusiasm of some friends and members of the company, it was because I was still put off by the first and last acts. For the time being, the matter rested. I had learned that Odets was worth encouraging.

On the whole, the summer was a very fruitful one, despite hectic personal upsets for various people. My own work on the Odets play and a brief period of rehearsal of a German play about the theatre called *Gallery Gods* counted for little. My reputation that summer was bad. (Kirkland and others repeated the phrase: "The Group has only one director" — and they didn't mean me!) But apart from this, our speech instructor had had a breakdown; our dance instructor had been a failure. Max Gorelik clamored for security and a seasonal contract. The gossip columns in the New York papers kidded us, and made disparaging remarks about our services as "entertainers." But nearly everyone worked very hard.

Men in White was a hit. Though this was surprise enough, the notices, with a few exceptions, were breath-taking. In the *New York Times* Brooks Atkinson wrote: "After two years of real hardship, the Group Theatre is not only still in existence, but still determined to keep the theatre in its high estate. This time they have a play worthy of their ambition, and they have adorned it with the most beguiling acting the town affords. It is a good brave play and it is just the play to summon all the latent idealism from the young players of the Group Theatre." Joseph Wood Krutch called it "a work of art."

For us in the Group the play had an entirely different value. It was our most finished production. Strasberg had given it a dig-

The three directors, Dover Furnace, New York, summer 1932.
LEFT TO RIGHT: Harold Clurman, Cheryl Crawford, Lee Strasberg.

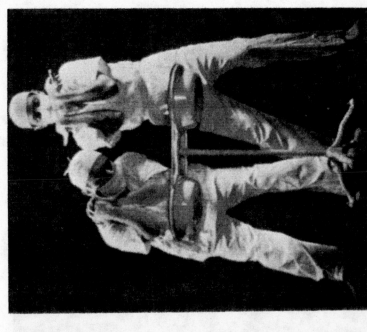

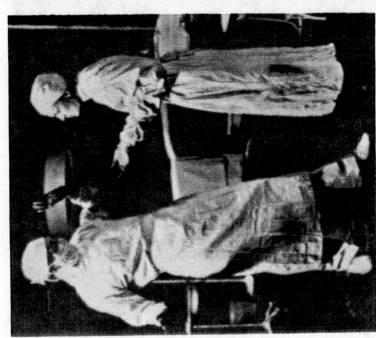

Scenes from *Men in White* by Sidney Kingsley, 1933. (Direction: Lee Strasberg. Setting: Mordecai Gorelik.)
LEFT: Alexander Kirkland, Margaret Barker. RIGHT: J. Edward Bromberg, Alexander Kirkland.

nity, a distinction all his own. For a fusion of all the elements of
the theatre this no doubt was his masterpiece. The settings were
another example of Gorelik's unusual talent for combining the
discoveries of certain abstractionists with the uses of a functional
and expressive stage design.

For the first time in its career the Group now had to face the
consequences of success. When I speak of success, I speak of organizational and moral success. The top salary was still $200
weekly, and this only for three or four actors. The three directors,
aside from $1,500 they divided between them, received no more
than $50 a week. The Group controlled only 22½ per cent of the
profits, which was used chiefly to buy plays and to guarantee our
next summer.

As a result of our success, two things happened. One was the
emergence of a backer brought to us by John Wildberg, a lawyer
who practiced show-business. The backer was D. A. Doran, attempting escape from Hollywood, bringing with him funds from
one of the owners of Twentieth Century-Fox. Concurrently John
Howard Lawson, disappointed over the Guild's out-of-town failure with his *Pure In Heart* and having difficulty with them over
his most recent play, *Gentlewoman*, decided to let us do the latter
play immediately.

D. A. Doran, then, was to be co-producer of *Gentlewoman*. The
title role was assigned to Stella Adler; Morris Carnovsky was to be
replaced in *Men in White* by Luther Adler, and one or two other
people with minor parts in *Men in White* were to play more important roles in *Gentlewoman*.

Before continuing with the story of this production, however, I
must retrace my steps a bit and take up the question of how the
Group actors faced success. Instead of making them complacent,
it turned their minds more insistently to a wholly new and rather
elevated source of disquiet. They began to suffer a special brand
of inferiority complex. Their conscience was troubling them over
the fact that we, the first to have spoken of a theatre with social
significance, were making money with a play that to our more
intimate critics was on the level of a *Saturday Evening Post* story,

while downtown the Theatre Union had already put on *Peace on Earth,* an anti-war play, and were preparing *Stevedore,* a rousing play on the Negro problem.

When Charles Walker and his wife had come during the spring of 1932 to interest me in their project for a theatre to do "proletarian plays," I did not oppose the idea, but I doubted that such a theatre would be able to survive on a professional basis for any length of time. Later when this theatre was in process of formation, I heard that Molly Day Thacher, Elia Kazan's wife, regarded it, rather than the Group, as the hope of the new people in the theatre. The Group, she felt, was too much concerned with "psychology," whereas the younger crowd was bent on more material and therefore more real matters.

And lo, it had come to pass. The Theatre Union was on the firing line on Fourteenth Street, charging no more than $1.50 for the best seat, while we were "safe" on Broadway with the contemptible carriage-trade price of $3.30.

Clifford Odets had begun to give classes for the younger actors around the Theatre Union. A few members of the Theatre Union board regarded him with suspicion, for they feared he might indoctrinate these rugged innocents with some of the noxiously sentimental and introverted doctrines of the Stanislavsky or Group systems. For his part, while Odets felt that the Group was artistically more mature, he was intrigued by the downtowners, for with them he might become something of a leader, a teacher. Besides this, the slogans of the Theatre Union were more daring than those of the fence-sitting, hair-splitting Group.

At any rate there was unrest in the Group. Part of this was due, no doubt, to lack of activity for the small part actors. For many actors, being in a successful show is activity enough. It is to the credit of the Group actors that this was not so with them.

One of Bobby Lewis's activities at that time had a historic aftermath. It seems that the producer of the current hit *Sailor, Beware!* had asked his actors to take a cut in salary at a time when the actors were certain that the show was running at a profit. They petitioned Equity to intercede for them, which Equity failed to do. Bobby Lewis got wind of this and enlisted the interest of a

few other Group actors, who in turn consulted with players from
other companies.

This movement on behalf of the *Sailor, Beware!* company developed into a critical examination of Equity itself. The leadership of that organization, it seemed, had grown stodgy and remote from its membership. The atmosphere of reform, which was
everywhere prevalent under the new national administration, expressed itself here in a series of demands on Equity: demands for
a "cut board" to protect actors from unscrupulous managers, for
rehearsal pay, and for other similar corrections of theatre practice. The leadership of Equity, struck as if by a squall by this disturbance of its peace, reacted with the fear and resistance characteristic of stagnant authority. They saw red and screamed
bloody murder. A dissident body, calling itself the Actors' Forum,
rose within Equity's sleepy ranks. They called special meetings
at which Heywood Broun made jolly speeches; they enjoyed up-
setting the apple-cart and making the feathers fly. It was the fun
of the thirties. Though the Actors' Forum was obliged to dis-
solve, it helped bring about a number of changes from which
every actor profited.

Egged on by a sense of emulation and frustrated by his inability to place his play *I Got the Blues* with us, Odets began to
write another, which he called *Paradise Lost.* I recommended *I
Got the Blues* to an agent. The agent was skeptical of my recom
mendation since we had not accepted the play ourselves. Shortly
after, the play was bought by Frank Merlin.

With the $500 acquired through this sale, Odets at once bought
a large Victrola and a few cases of whisky. He moved from Lee
Strasberg's scanty apartment to one on Horatio Street adjoining
a stable — a fact that chagrined his father no end.

The other actors who were neither writers, teachers, nor directors attended lectures, took courses, tried to gather fresh information. While a year before, in the depths of the depression, the
actors were making vain attempts to continue their acting classes,
now, shortly after President Roosevelt's experiments had begun
(the NIRA, etc.), they sought social knowledge. If, as I had always insisted, the artist is intimately related to the society in

which he functions, the actors were going to investigate more specifically the anatomy of their own society. Some began to study
economics — with what real success I never learned. Others attended the entertaining talks of John Strachey, whose book *The
Coming Struggle for Power* had caused something of a stir among
the intelligentsia as well as in the editorial offices of the Hearst
press. Political debates became popular: the editor of the *Daily
Worker*, for example, challenged the avowed fascist Lawrence
Dennis. The subject of their debate was announced as "Communism or Fascism" — an altogether misleading formulation of the
social problem, but sufficiently sensational to provide headline excitement and good box-office.

What precisely was learned from all this is of little import here;
the fact is that our actors began to question themselves, their
work, their theatre. They seemed to hanker after barricade dra-
matics, a sense of being in the fight rather than on the side-lines.

When Lawson's *Gentlewoman* was read to our company, they
were fairly enthusiastic. The play dealt with a sensitive, educated
woman of wealth who had grown neurotic through emotional dis-
use and lack of connection with the world. She is attracted by a
poet, both envious and contemptuous of her class; they have an
affair in which both hope to resolve their lack of fulfillment. He
wants the stability which she represents to him; she wants to share
the strength, courage, and daring that he symbolizes for her. He
learns through her that he is incapable of a steady relationship —
he has not yet found himself — and she learns through him something of the objective world which cannot be known except
through actual confrontation. He goes out to mend his soul
through work; she is left with the conviction of a future teeming
with trouble and the promise of a truer life.

The play possessed real qualities of emotional eloquence and
social understanding. But it lacked thematic and dramatic definition. It was a symbolic poetic work forced into the mold of a
drawing-room drama. Lawson himself at the time was a little like
both his protagonists, deeply in sympathy with the gentlewoman
of the past, brutally impatient with the softness that made him

cling to her, aware that he could not long dwell within this dual consciousness, eager for the conflagration ahead that would ultimately burn and temper all to a new wholeness and strength.

Every aspect of the play betrayed an ambiguity that derived from Lawson's intense groping. The social problem that was the center of the play's meaning could not be identified with any particular situation, for what was clearly visible struck the audience as merely the depiction of a rather stupid love affair.

Gentlewoman represented Lawson in a kind of halfway house on a nameless road leading to an unknown destination. It reflected a time when the confusion created by the stock-market crash and its sequel left the middle class with prayers and imprecations on their lips, but no clear answer in their mind or heart. They were waiting — and most of them didn't even know that.

The press was bad. The reviewers had no idea what the play was about, and didn't care. Lawson, they said, was maundering; his people were disturbed souls whose babblings made no sense. The Group directors were indignant at this reception of the play. We wrote letters of protest and even ran a paid ad in which we reminded everyone that the same author's *Processional* had also been underestimated when first produced. This provided fair game for the theatre columnists, who retorted easily enough that they still didn't think much of *Processional,* while granting that Lawson might continue to be described as "promising."

I believed in Lawson's talent. To prove it, I advanced him a thousand dollars on his next play — the one he had told me about in 1932. It was to be his most ambitious work.

Lawson interested the radicals, who nevertheless trounced him as mercilessly as the uptown boys. While the latter deplored his confusion, the former were positively enraged by it. Lawson accepted the invitation extended by a radical literary club to speak to them on his plays. Before he could take the floor, he was bombarded by a host of indictments, the burden of which was that though undeniably a writer of parts, he was *confused.* The word "confused" was repeated so often by so many that it took on the quality of an anathema.

When Lawson rose to speak, I was shocked to find him not only humble but apologetic. He talked like a man with a troubled conscience, a man confessing his sin, and in some way seeking absolution. He wanted his present critics to like him; he wanted to live up to their expectations, fulfill their requirements. He knew his plays were faulty; he was seeking in his heart and mind for the cause and remedy. I too knew the faults of his plays — although wiser about them in retrospect than I was at the time of their production — but I could not bear to see him refuse to defend the qualities they had, rare and valuable qualities which his critics spoke of patronizingly as if they were common and easily come by.

Someone hinted that what Lawson needed was closer contact with the working class. Lawson readily admitted this, and soon went on a trip to cover the Scottsboro case for a Left paper. He was arrested almost immediately and returned at once to New York. He set to work on his new play, but made no headway with it. He went to Hollywood to earn money, returned, and began to consider seriously the source of his weakness. He sought ideological clarity.

We tried to make a fight for *Gentlewoman*, so that it might not die in nine days. We asked the actors to cut their salaries so that we might prolong the play's run. I encountered resistance. One actor explained his refusal to accept a cut on the grounds of his disappointment with Lee Strasberg's direction of the play. I had always held that the artist had as much right to fail as anyone else, that very few artists worthy of the name had ever produced a steady stream of pleasing work. There were other complaints: we had wasted money on a "confused" play; we had erred in employing some non-Group actors.

The season of our success was thus strangely troubled, a season of subterranean growth and greensickness. All sorts of minor eruptions gave evidence of transition. Max Gorelik, for example, who had designed most of our productions, had insisted that nothing less than a contract for two productions would satisfy him. When we were about to do *Gentlewoman*, he heard a rumor that we were contemplating engaging another designer. He was in a dither and hastened to our office, armed with his wife. He wanted further guarantees. We were "exploiting" him. Furthermore, the directors were "exploiting" everyone in the Group. It mattered little to him that he had been the only one of us to be paid for his work on *Big Night*, and that even now the directors were among the Group's lower-bracket members. Facts were of little account: we were "bosses" and bosses "exploit." We were "exploiters." So infatuated was he with the word, that I soothed him by saying "Yes, we are bosses and exploiters. Now what do you want?"

He was delighted that he had at last wrung this damning confession from me. He wanted to present his case to the Group actors. This was granted. He also wished to have impartial witnesses — Lawson and other friends — attend this hearing. This also was granted.

We met on the stage of the Broadhurst after an evening performance, and Gorelik was given the floor. The gist of his speech was that while the three directors were people of some ability, they were not entirely trustworthy. He demanded first that he be made a member of the Group, with the same privileges as the actors; and he wanted all Group members to have access to the books of the organization, the right to formulate policy, and so on. The actors recognized his naïve wrongheadedness and tried to reason with him. They had confidence in their directors, they affirmed, and began to explain why. Among other things, Art Smith pointed out that in the Group he could "go over and punch Harold in the nose, and not be fired for it." A peculiar example, I thought. Gorelik made little headway as he concluded that the directors had cast an evil spell over the actors' minds.

The actors' state of mind was not quite so simple. They were doggedly loyal and anxiously critical. When we read the first rough draft of Melvin Levy's play *Gold Eagle Guy*, which we were to produce in the fall of 1934, they did not disguise their disappointment. It was not so much that they believed it a poor play, but it was not hotly contemporaneous in subject matter or feeling. I decided to analyze the whole subject of the Group's discontent. I wrote a forty-page paper in which everything — their dissatisfaction with our "conservative" policy in plays, their uncertainty as to whether they were given sufficient opportunity as actors, their feeling that there was something wrong with the salary arrangement — was fully discussed.

In this paper I pointed out that our aim was not and never had been to become a political theatre, but to be a creative and truly representative American theatre. This was no easy matter, because what had to be taken into consideration was the whole complex of facts that went into the making of a theatre: the state of our audience, the question of backing, the actual availability of new play scripts. With the success of *Men in White* we were in a position to look forward to the solution of some of our problems; that is, to co-ordinate the various elements that went into the making of a theatre in such a way that ever more significant contributions — artistic and social — might be anticipated by us. To the partisans of the new Leftist manifestations on the stage, I remarked that just as we had done the first depression play in *1931* — not from any political bias but from a sense of what was going on in our day, so in the future we would do more socially conscious plays than any other theatre then functioning. "But remember," I added, "it was no whim or eccentricity that made Gordon Craig say: 'It takes ten years to build a real theatre.'"

Lee Strasberg had decided to visit the theatres of the Soviet Union; so had Stella Adler. My paper, which cleared the air of certain lethal gases, was read to the Group on the eve of their departure. I was eager to follow them, but was delayed by duties and debts. Finally I found a way to make it.

The day before I sailed, the actors put forward a few practical suggestions. One of them was to give a number of people who had played all season in *Men in White* two weeks' vacation with pay. Early in the season the directors had forgiven all the actors' debts to the Group in an attempt to repay the actors for the many sacrifices they had made in harsher seasons. The present suggestion did not altogether please me. I asked how this arrangement could be made practicable without overtaxing the Group treasury. One method was to stop paying Stella Adler her $200 weekly now that she was on her vacation abroad. I submitted that this was tantamount to penalizing her for not having been fortunate enough to be cast in *Men in White*. Was she to be the exception to our rule to pay an actor his or her salary as long as a Group production was running? I was answered that my point would hold water if Stella had remained in New York and had agreed to understudy or perform some equivalent professional function. If we insisted on paying her now, it meant she had been placed in a special category — she was a star in the Group. I refused to be moved by this counterargument, which showed traces of a petty vindictiveness. As far as I was concerned, the question was closed. Clifford Odets asked me whether I intended to ride roughshod over the actors' feelings. I answered: "Yes."

On my arrival in Moscow I heard that the actors had carried out their plan — no doubt with Cheryl Crawford's assent — and that Stella's salary was no longer being paid. Stella was incensed over this, and I defended the Group's action. The matter was soon forgotten. We were in Moscow; a new world faced us.

CHAPTER ELEVEN

Transition

MY stay in Moscow was very brief — ten days. What impressed me most in the theatre was the variety and scope of the repertoire, the incredible richness of the productions, the excitement and enthusiasm of the audiences. Maturity of technique, clarity of purpose, the gusto of play, and a colorfulness beside which the theatres of the west were drab, inspired the spectator with a feeling of elated energy. On leaving I determined that I would return to Moscow when I could see it at greater leisure.

On the way home I stopped off in Paris. There was something wrong here that I could not quite make out. There was a certain grimness I had never observed before. There had been riots in

February, about which jokes were cracked in all the revues. The business man at the café sat behind his paper with an air of holding out against some menace he wanted by all means to avoid or suppress. It was probably not so much the Nazis as the Popular Front.

My passage through Paris was made memorable by my meeting with Stanislavsky. I had not known he was in Paris. When I visited Copeau, who was then dramatic critic for a literary weekly, he told me that Stanislavsky was in town and that I ought to meet him.

Stella Adler and I called on him. He spoke at once of what was uppermost in his thought: the theatre. Every afternoon he went out for a few hours to get the sun in the Bois de Boulogne. He had been suffering from a heart ailment and had been spending the past year in Italy under the care of a physician supplied him by the Soviet government. Stanislavsky asked us to accompany him to the Bois. Stella and I asked many questions. Stanislavsky answered all of them cordially and carefully. He asked us to come again. We went to the Bois again the next afternoon to take up where we had left off the previous day.

Stella Adler had been worried for three years over certain aspects of the Stanislavsky system or method. She no longer found any joy in acting, she avowed; perhaps this was due to that cursed method. Stanislavsky said immediately: "If the system does not help you, forget it. But perhaps you do not use it properly." He offered to work with her on some scene that she had found difficult.

Day after day we returned. I was growing restless despite my deep enjoyment of these conversations. Stanislavsky was not only a great man of the theatre but a fine human being, strong and simple, urbane and warm, thoughtful and relaxed. Yet I felt I had to get back to New York and the Group. Stella urged me to stay on. I left. She continued seeing Stanislavsky daily for five weeks, during which time she worked with him on a scene from *Gentlewoman*.

The Group spent that summer in an enormous house on top of a damp hill in the Catskills. Our colony consisted, as the *New*

York Times put it, of "8 dogs, 21 victrolas, 3 radios, 14 motor cars, a complete library of symphony records, a lot of books on the theatre, 4 colored waiters, Alexander Kirkland's dog who has lost all his fur." The profusion of animal life brought on an epidemic of ringworm among us.

We rehearsed Melvin Levy's *Gold Eagle Guy*. A new apprentice was the fervid Jules Garfield. Morris Carnovsky gave a speech class based mostly on the reading of verse, and I gave my first formal class in playwrighting. My method was to analyze dramatic technique from the Greeks to Sean O'Casey. Among the students were Alan Baxter, Art Smith, Roman Bohnen, Elia Kazan, and Odets. These classes were continued through the winter, and were resumed with new people in 1937.

The outstanding artistic feature of the summer was the influence of Stella Adler's report on her work with Stanislavsky. To put it bluntly, she had discovered that our use of the Stanislavsky system had been incorrect. An undue emphasis on the "exercises" of affective memory had warped our work with the actor. Strasberg's first reaction to this declaration was the charge that Stanislavsky had gone back on himself. Later, however, he decided to take advantage of the suggestions furnished by Stella's report, and to use what he could of the "innovations" in Stanislavsky's method. Stella herself began to give classes that summer.

Strasberg had been most impressed in Moscow with the Meyerhold productions, as they had always held a theoretical fascination for him. In his production of *Gold Eagle Guy* he displayed a greater concern with movement and the expressive value of physical materials than he had ever had before. There was a certain factitious side to this, however. Strasberg, as I have noted, had a very special talent, so that even his early teaching of the Stanislavsky method was peculiarly his own. The "improvements" of recent import tended to weaken Strasberg's grip on his own method.

The effect of my Moscow trip was to release me. For four years I had lived, theatrically speaking, in Strasberg's shadow. My failure to achieve my own style of direction derived from my falling into an imitation of Strasberg's method. The variety of Soviet theatre styles helped me find myself by showing me concretely

how many possibilities there were. But this only became clear to
me the following winter.

Another striking aspect of our summer was the desire for social
action that seized some of our people. At this time it had a pre-
dominantly comic quality. Our neophyte radicals wanted to fix
everything. Theirs was a veritable itch to unearth monstrous in-
justices they could be indignant about, to find causes they could
espouse, to seek battles they could join.

The mayor of a small New England town had committed some
transgression against democratic procedure: we were exhorted
with something like an anguished sense of injury to send wires of
protest. Here, there, everywhere, some social foul play needed
our remedying. One or two people suddenly became trade-union
experts. What knowledge they lacked they could pick up by in-
viting veterans in this field to visit them. An exchange was effected: the actors were given this all-important information while
the astonished and delighted trade-unionist would become acquainted with our cultural pursuits and unusual environment.
Nor did all this learning go for nothing. Not only was Gorelik's
charge that the Group directors were conspiring against the
United Scenic Artists given close scrutiny, but I discovered that
even our own kitchen staff was being propagandized. It appeared
that the directors were at it again — exploiting the help. It is true
we were mostly good guys, but as directors we had the blindness
of bosses.

During the run of *Men in White* Cheryl Crawford, together
with our "audience manager," Helen Thompson, had discussed
the possibility of a Group season in Boston with Mrs. Roland
Gage Hopkins of that city. We opened there in October 1934 with
Men in White, followed by a revival of *Success Story*, which in
turn was followed by the premiere of Melvin Levy's *Gold Eagle
Guy*.

The guarantors for this season included the presidents of Rad-
cliffe College, M.I.T., Tufts, eight representatives from the Har-
vard faculty, the chairman of the Boston Opera Company, heads

of thirteen preparatory schools, bankers, journalists, and other prominent Bostonians. The arrangement of all this in its detail was something of which Lee Strasberg and I particularly were hardly aware — our heads were in the clouds. So we were equally unaware of the real-estate chicanery that landed us finally in the vast and miserable Majestic Theatre, a house utterly unsuited to our program.

Men in White was moderately successful; its release as a picture prevented greater popularity. *Success Story* was received with critical respect. But the advent of Hitler and his malignant creed affected the reception of the play badly. Many who saw or heard about the play, whose central character was a demoniacally ambitious Jewish boy, could not help feeling that the appearance now of such a character on our stage was, to say the least, ill-timed. For this reason, and because our large physical production of *Gold Eagle Guy* needed much rehearsal, we cut the run of the Lawson play short.

At this juncture Clifford Odets came to me one evening with an outline of a one-act play he contemplated writing for the New Theatre League. The League was looking for plays that workers might put on at any meeting-place or hall. The scheme of the play, Odets explained, was related to that of the minstrel show. A meeting is called among taxi-drivers to decide upon the question of a strike. They are waiting for a leader who never appears. In the meantime a series of characters rise to tell why they are in favor of striking. Their stories make the body of the play, the decision to strike its climax. It sounded very promising, I told Odets. On this he disappeared like a flash — and wrote *Waiting for Lefty* in three nights.

He did not mention the play to me again. He consulted the actors, read it, and advised with them on it. Perhaps he was saving it, showman fashion, for a bombshell effect on the Group directors.

He did speak to me, however, about his present state of mind, the feeling the times evoked in him. He wanted comradeship; he wanted to belong to the largest possible group of humble, struggling men prepared to make a great common effort to build a better world. Without this, life for him would be lonely and hopeless. In the Group Theatre he had found kindred spirits, intellectual stimulation. But we were artists. Now he felt the need to share his destiny with the lowliest worker, with those who really stood in the midst of life. I sympathized with him fully, but I cautioned him against immediately translating his sentiments into acts the consequences of which he might later either shrink from or find himself unable to sustain. In the sphere of action, withdrawal or vacillation often leads to compromise, disappointment, confusion. One may belie oneself through ill-considered boldness as through false humility. But none of my homilies could have the slightest effect on him. He was driven by a powerful emotional impetus, like a lover on the threshold of an elopement.

When the company read *Waiting for Lefty* in the cellar of the Majestic Theatre, they were struck by its originality and fire. They rehearsed it in their spare time. Luther Adler told me with a quiet glow of pleasure: "Harold, the Group has produced the finest revolutionary playwright in America."

In the meantime *Gold Eagle Guy* had its Boston opening. Rehearsals had become increasingly difficult in their final phase. The actors had never been much impressed with the play, and Strasberg was worried over it. Backstage Luther Adler, referring to the play, said: "Boys, I think we're working on a stiff."

The New York press on the whole was remarkably cordial to *Gold Eagle Guy*. Designed by Donald Oenslager, it was visually very handsome. It had energy, color, and a degree of racy Americanism. The script, however, was basically deficient in dramatic flare and tension, loosely knit, and lacking in genuine emotion.

The public was perhaps more astute than the press. The play did not go, though we beat both play and public on the head to stir them to some semblance of life. Difficult days were facing us again.

About this time, I had another of my almost perpetual philosophical disputes with my father. He was a critical man, often relentlessly objective and impersonal. He told me now, as he had hinted before, that the Group was doomed to failure. His prediction took full account of our talent, conscientiousness, determination. He knew of the praise we had earned, even the money. *Men in White* had been awarded the Pulitzer Prize. But, he pointed out, we held to a collective ideal in a competitive society; we harped on the Idea in an impatient, money-minded world. I insisted we could go on and achieve a measure of success. "It's a very hard job," he warned. "It's an impossible one," I answered.

The Group did fail in 1941. But in 1935 it was on the eve of its most memorable and significant accomplishments. Who was right, my father or I?

The Group directors met. It was suggested that we close the season. We had played six weeks in Boston and eight in New York. We could do no more. I admitted that we were in a bad spot, but a way out could be found. If we quit now, we were through. The company, I said, demanded an act of faith from us, and holding on for the rest of the season, despite every hardship, was the only proper response to this demand. As I spoke, Strasberg kept reading or pretending to read a newspaper. This was his way of masking his feelings and preserving his patience.

He put his paper down and as calmly as possible explained that he and the Group were well acquainted — in fact, a little tired — of my breathless professions of faith. The truth was we were now restraining people from earning a living. Nearly everyone had offers to work elsewhere, while we had nothing concrete to offer except more heroic tirades. It was a physical impossibility for us to keep on this way: we should soon all be headed for the hospital or the psychopathic ward.

This is exactly how Strasberg had spoken after *Big Night*. Now there was even greater justification for his state of mind, yet I could not see eye to eye with him. Perhaps this was so only because I was not as tired now as he or Cheryl Crawford; perhaps unconsciously I sensed that in 1935 we were entering a more favorable period than the spring of 1933 had been. Yet their failure to be moved by my exhortation appeared to defeat me. We were going to close our theatre for the season. Only it was I, and not they, who was supposed to announce this to the actors.

On several occasions early that winter I had brought up the possibility of doing Odets's *I Got the Blues*, now renamed *Awake and Sing*. The more I thought about it, the better I liked it. In a careful production it could be given real distinction. Strasberg disagreed with this. He was troubled by the play's frequent bad taste — as, for example, when in the play's early version Bessie Berger not only abused her father but slapped him. A few minutes before the meeting at which I was to announce our cheerless decision, I asked again whether it would not be a good idea to do Odets's play. Cheryl Crawford remained silent — she was undecided — while Strasberg repeated his objections.

I addressed the actors in the basement of the Belasco Theatre. When I had finished, a moment of silence ensued. Suddenly Stella Adler scornfully told me that it was the most abject weakness for the directors to close our season in January. It was not what the actors wanted to hear; they wanted to be told that, by hook or crook, we would continue. The entire company applauded; each actor took up where Stella had left off, and threw the gauntlet down to the directors. Strasberg said: "If the directors had come to you with the decision to continue, you would have protested." "We resent that," Walter Coy retorted.

The actors had won the day. Only the first step had been taken, however. Now that we had decided to keep our theatre running, the question of what play we would produce remained. A number of suggestions were made, and the actors planned to review every available script that offered them the possibility of another production.

Odets spoke up on behalf of *Awake and Sing*. (He had already finished two acts of *Paradise Lost*, which I had read on New Year's Eve 1934, but it needed more work and time for completion.) Odets pointed out that he had cut the first twenty pages of Act One, that I had always like the second act, and that the third could be revised. He himself offered to raise the money for the production. Exasperated, Strasberg broke out fiercely: "You don't seem to understand, Cliff. We don't like your play. We don't like it."

During the next two weeks a number of scripts were read. In my own mind I had already decided that *Awake and Sing* would be our next production. But I wanted the actors to affirm my choice, or at any rate to appear to force it. While the actors were reading all the other scripts, I told Odets that we would certainly do his. Finally Odets read *Awake and Sing* to the company. I did not attend the reading myself, but I came in just as the last words of the play were being spoken. The actors' faces were aglow. Enthusiasm was unanimous.

The next day I told Cheryl and Lee that we should do *Awake and Sing*. There was no debate. I also announced that I would direct the play. Strasberg said: "It would be very beneficial."

During the run of *Gold Eagle Guy* Cheryl had told me that Lee believed that the actors were losing faith in me because I had not yet directed a play. I answered that though this was probably true, I would direct only when I felt it was right for me to do so, and was not going to be frightened into it either by suspicion from the outside or by a sense of inferiority within. I had been prepared for this statement from my director colleagues since about the same time Stella Adler had told me, in a way that really hurt, that because of my failure to direct any of the Group productions I had proved myself a thorough disappointment.

Clifford Odets and I had shared our days of dejection together; we had become close friends. Some weeks before the events just recounted, Clifford, slightly high with brandy, had thrown his arms around me in front of the Hotel Brevoort, where I lived at the time, and cried: "Harold, I love you like a brother."

I was also brother to his play. On the closing night of *Gold Eagle Guy*, after the final curtain, I announced that our next production was to be the work of our own Clifford Odets. The actors gave forth a shout of joy and threw their costumes in the air. It was as if we had been working and waiting for this for four years.

PART IV

CONSUMMATION

CHAPTER TWELVE

Awake and Sing

ALTHOUGH *Awake and Sing* was a modest one-set play, Odets was unable to raise the money to produce it. Neither was I, when I addressed myself to backers interested in the "better things" in the theatre. The play, which showed people grappling with the petty details that mess up their lives, seemed in script form to make an unpleasant, harsh impression. The pettiness and mess were more apparent than the play's tenderness and pathos.

I decided to appeal to Franchot Tone in Hollywood. I called him by phone, and told him we needed $5,000 to produce Odets's play. He asked me to send a script on to him for reading. I promised to do so, but I insisted that he send the money without waiting for the script. Franchot laughed and agreed.

Though we now had the money to put the play on, no provision had been made to defray the cost of moving the heavy *Gold Eagle Guy* scenery from the stage of the Belasco, where the new production was to be housed. Part of Franchot's money had to be used to pay for this operation. Cheryl Crawford was obliged to raise another $1,500 to compensate for this unforeseen expense.

Rehearsals proceeded with remarkable efficiency and harmony. Boris Aronson, an artist whose talent had always interested me, was engaged to design the set. Stella Adler, though she first shrank from the idea of playing an unglamorous woman of fifty, took up the challenge because I suggested that perhaps after all she might not be able to do it. She wanted to prove that she could act virtually any role, no matter how removed from her in type.

Though it is true that everything at this time was done *con amore*, a few trifling circumstances cast shadows to highlight the generally creative atmosphere of our work. During the first week of rehearsal Bromberg asked if we could release him for an engagement in Hollywood, since his part in our play was only a secondary one. When I rejected the very thought of this, he said no more about it.

I was living with Odets on Horatio Street, and after rehearsal he kept me up nights to discuss the progress of the play. (We promised each other that if the play prospered at all, we would move to more respectable quarters.) I hardly slept at all. Because of over-concentration and the rapid pace of production – the play was rehearsed less than four weeks – I was in a state of almost complete exhaustion as opening night approached.

There were only nine members of the Group company in *Awake and Sing*. Most of the others were busy with rehearsals of *Waiting for Lefty* under the direction of Sanford Meisner and Clifford Odets. It was to be given at a benefit for the *New Theatre Magazine*, unofficial organ of the new insurgent movement in the theatre.

Sunday night, January 5, 1935, at the old Civic Repertory Theatre on Fourteenth Street, an event took place to be noted in the annals of the American theatre. The evening had opened with a mildly amusing one-act play by Paul Green. The audience, though attracted by the guest appearance of a good part of the Group company, had no idea of what was to follow.

The first scene of *Lefty* had not played two minutes when a

shock of delighted recognition struck the audience like a tidal
wave. Deep laughter, hot assent, a kind of joyous fervor seemed
to sweep the audience toward the stage. The actors no longer
performed; they were being carried along as if by an exultancy
of communication such as I had never witnessed in the theatre
before. Audience and actors had become one. Line after line
brought applause, whistles, bravos, and heartfelt shouts of kinship.

The taxi strike of February 1934 had been a minor incident in
the labor crisis of this period. There were very few taxi-drivers
in that first audience, I am sure; very few indeed who had ever
been directly connected with such an event as the union meeting
that provided the play its pivotal situation. When the audience at
the end of the play responded to the militant question from the
stage: "Well, what's the answer?" with a spontaneous roar of
"Strike! Strike!" it was something more than a tribute to the
play's effectiveness, more even than a testimony of the audience's
hunger for constructive social action. It was the birth cry of the
thirties. Our youth had found its voice. It was a call to join the
good fight for a greater measure of life in a world free of economic fear, falsehood, and craven servitude to stupidity and
greed. "Strike!" was *Lefty's* lyric message, not alone for a few extra pennies of wages or for shorter hours of work, strike for
greater dignity, strike for a bolder humanity, strike for the full
stature of man.

The audience, I say, was delirious. It stormed the stage, which
I persuaded the stunned author to mount. People went from the
theatre dazed and happy: a new awareness and confidence had
entered their lives.

A series of *Lefty* performances was given every Sunday thereafter at the Civic Repertory Theatre — all of them benefits. Finally
on February 10 the press was invited to see *Lefty*, given together with the Group's experimental sketches.

The reviewers liked *Lefty* very much. At this time, after the
Theatre Union had done three productions, and the Jewish
workers' group known as Artef had won a degree of esoteric
fame, one or two commentators noted that "the progress of the

Scene from *Waiting for Lefty* by Clifford Odets, 1935. (Direction: Clifford Odets and Sanford Meisner.)

Scene from Amelia and Sarah Giffard's *Clifton Oaks*, 1925 (Director — Harold Clayman; Setting — Basic Acme, n.p.)

revolutionary drama in New York City during the last two seasons is the most recent development in the theatre."

Awake and Sing, which had been in rehearsal about ten days when *Lefty* was first presented, opened on February 19, 1935. It was accorded a very favorable but not sensational newspaper reception. In the *New York Times* Brooks Atkinson, after calling Odets the Group's "most congenial playwright," went on to say: "Although he is very much awake, he does not sing with the ease and clarity of a man who has mastered his score. Although his dialogue has uncommon strength, his drama in the first two acts is wanting in the ordinary fluidity of a play. . . . To this student of the arts *Awake and Sing* is inexplicably deficient in plain theatre emotion."

Awake and Sing was written out of the distress of the 1932 depression (not to mention Odets's whole youth). It was completed in 1933 and belatedly produced in 1935. Yet only when it was revived in 1939 did the same reviewer say: "When Clifford Odets's *Awake and Sing* burst in the face of an unsuspecting public four years ago, some of the misanthropes complained that it was praised too highly. Misanthropes are always wrong. For it is plain after a glimpse of the revival last evening that *Awake and Sing* cannot be praised too highly. . . . When it was first produced, it seemed febrile as a whole and dogmatic in conclusion. It does not seem so now; it seems thoroughly normal, reasonable, true."

Now when no one ever mentions the possibility or desirability of a repertory theatre, it might be pointed out that there can hardly be any true theatre culture without it, since most judgments in the theatre are as spotty and short-sighted as those Mr. Atkinson confessed. Indeed, the judgment of any work of art on the basis of a single hasty contact would be as frivolous as most theatre opinion. And, since I have paused to make the point, I might add that only by constant repetition through the seasons did the plays of Chekhov become box-office in Russia.

A bit of loose talk about Chekhov's influence on Odets cropped up in some reviews. Odets knew very little of Chekhov's work at this time, but quite a lot about Lawson's *Success Story,* in which he had served as Luther Adler's understudy. It was Lawson's play that brought Odets an awareness of a new kind of theatre dialogue. It was a compound of lofty moral feeling, anger, and the feverish argot of the big city. It bespoke a warm heart, an outraged spirit, and a rough tongue.

But the talk of Chekhov's influence on Odets's work was a minor note in the reception of his plays. Far more common was the bugaboo of Marxism or Communism. They constituted the specter that haunted the thirties. Rumor on these subjects was so prevalent that it reached even the daily theatrical columns. One reviewer, for example, spoke of "the simplicity of his [Odets's] communist panaceas." He preferred *Awake and Sing* to *Lefty* because in the latter "one finds Mr. Odets working now as a party member."

The Left press at the time of Odets's first success granted his importance, but was careful to make serious reservations about *Lefty*, spoke gingerly of *Awake and Sing* (in the *New Masses*), and called it "a come-down for the Group Theatre, an unimportant play whichever way you look at it," in the *Daily Worker*.

Odets became the central figure of the so-called Left movement in the theatre. But the relation of his work to Marxism or Communism was of a special sort not to be understood in terms of glib political commentary. The Marxist drift of the thirties no more "caused" *Lefty* or *Awake and Sing* in January and February of 1935 than *Lefty* and *Awake and Sing* caused the organization of the CIO in November of that year. All these phenomena, including also the NRA and the later acts of the New Deal (the National Labor Act and so on), were an outgrowth of and a response to a common dislocation that convulsed our whole society. They were all undoubtedly related, but they are by no means comprehensible if they are lumped together mechanically as if they were identical.

Odets's work from the beginning contained "a protest that is also prophecy." There was in it a fervor that derived from the hope and expectation of change and the desire for it. But there was rarely any expression of political consciousness in it, no deep commitment to a coherent philosophy of life, no pleading for a panacea. "A tendril of revolt" runs through all of Odets's work, but that is not the same thing as a consistent revolutionary conviction. Odets's work is not even proletarian in the sense that Gorky's work is. Rather is it profoundly of the lower middle class with all its vacillation, dual allegiance, fears, groping, self-distrust, dejection, spurts of energy, hosannas, vows of conversion, and prayers for release. The "enlightenment" of the thirties, its effort to come to a clearer understanding of and control over the anarchy of our society, brought Odets a new mental perspective, but it is his emotional experience, not his thought, that gives his plays their special expressiveness and significance. His thought, the product chiefly of his four years with the Group and the new channels they led to, furnished Odets with the more conscious bits of his vocabulary, with an occasional epithet or slogan that were never fully integrated in his work. The feel of middle-class (and perhaps universal) disquiet in Odets's plays is sharp and specific; the ideas are general and hortatory. The Left movement provided Odets with a platform and a loud-speaker; the music that came through was that of a vast population of restive souls, unaware of its own mind, seeking help. To this Odets added the determination of youth. The quality of his plays is young, lyrical, yearning — as of someone on the threshold of life.

It was nonsense for the New York *Sun's* reviewer, in order to challenge the validity of *Lefty*, to check with a taxidriver on his average earnings. *Lefty* was not basically about the hackman's low wages, but about every impediment to that full life for which youth hungers. Hence the play's wide appeal.

Perhaps Odets privately harbored the belief that socialism offers the only solution for our social-economic problems. Perhaps his desire to share a comradely closeness to his fellowmen might attract him to those who hoped to bring about a socialist society, but he must also have suspected that temperamentally he might prove a trial to any well-knit party. Instead of being an adherent of a fixed program, a disciplined devotee of a set strategy or system, Odets possessed a talent that always had an ambiguous character. If because of all this the regular press was misled into chatter about his "Marxism" while the Left press was frankly perplexed and troubled by him, it may also be guessed that Odets too was pretty much in the dark on this score.

On the one hand, Odets felt himself very close to the people — the great majority of Americans — even in his bent for the "good old theatre"; on the other hand, his heart was always with the rebels. But who precisely were the rebels, and what did they demand of him? Those he knew were a small minority, and they marked out a line for him that he could not altogether accept. After the first flurry of Odets's success had passed, everyone discovered a "change" in him. The conventional reviewers were glad; the Left was disconcerted. But, in the sense they had in mind, both were wrong — Odets had not changed.

Perhaps the truth is that the vast majority, to which Odets felt he belonged as much as to any rebellious few, had not yet created for itself a cultural clarity or form, not to speak of other kinds of clarity or form — had not, for example, yet made for itself a theatre in which he could function freely. Perhaps the "few" who often criticized him more harshly than anyone else did not know how much they had in common with those they professed to scorn.

Whatever later wisdom might declare, Odets in the spring of 1935 was the man of the hour. Theatrically speaking, the climax of the Odets vogue came with the production of *Lefty* as a regular show on Broadway.

Since *Lefty* was only an hour long, we had to have a companion piece to go with it. Odets himself supplied this by dramatizing a short story purporting to be a letter from Nazi Germany he had read in the *New Masses*. The play, written to order, was finished in less than a week. Cheryl Crawford directed it, and the setting was designed by an unofficial Group apprentice, Paul Morison, who had performed similar services for us at Green Mansions.

This twin bill opened at the Longacre Theatre on March 26, 1935 at a price range from fifty cents to a dollar and a half — something of an innovation on Broadway.

In order not to disturb the casting of *Awake and Sing*, all the actors not engaged in that play took over the production of *Lefty* and *Till the Day I Die*, which, incidentally, was one of the first serious anti-Nazi plays to reach the New York stage.

Odets himself played Dr. Benjamin in *Lefty* (originally played by Luther Adler), and on opening night his appearance was greeted by an ovation. This was the last acting assignment of his career. Lee Strasberg under an assumed name played a small part in the anti-Nazi play. In the new *Lefty* cast Elia Kazan, replacing Bromberg, was thunderously effective. Everyone was sure we had picked him off a taxi to play the part — our "discovery" from Constantinople, Williams College, and Yale!

The new play was respectfully received though the *New York Times* reviewer thought: "If you want to register an emotional protest against Nazi polity, Mr. Odets requires that you join the Communist brethren" — a rather peculiar interpretation of a play that at most called for a united front against Nazism. But the plea for such a front in those days was chiefly associated with Communists.

The play actually was a rather old-fashioned piece of theatre in a style that derived from the swell of Odets's sentiment, an unavowed inclination toward romantic drama, and a feeling for social currents. It was a little artificial, yet not without some qualities of youthful sweetness and idealism.

Awake and Sing never made much money. Odets believed the failure of *Awake and Sing* to become a box-office smash was due to the Group's lack of business ability. He was wrong; the play attracted an important but small part of the theatre-going public: those who bought the cheaper tickets. *Lefty* and *Till the Day I Die* were seen by a devoted and intelligent public still too small (and poor), alas, to furnish box-office comfort.

Yet, except for their bewildered backers, the plays were an enormous success. They were the talk of the town, the thing-to-see for all who wished to remain abreast of the times. If we hadn't known this through reviews, interviews, public clamor, and an excited correspondence, I at least should have guessed it by the constant buzzing of the phone in the University Place apartment I shared with Odets.

The lion-hunters were on the trail. Actresses, publicists, bankers, novelists, editors, wanted to meet the boy wonder. There was a difference in his situation as compared to that of a young writer like Thomas Wolfe, who was similarly sought after on the publication of *Look Homeward, Angel.* The difference was that while Odets was regarded by many as the dramatic find of the day, he was in addition that new phenomenon, a radical, a revolutionary, a Red.

An interest in an important new playwright was altogether normal for people like Tallulah Bankhead, Ruth Gordon, Beatrice Lillie, Helen Hayes, Charles MacArthur, Clare Boothe (Luce). But when Bernard Baruch began to examine him, when Edna Ferber asked that he be invited to a party that she might simply "take a look" at him, when Walter Winchell sought him out to have him explain the meaning of Communism (only to decide that he preferred to get the information from the "top man," Stalin himself), we were confronted with a sign of the times as significant as it was comic.

Odets was in a whirl, pleasant at first no doubt, a little terrifying later. He bought himself more records and virtually doped himself with music. Little girls he had known in the days of our jaunts to Stewart's Cafeteria on Sheridan Square now approached him timidly (or suspiciously) and asked him if they could still speak to him. This infuriated and bruised him. He began to feel rather shut off, isolated.

At the time *Awake and Sing* was written, a Hollywood scout offered him $500 a week on the gold coast. Odets asked me if it wasn't "unrealistic" to refuse it. I replied that it wasn't, if for no other reason than that he would be offered more later. When, despite all the acclaim, his earnings were relatively modest, though greater than they had ever been before, his agent called to tell him that MGM was willing to go as high as $3,000 weekly, perhaps even higher. Like a conspirator he whispered that he might be willing to consider it.

I overheard this conversation and was troubled by it. When I was at sea on my way abroad in April, I wrote him a letter confessing my reaction. It was his duty to himself, to his colleagues, and to his audience to go on writing plays. The three first plays, and the recently completed *Paradise Lost,* were a mere beginning. Odets answered that he was happy I had written him as I did. Indeed such criticism as my letter implied was always welcomed by him: it made him feel responsible. In 1937, after the success of *Golden Boy,* when I wrote him a letter in which I was very severe with him for not making better use of his time than he was wont to do at such periods, he said to me: "I received your letter. I loved it." Perhaps not all artists are so, but many flourish only when they feel a concern for their work that is eager, jealous, essential.

People from all over the country swarmed into our offices. They wanted to join us, they said, because they were in sympathy with our aims. It was often a rude shock to them when I pointed out that we were a theatre, not a cult, and that talent was still the first requirement for work with us.

The actors were now riding the crest of the wave. I do not mean this in any material sense, since most of the Group had as vague an understanding of their own economic situation as I did. They never worried over money except when they were broke, in which case a few dollars in their pockets would make them feel affluent again. They were thriving with a sense of fulfillment, the feeling that they were part of the main current, which to an extent they had helped create.

Our activity was incessant. A few of our people made experimental films with Ralph Steiner. Others helped direct plays for new groups. Kazan, for example, did this for the Theatre of Action, which produced *The Young Go First,* a play about the CCC camps. We arranged a symposium of lectures at the New School for Social Research. Lee Strasberg gave a course on stage direction at the Theatre Collective School. At Mecca Temple Morris Carnovsky did a monologue by Odets called *I Can't Sleep,* one of the pages of Odets's work most significant for its indication of the source of his inspiration — the troubled conscience of the middle class in the depression period. At the same time a playlet by Art Smith called *The Tide Rises* based on the San Francisco marine strike used the talents of the younger people in the Group and showed the Odets influence already at work.

New theatre societies were being formed all over the country to give the three Odets plays. Group Theatres shot up like mushrooms: in Chicago, Hollywood, New Orleans, San Francisco. A Negro People's Theatre was set up in Harlem to give *Lefty* under the direction of our own Bill Challee. All in all, *Lefty* was being done in some sixty towns which had never before witnessed a theatrical performance. Thirty-two cities were seeing the twin bill of *Lefty* and *Till the Day I Die* at the same time.

Even suppressions, bans, arrests on grounds of "unlawful assembly" or "profanity," served to increase the play's prestige. These occurred in Philadelphia, Boston, New Haven, Newark, Dorchester, Chelsea, and Roxbury. On the west coast Will Geer, managing a small enterprise that had announced *Till the Day I Die,* received a menacing note: "You know what we do to the enemies of the New Germany." He produced the play, and was severely beaten up by Bundist hoodlums. In New York Odets put an extra heavy lock on the door of our apartment.

From a political or sensational standpoint, all this came to a boil when Odets went down to Cuba as head of a committee to study labor and social conditions, with emphasis on the status of students under the reactionary Mendieta regime. The visit — under the auspices of the League of American Writers — was supposed to last two weeks. It lasted a few hours; on the arrival of the S.S. *Oriente* the entire committee, composed of timid little white-collar workers and teachers, were arrested as "agitators."

The story made the headlines. Telegrams of protest were sent, meetings held, petitions signed. When I heard that some of the Group actors had called a protest meeting for the acting profession and saw one of them haranguing the small audience, beerhall fashion, I became almost as annoyed as I had been amused.

Odets had been chosen to head the committee because in six months he had become a name. To be used in this way, flattered him and appealed to his Hugoesque imagination. He wrote a few amusing reports on the matter for the *New York Post,* made highly inflammatory statements, and sounded off generally like a gay hothead in the Parisian forties of last century. He soon became bored with his own busyness, temperamentally foreign to his introverted nature.

Odets's plays aroused interest not only in theatrical and minor political circles but in the literary world generally. The book-reviewers devoted columns to him: he was being read in the same spirit as were the novels of Dos Passos, James Farrell, Erskine Caldwell, John Steinbeck, Robert Cantwell, and Thomas Wolfe. The Group as a whole drew strength from this graduation from Broadway onto the larger American scene. It also drew some false conclusions from it.

This became evident in its reaction to new plays — for example, *Winterset*. Maxwell Anderson was contemplating letting the Group, for which he had an abiding affection, produce the play if it would cast Burgess Meredith in the leading role. Despite interesting production possibilities and a fine basic theme, it left me rather cold. I could not make myself comfortable in its atmosphere of an "Elizabethan" East Side! But, considering the state of American drama, it was not a play to be dismissed lightly.

We decided, therefore, to read the play to our company. With the exception of two or three people the actors were more averse to the play than I. Though its theme was Justice and its idea sprang from a prolonged pondering on the historic Sacco-Vanzetti case, they felt no immediacy, no true life in the play, only a filtering of these matters through a sentimental literary imagination.

Lee Strasberg did not so much disagree with this reaction as he feared its consequences on the course of our development as a practical theatre. Because he felt himself under a cloud at this time, he failed to fight for his opinion. Two years later, when I admitted to the company that we had made a mistake in not doing the play, for all our reservations, since the function of a producing organization cannot be equated with that of the critic in his chair, the company maintained the integrity of its character and expressed shock at my change of view.

Yet it must not be assumed from this that the actors had be-

come altogether complacent because of their newly won acclaim.
On the contrary, there was a strong urge to make further progress.
There was, for example, a movement afoot — led by Stella Adler
— to take group lessons from the Russian actor Michael Chekhov.
We all considered Chekhov a true acting genius, though the New
York press had been unable to recognize it. The actors felt that
they had achieved some measure of honesty and truth in their
work, but Chekhov's gift for combining these with sharply expressive and yet very free color, rhythm, and design was something
in which they knew themselves to be deficient, and which they
therefore envied.

The discussion that ensued among us on this subject — a few
suggested that Chekhov be persuaded to return to the Soviet
Union — was a mirror of the Group's varied and lively state of
mind.

Another type of discussion took place between John Howard
Lawson and me. Instead of completing the play for which we
had made him an advance, he had taken to writing a book. This
book was intended to guide and correct himself as much as other
playwrights who stood at a creative impasse. He planned to study
the leading thought of the various historic epochs and to trace
the manner in which this thought had been converted to dramatic
use by the playwrights of each period. Then by assessing his own
beliefs, by shaping them into some sort of system in tune with the
most solid social wisdom of the day, he hoped to arrive at a
methodology that would lead him out of the morass of his own
violent mysticism and emotional anarchy.

The writing of this book, the reasons that motivated it, the
changes within the author's mind during its writing, all were of
utmost concern to me. They reflected not merely a personal but a
typical drama in the æsthetic, moral, and social history of the
period.

All that was clear to me then was that in our friendly dispute it
seemed that I was advocating a greater reliance on the artist's
individual instinct, and Lawson was insisting on a greater adherence to rational analysis, coherent thought, and a firmer definition of technique and objectives. Our positions had apparently re-

versed since the days when Lawson was fulminating rather wildly and asking: "What do you mean 'art of the theatre' ?" while I had solemnly called for a more conscious approach to it. Nevertheless, I really made no issue of our debate, since I preferred to trust the testimony of works rather than the correctness of any idea.

That our success was neither universal nor equally gratifying to all who observed it, I began to suspect as soon as the first hurrahs began to die down. *Time* magazine, for instance, published besides its regular and, I believe, complimentary reviews of our three new plays a newsy report of Odets's career, which had to take the Group into account as the background from which Odets had emerged. It was all blithely factual, but there was a curious emphasis that was perhaps not accidental. The item stated that the majority of the Group were Jews (an untruth), and in another place conveyed the impression that from its inception the Group had nurtured the idea of making propaganda for a radical political philosophy. Thus our first production had been the Soviet play *Red Rust* (a misstatement of fact), and all our other productions that couldn't be interpreted in this light were either not mentioned at all or set down as subtle disguises of our fell intent.

Perhaps my announced intention of making another trip to the Soviet Union at this time served to strengthen the idea *Time*, and others, were trying to suggest. It looked even worse when Cheryl Crawford decided to join me on this trip. I expressed myself as exactly as possible when, in reply to a request for a statement from the magazine *Soviet Union Today*, I had written that, as a theatre man, I considered the theatre of the Soviet Union the most complete in our contemporary world, and added that I believed the Soviet Union was well on its way toward the creation of a truly modern culture. (What I meant by culture in this connection was the continuity of idea and sentiment between worker and artist, soldier and poet, philosopher and statesman.) With our leaving for Moscow, there was a certain amount of head-wagging and whispering.

CHAPTER THIRTEEN

Complications

FORTIFIED with the Group's gift of a new traveling bag and a handsome leather-bound journal in which the actors hoped I would jot down impressions of the trip, Cheryl Crawford and I set out to broaden our knowledge of the Soviet theatre.

In five weeks we saw some thirty-five productions, the most outstanding of which possibly were those of *Romeo and Juliet* at the Theatre of the Revolution and *King Lear* at the Jewish State Theatre. We found pleasure as well as instruction in Meyerhold's versions of *The Inspector General* and *The Forest*. Indeed, the impression of a sumptuous theatre pageant rich with color and meaning that I had received on my earlier trip was now renewed tenfold.

We met Stanislavsky and Meyerhold and kept them answering questions for hours. We visited Eisenstein, to whom we introduced Paul Strand, who because of our eagerness for the trip had been stimulated to follow us. We interviewed playwrights (like Afinogenev), scene-designers, and the directors of the most important theatres. We found all these people serious, cordial, and hearty. For theatre workers like ourselves, no more inspiring environment could be imagined.

It was natural therefore for Strand to ask me if I would like to remain in the Soviet Union. What I answered I find summarized in the diary I kept (May 1935), pieces of which were run in theatre publications on my return: "I have come to the conclusion that the question (though it has a real basis) is in itself a false one. It derives not from an enthusiasm for the Soviet Union, but is chiefly a sign of the weight of the American burden, the difficulty of the artist's task in America. But since life in these times is hard for any sort of decent person, I feel that whatever joy we take in life can only come from accepting this knowledge and then 'making the best of it.' By this I mean: appreciating, enjoying, and loving everything we find beautiful and good in life — defending it, working to preserve it, and, what is only right and natural, fighting for it. This joy we can have as much of in America as anywhere else. But even to appreciate, enjoy, and love truly, one must have first accepted the premise of our life's difficulty. The person who begins to yearn abstractedly for the Soviet Union is merely finding a new way to avoid this acceptance — by escaping into something that is not altogether real to him. When one has accepted the real, which is always difficult (in the Soviet Union as much as anywhere else), one is prepared to hope and to take joy — to be free. Something of this sentiment went into the making of the Group. It is also something I learned from the Soviet Union itself. It is well to remind ourselves of it from time to time. It has the seeds of growth in it."

During my visit, I was asked to draw up a report for an organization that was interested in fostering better relations between all the progressive theatre units in the world. I did so, and my main point was that what America needed was not so much the strengthening of its "Left theatre" as the sustaining of all those forces that would contribute to the making of good theatre of whatever description. The "Left theatre movement" had made great forward strides during the past season, but I predicted there would soon be a period of reaction against it — or, more properly, indifference — for the American public shunned certain labels even more than they feared what they represented. If the "Left theatre" was to have any future it would have to cease to be merely that and become the theatre of a "united front" — that is, a theatre with a wide appeal to all the best elements of our society, regardless of political sympathies.

The deepest impression I carried away from the Soviet Union was the sense of a *sane* people. Here were people who seemed to have been tempered by suffering and struggle into hard common sense, patience, tolerance, and determination. I could discern no bitterness in these people, no unreasonable fanaticism, no frustration. The little they had seemed what they could expect at this stage of the struggle. (That life was a struggle appeared the tacit assumption in every step they took.) They hoped for peace, but expected war. They were energetic, with calmness; convinced, with natural decorum; sure that the future, which might bring forth hardship, bloodshed, sacrifice, and at all times draw on their limitless capacity for work, would be a happy, indeed a glorious one.

Above all, there seemed in these people no conflict between the ideal and the real, between what their hearts dreamed and what their hands were doing. If the day-to-day fact was poor in comparison with the ultimate objective, it was because that objective was so great; but they had no trouble in seeing the relationship between the two. Every partial achievement, such as the opening of the Moscow subway, bore witness to that relationship and was illuminated and made meaningful through it. It was in this assurance that, no matter how humble their job, how far from perfection their condition, they were all actively contributing together toward an end their whole being desired that I sensed the people's sanity. I considered this the greatest Soviet triumph.

On our return Cheryl Crawford and I were given a gay reception. I read my Soviet Diary to the Group at two different sessions, and Cheryl Crawford described the outstanding productions in great detail at a third. Not only were our Group actors invited to these occasions, but many of our friends, actors from other groups, playwrights and artists who might find some interest in our experiences and impressions. There was a very warm feeling among us, a feeling of moving forward.

I was resolved nevertheless to moderate the Group's legitimate enthusiasm with some realism. The whole temper of the day, which led to brash statement, to a feeling of the inevitable success of all our ideas, to a sectarian insistence on the acceptance not only of our views but even of our vocabulary, was something that had to be controlled. Everyone, it seemed, was expanding into a highly vocal authority on art and life, theatre and culture, politics and the state of the world.

If this continued, we would become not only the pests of Broadway but very bad workers in our own domain. I called for self-criticism. I warned not only that we might soon be misunderstood but, what was worse, that we might get to a point where we no longer understood ourselves! Our purpose was "to become the recognized and honored first theatre of America," I told the actors. "This means that we must achieve the highest standards of excellence not only in such matters as acting, direction, stage-setting, costuming, and quality of plays, but in the variety of our productions, in a choice of repertoire that will truly represent all the creative aspects of our country, that will make use of the widest and deepest traditions to which as an American theatre we are heir. Furthermore, we must become a popular theatre, a theatre, that is, which any unspoiled normally sensitive person can come to and enjoy. . . ."

I went further and criticized the actors whose negligence in matters of personal appearance off stage or whose lack of courtesy in social relations had been detrimental to the progress of our organization as well as bad in themselves. I did not stop there. I warned the actors not to disparage the Group's work themselves, a tendency they indulged in even while retaining an overall Group conceit.

Clifford Odets at this point of our discussion burst forth with what sounded very much like abuse of the entire company. They were getting complacent, stuffy. The actors were making no progress within themselves. It seemed as if he were disgusted with them and ready to give them up as a bad lot.

Although what he thundered might appear an amplification of my own criticism, I could accept neither the tone nor the conclusions of his diatribe. I knew that the faults that our Group manifested were, in part, simply the hazards of growth; our excesses were distortions of what basically were the virtues of our company. In all living enterprise there are moments when every sound principle one enunciates, every good one espouses, will in the realm of action and in the context of reality give rise not only to misunderstanding but to falsity and to evil. There is no cause for despair or renunciation in this. Nothing grows otherwise.

We ran *Awake and Sing* and the double *Lefty* and *Till the Day I Die* program till the end of July. We decided on a recess for the summer weeks. We could safely make this our first real vacation, since we planned to tour with *Awake and Sing* and *Lefty* while we were rehearsing the new Odets play, *Paradise Lost*.

We also bought a play called *Weep for the Virgins* by Nellise Child, a new playwright. In almost every way this play became a kind of Group stepchild. When it was submitted, I thought it had something: it dealt with one of the least observed or understood sectors of our population — the backward elements of our working class. The central characters were a depressed family on the San Diego waterfront in which most of the children worked in a fish cannery. Everyone dreamed of escaping from these sordid surroundings — the father through the fantastic hope of acquiring a frog farm, the mother through her three daughters, who might do something with their lives by the fabled path of Hollywood. The play, in many ways unusual and talented, had a certain wry humor and understanding. It was incompletely organized, however, unsure in technique and point of view.

We were considering this play without taking any decisive action. Strasberg, probably disappointed over the fate of *Winterset* in the Group's councils, said a little sadly that we "considered plays but did nothing about them." This challenge on Miss Child's play made me answer: "Well, let's do it." The acquisition of this play, which might be described as an organizational oversight, is not a reflection on its merits, but the mark of a production that at almost every step was characterized by neglect. I do not remember how it was financed. No one, so far as I can remember, worked on the revision of the script prior to rehearsals. I was to direct *Paradise Lost* and Lee Strasberg refused to direct *Weep for the Virgins* or even to co-direct it, not from any dislike of the play but because after *Gold Eagle Guy* he had retired into a state of impassivity. The play thus fell to Cheryl Crawford, whose confidence in her powers as a director had probably diminished after *Big Night* and not been altogether restored by her work on *Till the Day I Die*. The settings for *Weep* were to be done by Boris Aronson, who was also engaged to design *Paradise Lost*. Although the designs for these productions were marked by Aronson's talent, both suffered through this combined arrangement.

We reopened *Awake and Sing* and *Lefty* in September, played them for a week at the Belasco, and then took them to Philadelphia, where they remained for five weeks. There we began rehearsals of both *Weep for the Virgins* and *Paradise Lost*. The company was rather entertained by the quality of *Weep*, and deeply moved by two acts of *Paradise Lost*.

Before I left for my trip to the Soviet Union I had made several suggestions to Odets for revisions of his play, particularly its last act. He agreed with my suggestions, but on my return six weeks later I found he had not written a line. After the busy season of his first success he found it difficult to concentrate. He did not rewrite the third act of his play till we had been in rehearsal three weeks.

Despite the actors' enthusiasm for the new play, the first days of rehearsal were rather painful to me. Many of the cast were not satisfied with their roles, and Odets too was worried. Morris Carnovsky would have preferred to play the part assigned to Bohnen, and Odets would have agreed to the change, as Carnovsky's playing another idealist would emphasize the play's resemblance to *Awake and Sing*. Luther Adler wanted to exchange parts with Meisner. Bromberg was bitterly disappointed at being chosen for *Weep* rather than for the Odets play; and Stella Adler didn't want to play at all.

Stella's objections were the hardest to overcome. She had played the mother in *Awake* on a dare; she didn't wish to repeat this tour de force, since by doing so she might become identified with this sort of role. Her objections were wholly sound for the theatre world we lived in; but it was my desire to combat the practice of that world, and by this time I was convinced that it could be done. Theatrically speaking, the Group was to be a law unto itself and should not think of its actors in terms of the market. Our actors, in other words, would never be constrained to go out again and play for commercial managers who would judge them solely on the basis of type; they would stay within the fold, where they would be cast in such a variety of roles that experienced theatre-goers would appreciate their versatility. So I insisted that Stella play the part for which she had been cast.

When these difficulties were settled, the actors thought the rehearsal period of *Paradise Lost* one of the times I was most in the vein. For once I worked with little feeling of pressure external to the work at hand. Metro-Goldwyn-Mayer had put up $17,000 for the production — for reasons entirely mysterious to me. But more than the freedom from financial worry, I was helped by a personal feeling for the play's material.

This might be explained by the fact that on my return from the Soviet Union, where I had been so impressed by the sanity of the people I met, I was almost equally depressed in New York by a feeling that I was living in a mad world. Wherever I went it seemed to me I observed an inner chaos. People hankered for things they didn't need or really want, belied their own best impulses, became miserable over trivialities, were ambitious to achieve ends they didn't respect, struggled over mirages, wandered about in a maze where nothing was altogether real to them. *Paradise Lost* seemed to me to reflect this almost dreamlike unclarity and, in a measure, to explain it.

The play, I told the actors, represented the search for reality. The little people of the small middle-class world were fumbling about in an environment they didn't control or understand, their hearts full of fond dreams, their eyes beclouded with illusions inherited from the past, while their hands groped in a void that was full of terror. When facts finally confronted them with unmistakable concreteness, they were the facts of bankruptcy and destitution, a house empty of all its foolish and kindly furniture, forever shaken and damaged in its ancient comfort. Nothing was left these people except their basic sweetness. With this and a little courage to continue life and to learn that their plight was not unique, new hope might be born and a new happiness be achieved.

Opening night was a sensation of general enthusiasm and controversy. The press, with a few exceptions, was very disappointing and disappointed. Instead of a play neater than *Awake and*

Sing or bolder than *Lefty, Paradise Lost* was a fuzzy piece of a wool-gathering quiet.

To complicate it all, Odets, at the request of our publicity representative, Helen Deutsch, had written a short article to point out the similarity between the middle class of Chekhov's plays and his. This article, the very existence of which was unknown to me, had been submitted to the reviewers before the play's opening. It proved to be a great mistake. Nearly all the reviewers made the Chekhov analogy the starting-point of their morning comments. "Clifford Odets is entitled to his Chekhov interlude. *Paradise Lost* is more an exercise in style than an organic drama."

This was not all. Joseph Wood Krutch, who had written the woeful *Modern Temper*, had praised the acid comedy of our *Big Night*, had found merit in the viciousness of Caldwell's *Journeyman* and talent in the messiness of our *Weep for the Virgins*, was offended by the heartbreak of *Paradise Lost* and rose to defend the innocent denizens of the Bronx, which he assumed to be the play's locale. It struck me that what irritated him most in the play was not its gloom but its hope. He called his review "The Apocalypse of St. Clifford" and he concluded it with the diagnosis: "Odets has lost his reason from too much brooding over the Marxist eschatology."

The Marxists — whom the nice reviewers of the thirties referred to as to some society of blackhands — were, strangely enough, as divided on the play as their more respectable brethren. Two or three Left journals kicked it around unmercifully, and only one of their reviewers, who divided his time between the *New Masses* and *Collier's*, was at all kind.

The play had a certain under-cover popularity; many people were devoted to it without being explicit about their reasons. Clifton Fadiman summed up the situation regarding the play when he wrote: "As it is practically impossible to make oneself heard amidst the hurly-burly of the Odets controversy, this department wishes merely to mutter doggedly that with all its faults . . . *Paradise Lost* is a pivotal American drama."

From the standpoint of the press and the big public, the nays had it. We were going to fight. I drafted a kind of protest and rebuke of the press which was widely published and, in several instances, answered. We ran ads proclaiming our belief that "Odets' Paradise Lost is a great and important play. We are proud to present it."

This campaign helped a little, and with the inevitable recourse to salary cuts we were able to maintain the play on the boards for nine weeks.

The Odets phone on University Place was now silent. The lion-hunters were in search of new quarry. Within a single year the burning interest that might just as well have been applied to a radio crooner, a vulgar evangelist, or an addle-brained aviator had consumed itself, leaving its object alone with a constantly turning Victrola disk.

For purposes of publicity Odets at this time wrote a rather amusing and naïve biographical piece:

The young writer comes out of obscurity with a play or two. Suppose he won't accept the generous movie offers. Why, that means he's holding out for more. Suppose he accepts — an ingrate, rat, renegade. If he won't wear evening clothes, that's only because he's trying to be different. But when he wears them, you may be sure he's turned capitalist overnight.

If he's written two plays about the same kind of people, everyone knows that that's all he can write about. But when he writes about a different class, he is told to go back where he came from and stick to his cast (or caste).

He gets party invitations and when he won't accept, he's too serious. But when you see him at a party or a bar, you knew all the time he was a playboy.

Suppose he rapidly follows one play with another, why he's writing "quickies"! But if they come further apart, it is a sure sign he's already written out.

If the reviewers praise him Tuesday, it's only because they're gentle, quixotic fellows. But watch them tear him apart on Wednesday! . . . The young writer is now ready for a world cruise!

Odets was now ready for a world cruise. For a New York playwright this means almost inevitably Hollywood. From success or
failure the playwright's escape is Hollywood. Had Odets been a
poet, a painter, a composer, even a novelist, the step to Hollywood would not appear so inevitable. The reason for this may be
that a serious worker in the arts outside the theatre not only is
rarely afflicted with the sudden and dizzying success of a playwright, but rarely lives in expectation of such a success. In a sense
the serious artist — particularly the painter, poet, or composer —
takes a vow of humility and poverty on entering upon his career.
His work is not likely to pay off in big dividends. He does not
dwell too close to the market-place. The theatre is in the very
heart of the market-place, where a feverish and fabulous exchange
of goods seems the essential drama. The playwright cannot but be
affected by it. If he has had some success, why not more? If he
has had little success, and greater rewards for his efforts are open
to him in Hollywood, why not take advantage of the situation?
This thought-process is particularly typical of the more recent
playwrights, since respect for the stage as a medium and the tradition of the serious playwright as an autonomous artist are rapidly waning. The mortality rate among playwrights under forty
is extraordinarily high.

Odets, as I have said, had made comparatively little money in
1935, although it was more than he had ever made before. Being
completely without a sense of sober economy, most of his money
had been spent on gifts to friends, relatives, and worthy causes,
not to mention an indulgence in extra-good wines and foods,
which he loved as much for the opportunity they offered him for a
large conviviality as the pleasure they afforded in themselves.

Despite the honest source of the income, and the benevolent
occasion for spending it, the newly successful playwright, it may
be said, disposes of his earnings as a robber does of his loot.

Odets's relationship to Hollywood at that time was uncertain. It
meant all things to him because it was not real to him. It meant
money — and that was only partially real to him. In the Group in
those days Hollywood was the symbol in the show world of
money-making unrelated to any other ideal. It was so remote to

us then that we hardly took pains to scorn it. We saw movies occasionally, and liked them perhaps, but we rarely thought of how or where they were made or that we or any of our kind might be connected with their making.

One evening when I was discussing some now forgotten subject with Stella Adler, she sailed into the conversation with the astonishing reflection: "I feel that I need to sin, and you make me feel I have no right to." Odets, pacing about the room to his own rhythm, stopped suddenly, turned, and fairly shouted: "She's right! She's right!" I looked up and found a faint smile on his face and an accusing finger pointed at mine. For Odets at this time Hollywood was Sin.

He was going to Hollywood on a trip — to look around. The actors knew what this meant. Though he would send back money to help pay the company a fraction of their salaries, they could not help feeling unhappy about it, when they were not resentful. For they could not move about freely and still play *Paradise Lost*. They had to remain in New York, on the cold stage of the Longacre Theatre, and act for hardly more than twenty-five dollars a week. They wanted me to dissuade Odets from going to Hollywood, to exercise some moral authority over him — if need be, to shame him.

Naturally, I refused to do this, if for no other reason than the futility of such an attempt. I believed, moreover, that Odets would never reach any maturity as a person until he had exercised his right "to sin," and either survived or succumbed to its effects. Sometimes I imagined he wanted me to stand in his way despite himself, to protect him against himself. It was a practice that I had engaged in to some extent from the first days of the Group, but it is a practice I found wearing and profitless for all parties.

CHAPTER FOURTEEN

Treading Water

WITH the production of the first four Odets plays the Group had proved its basic theatrical tenets: the values of a permanent company, the difference between the results of pick-up companies and those of a troupe integrated by a common ideal and technique, the influence that such an organization could have on creative writing.

With the production of *Awake and Sing* I had remarked: "Now the Group has put on long pants." But this sartorial change does not yet make a man, and our problem after *Paradise Lost* was to achieve some of the steadiness that befits man's estate. Something stood in the way. We were not sure what it was. Each season that followed brought with it an attempt at a new solution, and though each attempt brought certain benefits, none of them proved conclusive.

At this point the Group was stronger as a symbol and as an influence than it was as a theatre. The Group's merits could be measured more by what was going on outside its confines than by what it was doing itself.

Not only were such small groups as the Theatre of Action continuing their limited though interesting work, but new groups such as the American Repertory Theatre (which never was one) were being hatched and making such contributions as the production of *Bury the Dead* by Irwin Shaw. The Group Theatre offered to produce this promising first play (hailed in 1936 as "better than Odets"). But Shaw, very young and impatient, wanted an immediate production, and we had just contracted a strange liaison with Milton Shubert to do a production with him.

In the far reaches of the country new organizations were set up to do the kind of plays the Group had made the mode of the day. The life of such groups was usually very short, but even so, they prepared the way for the broad theatrical activity that the Federal Theatre Project was soon to engage in.

In New York the children of the Stewart's Cafeteria at Sheridan Square had moved over to the Stewart's Cafeteria at University Place. Just as the former Stewart's had been the meeting-place of the disconsolate and groping, the new Stewart's was the hangout of those who had found some direction through such organizations as the Group and the Odets cycle. The young people who gathered here were still very poor and generally jobless, but they all had some sense of where they wanted to go, what they wanted to achieve, where to study, what to read, whom to look to for possible guidance. Their faces were a little brighter, their eyes more eager. They still wasted time and stayed up too late, but this was because they were standing in line before a door that had not yet opened to them. Their ways were still somewhat on the bohemian side, but bohemia was no longer their ideal. Concretely many of them became active in a year or two in all branches of the WPA; and new dance groups, film groups, literary and journalistic enterprises were formed from their number. Today many of them, though isolated again, have achieved position.

Certain minor episodes within the Group itself stand out in my memory as significant of the peculiar period of floundering that followed the opening of *Paradise Lost*, to continue to the fall of 1937.

Some of our actors — particularly Bohnen and Luther Adler — wanted to get a Group paper started. This had been a dream of mine, but the actors had rightly become impatient with my habit of treasuring dreams that did not develop into plans. They took matters into their own hands and published a rather cute house organ they called *The Flying Grouse*. It was got out on mimeographed sheets and was distributed to friends of the Group on a very limited scale.

Besides cartoons and sketches poking fun at the infinite variety of Group extravagance, the first number of this sheet — there were only two issues, since by the time the second appeared we were on tour in Chicago — contained a short piece by me which the editors introduced under the sarcastic title "Der Heilige Geist."

Another episode: in the course of the *Paradise Lost* run an actor whom we had been warned when he joined us was addicted to drink had gone beyond bounds during a performance of that play. He could neither remember his lines nor be prompted. We had censured him before and docked him during *Men in White* for inability to perform, but there had to be a showdown now. Bohnen called an actors' meeting to decide what to do. The individual in question was a person who had virtually no life beyond the stage. After some investigation it was resolved that our unfortunate colleague was to receive the best medical attention available at a sanatorium that had treated such cases with great success. The cure took six months and was extremely expensive. The actors offered to foot the sanatorium's bill by giving bimonthly performances for the patients at the sanatorium. The arrangement was made and carried out. When our actor, much improved, returned to us, he was cast in the leading role of our forthcoming production.

Symptomatic too was the reaction in our Group to resignation of its members. A shock of hurt and anger struck the Group when one of its stronger pillars, Joe Bromberg, announced that he had signed with a Hollywood company without first informing us of his intention to do so. When we remonstrated with him for not having discussed his plan with us, he confessed he had been afraid to, for then he would not have had the heart to carry it out. My answer was a high-flown epithet designed to insult. When the actors heard of Bromberg's action, some of them behaved as if they wished there was some high tribunal where a terrible justice might be meted out.

I was fatigued, disappointed, and in another one of my periodic personal crises after *Paradise Lost*. We had made great financial sacrifices (despite Odets's help) to keep that play running. We needed to put on another play immediately — something for which it would not be too difficult to raise money. If it had come to us a little earlier, the next production, as I have noted, would have been *Bury the Dead,* although there proved to be great difficulty in getting backing for it.

Milton Shubert of the Shubert dynasty had bought a play he had seen done in the tiny but intrepid Hedgerow Theatre in Rose Valley, Pennsylvania. Shubert offered us the money to put this play on for him. It was a new dramatization by Erwin Piscator of Dreiser's *An American Tragedy.* It was called *The Case of Clyde Griffiths.*

I did not care for this play. It was schematic in a cold way that to my mind definitely went against the American grain. "Drama with a pointer" one reviewer aptly called it. In other words, a play of instruction to demonstrate a thesis. It was nevertheless technically intriguing and capable of being fashioned into a novel type of stage production. I decided not to say no or yes in the deliberations over this play. Lee Strasberg thought it had a popular "boy and girl" aspect that I had overlooked.

We did *Clyde Griffiths* with Lee Strasberg as director. We wanted Mordecai Gorelik to design it, but the Shuberts had a contract with a designer and insisted on our using him. The set — unimaginative, unwieldy, and without style — was almost universally praised by the press, as was the production as a whole.

I was in a sardonic, almost anarchistic mood at the time because of a sense of the Group's failings, heightened by personal unhappiness, so I may have looked with a jaundiced eye on the rehearsal proceedings. Quite objectively I saw that Strasberg was working with little conviction and half his talent. But half his talent was enough to give the production a certain fluidity and sensitivity, an aura of quasi-nobility, that were distinctive on the Broadway scene.

We had become so much an "institution" or an "academy" from the standpoint of acting and production that though the reviewers generally detested the play they repeated their conviction that we were "the most expert producing organization we have." In fact, I could not but look upon the reception accorded the production with some irony as I thought it inferior, despite an outstanding bit of stylized acting by Bobby Lewis and the other qualities I have noted, to a number of our other productions.

The reason for the reviewers' dislike of the play, however, was not that it was a poor piece of writing, but that it interpreted the plot of *An American Tragedy* (called an illiterate novel by one of the top reviewers) in terms of the class struggle. The Piscator dramatization employed a Speaker, who dunned the audience with a single refrain: "We have given a name to Fate. It is the Economic System." It made many of the reviewers hot under the collar. They grew somewhat shrill as they countered with the belief that Clyde Griffiths did not represent the effects of our society on a young uneducated boy, but that he was "a contemptible coward, a cheap and snivelling character." Something of a philosophical social controversy was thus aroused by the production, which was probably all to the good, and the play found its champions as well as its detractors. But, it seemed to me, both sides were wide of the mark, and we were both blamed and praised for the wrong things. We were now smack in the middle of a period in which there was perhaps more shouting than knowledge, taste, or reason.

We did not help matters much ourselves. There was a ridiculous line in the play — which should have been deleted — that made a snobbishly Leftist reference to wearers of dinner clothes. This, of course, was picked up as an example of the play's and the Group's erroneous — not to say subversive — philosophy of life. Strasberg suggested that I write a letter making clear that the Group was not to be held accountable for all its playwrights' ideas or tastes. I wrote the letter, which was signed by Cheryl Crawford. It was a prime example of collective bungling in both the tactical and the ideological sphere. Yet it is so neat a revelation of the cross-currents of the time that I must quote it in part: "Certain remarks in a few reviews of our recent productions make us wonder whether our general approach to the theatre is not being taken with an almost mechanical literalness, so that the detailed opinions of our playwrights are believed to represent our own opinions point by point. We have produced plays by Paul Green, Maxwell Anderson, J. H. Lawson, Dawn Powell, Sidney Kingsley, Clifford Odets: in other words dramatists of varying personalities and credos. . . . We believe, as you do, in a varied,

rich theatre that neglects nothing in the unmeasurable gamut of
human experience and imagination, and we believe too in allowing our collaborators — playwrights as well as others — the privileges of their own idiosyncrasies, prejudices and partisanship. As
a theatre we cannot be held responsible for all of them and a
quarrel with Mr. Dreiser or Mr. Piscator, for example, cannot
legitimately be made into a quarrel with the Group."

The reviewers commented on this letter, granted it a point, but
feared (or jeered) that we were straddling. Everyone now, including the most conservative commentators, insisted that we
stood for something! An anonymous critic said the letter betrayed
the difficult and often foolish position of people in the middle
trying to appeal to all publics. This was an astute analysis, but
the fact remained that though we did have a real point of view,
it did not coincide with the narrow interpretation then put upon
such bloodless designations as "Left theatre."

In a general and loose way I might have defined my attitude on
the problem involved here by saying with D. H. Lawrence: "The
essential function of art is moral. But a passionate implicit morality, not didactic. A morality which changes the blood rather than
the mind . . . changes the blood first. The mind follows later,
in the wake. . . ."

The Group actors were never really certain of my meaning in
this regard. Thus to my acute distress I heard one of our actresses
in a discussion say: "Harold hates art," while others thought of
me as an old-fashioned æsthetic idealist. Still others — like Alexander Kirkland — protested that our play program meant nothing at all beyond the fact that we did the best dramatic material
available. One or two others occasionally threatened to leave the
Group if we didn't do more "harmless" plays — plays without a
stigma: for example, the classics or just "good theatre." All of
this, it is necessary to remember, represented the Group, and all
of it possessed a more unified meaning than many realized.

But "ideology," for all its importance and the large part it
played both in our discussions and in the views, favorable or
otherwise, held of us by a good portion of our public, was not

our main problem. Our main problem was continuity of activity
or the means to provide our company with work and livelihood.

Failing this, there could be no stability in any phase of our
work. Immediately after the closing of *Clyde Griffiths* we were
offered an easy way of making money. The Group company went
on the air with a sketch by Odets based on the life of Sarah Bern-
hardt. The suggestion that we earn our livelihood by giving radio
performances had been broached many times. It seemed a sensible
solution to our money worries. But there was much resistance to
it. While all the Group actors had more or less come to accept the
modesty of Group salaries and the sacrifices of Group casting,
they accepted them only for the theatre — that is, for our legitimate work. If they were to do radio or any other work not actually connected with our productions, they preferred to work on
an individual and competitive basis. While this would have protected certain individuals, it did not offer safeguards to the organization as a whole. We feared too that the more protection
we found in outside activities, such as radio, pictures, or even
teaching, the less time would there be for our real work. When an
artist or a group of artists has made some sort of success — and
the Group by now had definitely become a name — all sorts of
opportunities are open to them. These opportunities, however,
rarely lead to more work of the sort that won the artist his name.
They lead to commercial by-products only tenuously related to the
artist's talent.

We made a spring tour of *Awake and Sing*. Two friends financed
the venture, and it opened in Baltimore late in April with the
original cast save for Bobby Lewis, who replaced Bromberg. Baltimore liked *Awake and Sing*, as did Chicago, which followed
on the route.

In Chicago, however, the actors were badly frightened the
opening night, as the audience never once laughed at a play that
had become as well known for its humor as for its pathos. The
company was certain it had made a fiasco of one of its favorite
productions. It turned out that the Chicago audience had been so
impressed by the advance publicity of the Group's seriousness and

the zealousness of its playwright Odets that they believed laughter on this occasion might appear unseemly. The reviews were enthusiastic, however. "Odets Strikes the Drama Like Sandburg Struck Poetry" ran one headline. Business was fair. And the audience after the opening night laughed appreciatively.

In the ease of Chicago's spring — Michigan Boulevard can be incredibly exhilarating — I turned to thoughts of the future. Playwrights! We must have more playwrights. There was a young man in Chicago who had written a very promising farce. I looked him up — Ardrey was his name — and encouraged him to write more. He had an idea for a play about a railroad man. I wanted to see it. But now that I was in Chicago, I thought of investigating what Odets was up to on the coast and of finding out if any of the other refugees from the theatre might not be led back. I set out for my first trip to California.

CHAPTER FIFTEEN

Millennial Interlude

WHEN I arrived at Odets's place in Beverly Hills, I was immediately struck with its overpowering pleasantness. On my first walk I thought I had suddenly moved into a new never-never land. When I met Eddie Robinson outside his imposing property, he nodded toward it and said: "This is the millennium," and grinned like a pumpkin.

What was new with my friend Odets? "I have fallen in love with the best actress out here," Odets told me immediately. "Luise Rainer," I guessed. I guessed right. She was the season's sensation.

Odets had begun writing a new play. That was important. I urged him to concentrate on it, as his picture, *The General Dies at Dawn,* was already in production. When I met Luise Rainer, I

urged her to press him to work. She was making *The Good Earth*
then, and she took me at my word. Odets was rather nettled. But
he continued writing.

Hollywood was buzzing with murmurs very similar to those I
heard in New York. The screen writers were trying to form a
strong guild and were running into difficulty not only with studio
executives but with many from their own ranks. It sounded like
the beginnings of every trade-union movement, except for the
wage levels involved here. Phrases flew, innuendoes became in-
sults, and everyone looked alert. Odets, annoyed and flattered,
whispered to me that at MGM he was thought to be the source
of all the trouble.

Waiting for Lefty had been done with some éclat down at San
Pedro, the Los Angeles harbor and workers' district. Now there
was a reading of Irwin Shaw's *Bury the Dead*. All the stars were
burning to finance it and to play in it. When it was done later by
an organization calling itself the Contemporary Theatre, very few
of those who had responded so inflammably to its reading financed
it, and none of them played in it. There were also gatherings at
which discussions on the prevention of war took place. At one
of them Odets rose in mighty wrath and spoke unintelligible
words (of which I fancy he was quite proud) to counteract de-
lusions and softness.

I had little time to study the local mores, however; I had to get
to business. Theatre people alone concerned me. I met Franchot
Tone again. He wanted to know about his failure to realize any
money on *Awake and Sing*, and I tried not to be sheepish in admitting our mismanagement. He did not take the matter amiss
however (in these questions he always alternated between pee-
vishness and indulgence). Basically Franchot was an idealist, and
he still idealized Lee Strasberg and me. Though in the long run
there is more peril than pleasure in being idealized, I was at the
moment the beneficiary of Franchot's warmest hospitality. I was
the (awkward) prophet of a religion centered in the theatre.
Franchot's wife, Joan Crawford, was prepared to believe. Some
day, Franchot intimated, he would return to the theatre, and, at
the time, theatre was synonymous to him with the Group.

I made propaganda among young and older playwrights, new-comers and some already forgotten. I spoke to novelists who had written no plays, to playwrights who had fled Broadway as though scalded. To all of them I held forward the promise of a young theatre in quest of their word. They were almost all interested, while they retained something remote about them all the time. Some seemed to be saying: "Shake me! Shake me! It might do me some good"; others: "I feel a faint stirring. I wonder if it is necessary."

Above all, Odets interested me. He appeared slightly somno-lent, and at the same time at war with himself and the world. At every turn he was fighting on behalf of the Group and its values. Fighting strangely. He wanted everyone to know that what the Group believed in was *right*, that the Group people were more talented than all others. Nothing provoked such a storm of pro-test as the suggestion that all Group actors would readily have left their organization if they had had the opportunity, like Tone and Bromberg. He pounded his fist on the table, grew red and wild-eyed. The columnist Sidney Skolsky liked to goad him on, out of professional guile and audience pleasure, and the novelist John O'Hara, who admired Odets's talent, provoked him out of cussedness and a suspicion of either "pretentiousness" or "reli-gion," which to him were almost the same thing.

What puzzled me was not Odets's faith, but his desire to make these people share it. I could not understand why he had to con-vince them, particularly since I knew that ultimately only the authority of successful action would impress them. It seemed a weakness in Odets to care so much for these people's approval. It was as if all his work, his thoughts and dreams were in vain if they did not recognize the validity of his claims. In my turn, I belabored Odets for hours because he had tried to sell his con-victions to those who, for one thing, were utterly unprepared to accept them in the abstract form of his tempestuous rhetoric. He had to believe more in himself and in his ideas rather than try to hammer the virtues of both into people's heads.

In failing to comprehend Odets's behavior I was being simple-

minded myself. I did not understand the closeness Odets sought
with these people he was bent on converting. He wanted their
admiration, their plaudits, their goodwill. He needed their love; or,
lacking that, power over them. Above all, he did not want them
to believe that if he thought as he did or wrote as he did, it was
because he could think or write no other way. If he was ecstatic
instead of being smart, it wasn't because being smart was foreign
to his nature, beyond his reach. No, what the boys of slick success could do, he could do just as well — nay, many times better.
Only he had chosen his way out of greater knowledge, deeper
thought, a finer sensitivity, honesty, and wisdom. His fierce attack was the tribute his hungry soul paid the powers that be.
He wished to be one with them — if in no other way, by winning
over them, by licking them. It was a profoundly human pattern
of adjustment through coercion. It is often followed by adjustment through self-abasement. It is an old drama, of which America offers fascinatingly new versions.

I could neither mock nor deplore this drama. Clifford Odets
was the voice of his day, reflecting, even more than he proclaimed
or knew, the urgent need of the people of his time and place.
That this was so the correspondence between his work and the
social-political scene gave ample proof. But the artist who is the
voice or the conscience of his time nearly always appears to be
ahead of it, often seems even to himself cut off from the very
people whose aspiration he expresses. While he serves as the people's antennæ, his very prescience places him in a position that
might be described as outside the main body of his contemporaries. The people, in bulk, may regard him as an oddity, may
believe him a trouble-maker representing a disturbing, wrongheaded minority. For the great masses of humanity, so far as their
consciousness goes, are nearly always conservative; they need
some sort of shock to make them aware of their actual situation
and the spiritual and even physical demands that their situation
should entail.

Despite his success (that in the theatrical scene might prove
only a seasonal affair), Odets still felt himself excluded, special.
He was not "accepted" in the sense that, let us say, playwrights

like Robert Sherwood, Philip Barry, S. N. Behrman, Sidney Howard, or George S. Kaufman were. Despite his pride in being what
the period was pleased to term a "revolutionary," he did not want
to remain a Left playwright. He wanted to be at the very center
of standard playwrights of quality. He wanted to be inside, not
outside that circle which the mass of Americans might regard as
their own. In this center was safety — not simply crude economic
safety, since in one way or another he would do very well, but
the safety that comes from feeling oneself part of a whole community.

That is why Odets was so immoderately vehement in Hollywood with characters whose critical opinion he might value in-
differently. That was why shortly after *Paradise Lost* he sat down,
with Elia Kazan, to knock out a pot-boiler in seven days — which,
of course, was no good from any standpoint. Odets was seeking a
home, a sure footing in a society of whose intimate soul he was
indeed an eloquent spokesman, but in which he still felt no protection, no warm, secure ties.

The Group for Odets was a kind of home and protection. That
was one of the reasons he was so ambitious for it. But despite its
tenacity it, too, rested on insecure foundations. If there was a
class in which he might have found a healthy soil to root himself in and gather strength from, it is clear he was unable to feel
it; it was not as palpable or real to him as he might have wished.

From Hollywood I wrote a letter to Stella Adler that she later
parodied, to the delight of the Group, who saw in this not only
a mild mockery of my peculiarities and theirs, but a quaint comment on our anomalous position generally. Today, indeed, I no
longer remember my letter, only the parody. According to this I
had written that "everyone in Hollywood lives in beautiful spa-
cious homes with lovely gardens, enjoying the luxury of princes.
Actors are paid fabulous salaries, work all year in pictures specially written for them, become the talk and toast of every community in the country. It's simply terrible. But in the Group! We
have no money, our success is momentary, we have difficulty in
finding plays, we rehearse under wretched conditions. We are not

sure we shall be able to pay our rent, we can't afford proper vacations, we are referred to in the press as an 'earnest band of young players,' the audiences flock to plays like *The Old Maid*, and glamour is associated only with the Lunts and Katharine Cornell. We quarrel, beat our heads against stone walls, shout, shiver, and shake. The Group is wonderful."

From Chicago the company went on to Cleveland in the throes of the Republican (Landon-nominating) convention of 1936. Business was poor and accommodations not only hard to find but very expensive. The company was delighted when it came upon comfortable private quarters where six or seven of them were to be accommodated for only thirty-five dollars per person. It turned out that there had been a little misunderstanding — what had been meant was thirty-five dollars per person per day! On the advice of our business manager, the production closed with a week in Newark, to business so bad that the small profit gleaned in Chicago was eaten away and a loss incurred for the whole tour.

These misadventures and the feeling I had that the Group was adrift, partly on account of a loose leadership, or the fear on the part of the directors — individually — to assume responsibility in the face of the constantly hazardous situation in the Group, prompted me to reconsider the whole matter of Group organization. I thought I might remedy the flaw in our setup by composing a sort of new Group constitution or plan whereby the benefits of a certain Group democracy might be combined with a strongly centralized leadership in the person of a single managing director. I drafted this plan on my way to New York, presented it to Crawford and Strasberg, and nominated myself for the job of managing director. They were altogether willing to adopt this arrangement now.

About this time there had arrived from abroad the composer whose *Three-Penny Opera* (on records) might have been described as a Group pastime. We befriended Kurt Weill, and Stella Adler insisted that he must do a musical play for us along lines he had made known in Germany. Weill suggested one day that he would like to do an American equivalent of the comic Czech war novel *The Good Soldier Schweik*, which had been dramatized and produced with success in Berlin. We set about seeking a dramatist to work on it with Weill.

On a visit to Chapel Hill to discuss a play about college life that Paul Green had submitted to us, I learned something about Paul's past that he had never before mentioned. He had fought overseas in the last war and had an intimate acquaintance with the American soldier of that day. I mentioned Kurt Weill's suggestion, particularly since Paul was fascinated with the element of music in the theatre.

When I returned to New York, I advised Cheryl Crawford and Weill that Paul would be the right man for the proposed musical play. When Paul Green informed us he was definitely interested, Cheryl and Weill went down to Chapel Hill to plan the play with him. All three worked out the scenario together in fairly complete detail. It was a Group project in the full sense of the word. It was also Cheryl Crawford's adopted child.

Being short of funds again, the Group decided to take a chance once more at another adult camp. This time it was the Pinebrook Club Camp at Nichols, Connecticut. We gave three performances a week and awaited the arrival of three playwrights and the scripts they had promised us. It was Decoration Day, 1936.

CHAPTER   SIXTEEN

Breakdown

AT Pinebrook my new plan, worked out to the last detail, was discussed for days. For a short time we regarded it rather naïvely as a cure-all. That the centralization of authority and executive decision was a good thing there could be no doubt, but for some reason we overlooked the fact that none of this had any bearing on the Group's basic difficulty. Lee Strasberg in a more or less formal speech explained why I was the right choice for the job of managing director. Just prior to this there had been some kidding about my new position, and Art Smith had said he would write a book about me entitled "The Group Theatre: The Man and His Works." Strasberg now said that though this was just a joke, he believed it true that because of my qualities and even some of my faults the Group Theatre had been founded. "If the Group Theatre has to be represented by a single face, I am willing to let it be the face of Harold Clurman." (When Strasberg and I quarreled a few months later, Strasberg remarked sharply that he was still prepared to stick by his statement, but he wanted to be sure that it was my face and not my backside that was representing the Group.) A new Actors Committee was elected by the Group as a whole. Its members were Stella Adler, Roman Bohnen, Morris Carnovsky, and Elia Kazan.

When Paul Green's script arrived, it was still in a very rough state. It needed much more work. Paul Green returned to Chapel Hill to do it. Next on the list of our plays was Odets's *Silent Partner*.

When Odets arrived on the premises, we gave him a party and he appeared very much moved to be back among his old companions. I read his new play almost immediately and found it at once his most ambitious and his most incomplete script. It had a great theme. Through a strike situation in an industrial area, identified as the twin cities of Apollo and Rising Sun, Odets showed an old order of benevolent capitalism that had grown lame, a new order of monopolistic capitalism that was growing vicious (or fascist), and a still unorganized and spiritually unformed working class. What Odets was trying to say was that the old world of money and power was fast becoming decrepit and desperate, while the new world of the future, which belonged to the mass of people, was in America still raw, unclear, undisciplined, mentally and morally clumsy. Between the two worlds, stood an Italian baker, representative of a more mature culture, and two young workers who were the strike leaders. These two men, brothers, represented two types of leader: the older, intellectual, introspective, slowed up by fear of evil-doing and qualms of every kind; the younger, all energy, fire, naïveté. They are both in love with a simple working girl. She is the future, the personal prize of all their efforts. At the end the older brother renounces the girl -- he is not strong enough to deserve her — and gives her to his younger brother, while their Italian friend (after the strike has been lost) sends the young couple out into life with his blessing, a new Adam and Eve from whom a better world will arise. The young people's hearts are clean, their spirit strong; they have only to learn more to become masters of their destiny.

No play of Odets had a wider scope, a greater variety of characters, or more exciting scenes. But the play, intuitively sound in its basic perception, was very weak in all its central characters and situations. The maturity that the Italian baker was supposed to possess was exactly the quality that Odets himself lacked. His play revealed more instinct than accomplishment, more rough substance than created form. I spoke to Odets at great length about this. If he could imbue these central characters with the life he meant them to have, this would be his most important play and he would indeed be the writer everybody hoped he would become. He needed to work hard rather than to push the play into production. Odets listened to me as if bemused. He was having his problems with Luise Rainer. He was somehow unsure of everything, more bewildered in a way than he had ever been as the obscure young actor of our crazy company. Odets was now his own greatest problem.

Finally the long-awaited Lawson play, *Marching Song*, arrived. It, too, was a play of labor strife. It struck me as cold, artificial, a creature of the author's will — lacking in spontaneity. Instead of telling Lawson this directly, I made a theoretical point: he wrote much more convincingly about the middle class, to which he belonged, I said. This was a half-truth (*Processional* dealt with the working class and was packed with lyric talent and imagination). But certainly plays like *Success Story*, which were much closer to Lawson's experience, though he had perhaps never been in an advertising manager's office, were far more alive than the present script, product of his study, conviction, and sense of duty.

Because I put what I felt so badly, Lawson was able to ask me: "Don't you think proletarian plays should be written at this time?" (*"Should be* written," I thought, was a very dangerous position for the artist to take.) I answered only: "Perhaps. But not by you." The Theatre Union did the play later in the year, the last production of its career.

Paul Green returned with *Johnny Johnson*, and it was put into rehearsal at the end of the summer, only a week or two before our return to New York.

In New York I found my job as managing director overwhelming. I relinquished the direction of *Johnny Johnson*, and asked Strasberg to take over.

Instead of being ready to open we had hardly begun to rehearse. As the script had only just begun to be presentable, backing for the play had not yet been secured. It was to be our most expensive production, and movie money (the support of the picture companies) was almost impossible to get now that the new Dramatists' Guild contract had caused a revolt among the picture executives. We had to provide the actors with some funds in lieu of salary and to raise money for the production as well.

For a while I lost courage. I asked the actors whether they wanted to risk the hazards of another winter under such pressure. Most of them had an opportunity to escape if they wished. Luther Adler, who was to play a bit in *Johnny Johnson*, was offered the role of the playwright in *Stage Door*. Kazan was being offered a part in a picture that Metro was making. Neither Adler nor Kazan was released. The actors hadn't the slightest desire to abandon the production of *Johnny Johnson*. They voted to continue, which meant that I had to get the production on somehow.

The building of the scenery had to be ordered, since further delay would necessitate postponing the opening of the play. There was no money up for the show yet, but our stage carpenter, Bill Kellam (who remained with us for years, as did our property man, Moe Jacobs), was willing to build on my word that he would be

paid. I ordered the scenery to be built, while I considered where
the money was to come from.

To keep the actors, I borrowed $1,500 from the picture director
Lewis Milestone. But $1,500 divided among 30 people will not
take care of them for very long. I asked Odets, who was out of
town, for another $1,500. I received a letter from him refusing to
let me have the sum; he wanted to teach me a lesson! I had
planned the summer badly — or not planned it at all. I did not
argue Odets's point. I simply insisted that, right or wrong, the
Group company by their devotion had helped him as a playwright,
and now that they needed his help he was duty-bound to give it.
Odets sent the money.

Bess Eitingon, who, you may remember, once offered to back
the Group to the tune of $54,000 only to be unable to find anyone
to receive it, now came forward with a good portion of the production cost — some $40,000. For the rest, Lewis Milestone en-
listed the support of his friend Jock Whitney, who flew from
Hollywood to attend one of our rehearsals. He invested $12,000
in the show. During the last days of dress rehearsal I had to beg,
borrow, and steal more money so that the play might open in
acceptable shape.

The rehearsals were held in a small theatre. Here the production seemed charming: informal, unpretentious and sweet. But
no house was available to us now except the Forty-fourth Street
Theatre, one of the largest on Broadway. I knew the large house
would be a disadvantage; it proved to be disastrous. Our actors'
voices sounded so small they were occasionally inaudible; Donald
Oenslager's sets, which had been designed larger than I anticipated, now appeared monstrous; the performances now looked
amateurish. In later years, when I explained some of the production's weaknesses as they betrayed themselves through the dis-
proportionately large stage and theatre, people asked me with
more impatience than commiseration: "Why did you take such a
house?" Take it! We had been shoved into it.

The first two previews of *Johnny Johnson* were the most distress-
ing experiences I have ever gone through in the theatre. The
large production — nineteen sets — and the orchestra had not had

sufficient time for rehearsals (dress rehearsals are costly). The actors were lost. After the first five minutes of the first preview half the audience left. By the end of the performance there were no more than twenty people in the auditorium.

The panic that ensues on an occasion like this has nothing to do with art. It is hysteria that combines the fear and shame of economic ruin with the humiliation attendant on a blow to one's pride. We had had such a hard time getting this play on the boards; and now — this! Something had to be done — fast.

At such times everyone becomes superstitious, "expert," confused, and weary all at the same moment. The director, especially when he is as sensitive a person as Strasberg, becomes a veritable sacrifice. Many of the musical numbers were cut — in a smaller theatre they need not have been — but what becomes most damaged in the process of saving a production in jeopardy is people's psyches. At one point during a midnight conference Strasberg shouted: "I know more about acting than any of you," and made feverishly irrelevant and disparaging references to the script and the music. As usual under such circumstances, everyone was patient and brave; but sanity and clarity never returned.

We received letters from Group admirers entreating us not to open. We made all sorts of futile gestures to save the show every morning when we were sleepy, exhausted, and only half recovered from the irritation and futility of the previous night's discussion. Actually each of the previews (or public dress rehearsals) showed an improvement. The improvement resulted from repetition of the show and might have been effected without any of the agonized after-the-performance vigils that wore away our forbearance and skill. In a way I did not understand what had happened or what was happening. I felt as if everything was giving way underneath me — not only the production, but six years of work.

Opening night was the greatest shock of all. The performance went smoothly, and the audience appeared wildly enthusiastic. It looked as if our disgrace had been converted into a hit.

The next morning brought still another shock. The press seemed very bad. I say "seemed" because in going over the reviews today

I note only two really damning reviews; the others are almost devout. There are two main causes for this discrepancy between the reviews and our reaction to them. There is first the matter of "business notices." A business notice is a review that may even be severely critical but nevertheless attracts customers to your play. (*Tobacco Road* was treated to notices of this kind.) Our *Johnny Johnson* press was critically favorable, but discouraged all except the cognoscenti from seeing it. For example: "The Group Theatre has sponsored the first departure from polite mediocrity of the season. If it is not all buoyant, that merely proves, in this column's opinion, that the aim has been high." (The economic pressure of play production nowadays is such that neither producer, playwright, nor actor is able to judge the validity of any criticism of his work since his response is attuned only to the business value of the notices.)

The second cause of our misjudging the critical reception of our play lay in our own special situation and the psychology that went with it. When we failed with a play that we thought deserved success, we were aroused and combative about it; when we failed with a play we were either uncertain of or that we believed we had bungled in production, we became very bitter with ourselves over it — far more severe, indeed, than our harshest critics.

Opening nights for this reason had become a more harrowing experience every year. Generally on Broadway the ever increasing financial hazards and stock-market excitement associated with play production make the failure of a play strike its producer like some crime he has committed, something he might be punished for with social ostracism.

Many people — including reviewers — thought highly of *Johnny Johnson*, so highly, indeed, that Burns Mantle included it in his collection of the "best ten" although he himself had thought the actors should have rid themselves of their directors for having chosen it. The Group actors were supersensitive about the notices because they themselves were profoundly, even exaggeratedly, dissatisfied with the production. They felt that the directorate had been at fault in the handling of the play. This in turn they regarded as a sign of trouble within the organization.

We put up a fight for *Johnny Johnson* because the company was very fond of this humorous and poetic play lamenting the world's path to war, and because there were many among both the press and the public to support us. But the running costs of the production were high. It stayed on some nine weeks.

The greater fight, however, went on within the Group itself. Relations between Strasberg and me had grown increasingly strained. There was no single reason for this. I found him extremely touchy and, what to me was even less pardonable, reluctant to admit his artistic shortcomings or difficulties, so that one felt oneself in trouble even in hinting at them. On the other hand, Strasberg was disturbed over my spells of "somnambulism." I was not entirely reliable. Above all, Strasberg felt it was my function as managing director of the organization to protect him, to ease his burden as stage director — something he believed I had failed to do. As he wrote me later, my value to the Group was to give it "its artistic and ethical line." He believed I ought to renounce stage direction until the day the Group was really settled. Cheryl Crawford agreed with him in all these respects.

No matter how bitter our feelings may have become, we tried to continue on our path. We respected our main task too much to allow any personal matters to stand in our way. We had hoped to do a new play by George O'Neil on which we had paid an advance. The play had not developed satisfactorily. We turned to Odets's *Silent Partner* even though Odets had failed to revise it during the summer. The actors, though disturbed by the evident clash of their directors' egos and all the hardships attendant on their Group career, still did not waver. Their need of such an organization as the Group was deep.

Without any idea where the money to produce it would come from, we put *Silent Partner* into rehearsal. Strasberg and Crawford did not believe it was ready for production. They were right, but despite my fatigue and desperation I hoped I might get it on just the same. Besides its inherent merits, the play was extremely timely. Though the Wagner Labor Relations Act had been passed in the summer of 1935, unions were experiencing great difficulties with some unregenerate employers. While Big Steel was to sign

with the CIO in March 1937 (we had reached the New Year of
1937), Little Steel was holding out savagely. Some of the more
brutal scenes of *Silent Partner* were to be enacted during the coming spring in the Chicago Memorial Day massacre.

Rehearsals continued for about three weeks. The Group office
was seething with unrest. The organization needed to be "saved."
Despite the major diseases we were suffering, we struggled valiantly over the minor ones. Joseph Verner Reed wrote us a letter
in which he conféssed himself disturbed at our failure to develop
any outstanding actresses to equal the men of our company. I
might have neglected this criticism at the time since it occupied
about as much part in my consciousness as a blister might to a
man with tuberculosis. Yet I answered it because I enjoyed the
irony of the situation. We were being highly praised just then
(in weekly and monthly publications) for our courage and artistic
integrity, while we were virtually at our last gasp both emotionally and economically. At the same time we were subject to
all sorts of well-intentioned and even intelligent criticism such as
Mr. Reed's.

I advised Mr. Reed that we were aware of the weaknesses of
our company and that we were anxious to remedy them, but that
on the other hand the general public and press were hardly aware
of our problems. For instance, in this matter of the women of our
company it was to be noted that for some reason most of our plays
had much better roles for men — our actresses certainly noted it!
— and that because of the nature of a small permanent company an
actress like Stella Adler was called on to play parts as varied as
Geraldine (*The House of Connelly*), Sarah Glassman (*Success
Story*), Gwenn Ballantine (*Gentlewoman*) and Bessie Berger
(*Awake and Sing*). If some of Broadway's women stars tried to
cover an equivalent range of roles, their limitations might be ex-
posed and their glamour diminish. As I wrote this I thought: "Our
situation does not permit us to satisfy our critics, who naturally
demand the best of everything, or ourselves — our actors, for example, who, in their own way, also demand the best."

Two of our lesser players at this point threatened to resign: the
Group was holding them down. One of these was an inordinately

self-conscious boy, the other an inordinately tense one. I had often wondered if they were capable of the progress from which they claimed we were barring them. I was relieved at this opportunity to let them try their wings. But I found Strasberg, who had no higher opinion of these actors than I did, pleading passionately with them not to leave the Group.

My amazement was even greater when Cheryl Crawford, impatient at my inactivity, put up a schedule of new classes under Strasberg which were intended to fill the void caused by our fears. The Group was on the verge of dissolution, and she imagined she could heal it with the palliative of fresh instruction.

The Actors' Committee were not to be bluffed. They sat down to state the actors' view of the Group situation. They drafted a document that was to become a landmark of our history. It was an entirely lucid, frank analysis of the Group's quandary. They tore our production of *Johnny Johnson* asunder to explore every false step that had been made by everyone in it. It was a very long paper, so I shall quote only the salient passages:

> *We are writing this paper so that the Group will go on.*
> . . . We are trying to find the truth regardless of personal feelings. . . .
> We all know that six years ago the Group was wrenched out of the American theatre by the sheer force of the directors' will. They, at that time, were undubitably the Group Theatre. Now six years have passed and the picture is different. *We* are sure that today the Group is no longer the three directors. . . . The Group Theatre is the thirty members (including the individual directors). Whatever superior talent and wisdom they might have today is no longer the *important factor* in holding the theatre together. . . . It is inescapable that the directors have not solved the Group problem. . . . The actors simply do not get any money out of the organization. . . . If any generalization should be made it is much more true to say that the actors by their dogged faith and belief in the idea of the theatre (which was planted six

years ago by the directors) are keeping each other and the
directors together. At certain points it has been absolutely
evident that what kept the Group was *their* determination —
seemingly unreasonable — that the Group must go on. . . .
There will be a Group Theatre no matter which of the directors resigns. . . .

There follows on this an analysis of the three directors in relation to the Group:

Lee Strasberg: There is no doubt that it was Lee who gave
the first artistic shape to the Group Theatre. For example, the
thing that most of the actors of the Group still call the Method
is in reality Lee's own method of work — at least up till *Gold
Eagle Guy.* In this respect, we believe that in actual influence exerted, Lee has been the greatest artistic force in the
American theatre during the last five years. Six years ago
with the inception of the Group, the revolutionary task was
his to do. He had to break down a whole tradition in thirty
different individuals and really necessitated (as it tended to
further harden and bring out) Lee's great courage, his dog-
gedness, his arbitrariness, his need to be right, his cold scorn
of artistic compromise, his clannishness, his removal from life,
his hysterical force (used as a threat) and above all the
brute domineering of his will. . . . Lee filled the need of that
time. . . . But today the same qualities that once were necessary seem unhealthy. We believe that Lee under the new
organization should be relieved for some time of all but
purely artistic tasks. . . .

Harold Clurman: To our mind, despite the fact that his
regime as a managing director is a failure, he is the logical
man for the position at the head of the theatre. It was he,
single-handed, who brought the Group alive into the world.
He is still the clearest and the most whole of the three directors, and in him the Group Idea still flourishes the most. . . .
But Harold has the gravest faults, which he is far from recog-
nizing himself. This is evidenced by the fact that during his
term as managing director *he did not create the theatre or-*

ganization that was his first and most important task. Harold really works only under the spell of inspiration, crumbling just before rising to heights. *He must have an iron-clad* and *completely worked-out plan.*

Cheryl Crawford: She's had six years of dirty jobs. We appreciate this, but she strikes us as a disappointed artist. She always feels she is wasting her life, that she is a "martyr" to the Group, that without her the Group would fold in a minute, and worst of all that no one appreciates her. She never stops trying to impress people with her own importance, the work she is doing, how what other people receive credit for doing is really her work. . . . We should get a business manager whom we really trust to take over these tasks. Cheryl's job lies in the creation of scripts like *Johnny Johnson,* tasks of general finance and promotion.

Finally the actors' paper concluded:

What's to be done?

First, we must assure the Group actors a regular, predictable sustaining income. At least one half the Group receive what for them is not even a subsistence wage. Another third live on a debasing wage level. The rest have either outside jobs or outside sources of income. Year after year debts pile up. As it is today the Group's continuance is impossible.

Second, the basic personal need for all of us, actor and director alike, is sufficient artistic exercise. . . . Often a whole year of one's life adds up to only one good part if one is lucky.

We believe we must take immediate steps now, to institutionalize ourselves as a Theatre. Next year, sweeping aside other desiderata, we must have our own theatre. With it, forty weeks of active and full production and performance. . . .

We have one tattered bond left between us all — a passionate concern for the Group idea. We have a choice:

Immediate Action — thus serving the Group through the

present personnel and present organization — following a plan
such as we have suggested

or,

an alternate possibility we have not discussed — Dissolution,
to allow a new and more fit Group rise from the ashes, to start
on a clean slate — reorganize fully, bearing in mind our mistakes.

Which Will Serve the Group Idea Best?

This paper — the writing of which I had encouraged, though
unaware of its details — was read to the assembled actors in the
absence of the directors. With their approval it was submitted to
each of the directors individually.

Strasberg, Crawford, and I met for a kind of war conference.
Two weeks before, Strasberg had decided to register a strong
protest against the failure of my office. After he had given full
vent to his statements, I suggested that he write me a kind of
memorandum in which he might express his considered opinion
of me, and I would do the same for him. He stopped me to say
that it was unnecessary for me to send him such a note, but that
he would oblige me by writing his. In a few days he did leave
me a résumé of his view of me, which included the criticisms of
me I have already mentioned.

Thus when Strasberg and Crawford met with me on the occasion of the actors' paper, the air had been cleared somewhat. It
seemed that the three of us were unified and had only to determine our relation to the actors. When asked what my attitude
toward them now was, I made a practical suggestion: "Since all
three of us are under attack, let us resign as a body of directors
and along with the actors reconstitute the Group according to the
new conditions that may obtain in the future."

I went on to say that rehearsals of *Silent Partner* ought to be
discontinued since Odets was now in Hollywood at work on a
new picture, and rehearsals had shown how much work the script
still needed. Moreover, I had decided to leave for Hollywood myself, where I would remain for six months. I was now too upset,

I added, to be clear about my future plans beyond that. This was perhaps not very helpful, but at the moment I could not honestly say more. My suggestion of a joint resignation by the directors was agreed upon.

We met with the actors and announced our resignation. The actors, both pleased and startled with the turn of events, took up the challenge of the directors' resignation by calling for a committee composed of the three former directors and a new Actors' Committee to draft an outline of future plans. All this would have to be done before I left for Hollywood, where, I repeated, I would remain for six months, though I offered no assurance of a return and no clear conception of the kind of Group I would be willing to work in in the future.

The truth is that I did not really know what was troubling me most, except for the fact that I was tired — very tired. My erstwhile fellow directors assured me the seat of my confusion was my troubled relations with Stella Adler, who had gone to the coast thoroughly fed up with the Group.

The few meetings our joint committee of directors and actors held at this time were an utter failure. Strasberg, irritated by my standoffishness, now hinted with icy heat that he and others might not be willing to wait till next June for my decision as to future participation in the Group.

The Group would go on, I proclaimed in an article for the *New York Times*, January 17, 1937. Our announcement that we would discontinue production activities till next season had been interpreted as the folding up of the Group Theatre as such — in other words, its finish.

In Hollywood, Odets, recently married to Luise Rainer, was irritated by my statement that we had stopped rehearsals of *Silent Partner* because it needed further revision, but when Jed Harris and others wired him for the right to produce it, he refused without equivocation. The Group would return, and they were to remain the producers of his plays. Theatre people were more often annoyed by than respectful of such loyalty.

When I left for Hollywood (accompanied by Elia Kazan, actor, friend, "disciple"), many of the Group company came to see us off at Grand Central Terminal. Lee Strasberg was there too, and he presented me with a gift — a rare edition of Ibsen's *Letters*. The future was blank and uncertain. I left New York with relief.

PART V

NEW PHASE

CHAPTER SEVENTEEN

We Run for Cover

I HAD no sooner arrived in Hollywood than I was engaged by Walter Wanger to assist in the making of a picture which Clifford Odets was writing and which our friend Lewis Milestone was to direct. Shortly after this, Wanger put most of the Group actors under contract in the hope of using some of them in this picture and farming out the others to various companies.

Exceptions to this were Stella Adler, who was put under contract to a Paramount subsidiary company. She compromised sufficiently with the new order of Hollywood to change her name to *Ardler!* Art Smith worked in Chicago as director and actor in the newly established Federal Theatre Project. Jules Garfield entered the cast of Arthur Kober's *Having Wonderful Time.*

Things looked bad for the Group's future. With the uncertain state of our organization and the collapse of the Theatre Union, it seemed pretty clear that our day in the theatre was definitely over. Certain commentators on the drama in New York wrote obituaries (under such titles as "Whither Revolt?") on the whole Left theatre movement, in which an I-told-you-so satisfaction was barely concealed. Undoubtedly this was partly due to the delight in burial so prevalent in theatre circles, but there was also the inference that this movement and its representatives were frauds and weaklings. Beneath their bluster, the chirping mourners did not see that some of the fire that appeared extinguished in organizations like the Group and the Theatre Union had gone into various elements of the Federal Theatre Project (reactionary Congressmen were able to see it); that productions like *The Cradle Will Rock* were its new manifestation; that even certain "academic" productions in reputable Broadway institutions were to owe most of their flare to the ignition provided by the younger and earlier groups.

When Odets saw Carnovsky, Bohnen, Kazan, and the others in the Wanger building for the first time, he burst into laughter, which Carnovsky joined without understanding. Odets perhaps didn't understand it himself, but he continued laughing and remarked only: "It's funny seeing all of you out here." He did not say why. Perhaps he was struck by the fact that in this wonderful country of ours, "poor guys" like ourselves, "outsiders" — the opposition, in short — were able to swim into the main stream of money, security, respectability.

Some of us spent many Sunday afternoons with Franchot Tone and Joan Crawford. Franchot was happy to play the host to his companions of old. To him we were clean spirits who brought light and warmth into his almost locked heart. Joan Crawford, a good sport, wanted to make friends with Franchot's friends. She thought at times of appearing on the stage, an ambition perhaps stimulated by Franchot. She wished to be able to follow him in all his steps, so that he might not be inclined to wander too far from hers.

In the afternoon we would chat, mostly about the theatre, play badminton, swim in the pool, dine, and see a picture in the projection-room, right off the pool. It was quite a pleasant routine that we followed almost every time we visited them. Once, while I lay afloat in the pool, basking lazily in the Sunday sun, Franchot

observed me with friendly malice and remarked: "The life of a
prostitute is pretty comfortable, isn't it?"

Work at the studio went well until Odets lost interest in our
script, and Milestone disagreed with Wanger on the casting of
the picture. Just as we were to go into production, the picture
was shelved. It was revived shortly after because Wanger wanted
to salvage the material on which so much time and money had
been spent. He asked me to recommend a writer who would re-
vamp the script, and I suggested John Howard Lawson, who was
having a hard time, financially speaking, in New York.

Lawson was engaged to re-do the Odets story. (Wanger's first
instruction to him was "not to improve pictures.") The story had
originally been a psychological melodrama laid in Paris. When
Wanger objected that its background was dated, Milestone had
countered that the most up-to-the-minute situation in which the
story might be placed was that of the civil war in Spain. So, many
months after the Group people had left Hollywood, the picture
Blockade emerged, to pursue a controversial course in many cities
of the world.

That this picture, to which none of us, except Odets and Lawson, made any contribution, had a semi-political base was thus
almost entirely an accident. But it was true that whatever interest
the subject had for its producer derived from the fact that Hollywood was then in the throes of a social consciousness of which
the Spanish situation was the fiery focus.

It was never clear to us in Hollywood at that time how much
or little the country as a whole was concerned with the Franco
coup against republican Spain. It appears today that a recognition of the importance of that struggle must have been far less
extensive than we supposed at the time. But then — and particularly in Hollywood, somehow — it was a flaming symbol not only
of the encroachments of Fascism, but of what might be called
more personal matters.

The writers, I believe, were the first in Hollywood to champion
the cause of the Loyalists. Spiritually speaking, a change of complexion had begun to show itself among the writers in the course

of the past two years (1935–7). Their little guild battles for recognition were both the cause and the effect of this sharpened sense of the world around them. Many of them, moreover, suffered the same peculiar sense of guilt or inadequacy that I had detected in other Hollywood characters. Those who came from New York and had labored in freer fields — the novel, the play, even poetry — were discomfited with the restrictions of the picture story. Though they had been driven by more than one type of need to their new refuge, they could not help feeling that there was something degrading in concentrating on trivialities in the face of a world that was palpably shaking under their feet.

Some sour commentators jeered that the Hollywood writers who had been worsted by the rigors of the creative life in the East now used their social preoccupations as a sop to their ailing consciences. Another theory among the cynics was that a vicarious participation in the Spanish fracas helped many a benighted Hollywood scribbler add stature to himself that he could not acquire through his work.

These leering interpretations were not altogether without truth, yet to accept them as conclusive would have been even more stupid than base. The fact that a man's relation to a big issue has a humble personal source need not diminish either the value of his contribution to it or the influence it will exercise on his life. It goes without saying that many whose hearts and pennies went out to Spain may themselves have been something less than heroic; it is even certain that much of the rapture with which many of the Hollywood crowd regarded the struggle against Franco had far less political knowledge behind it than was supposed. Indeed, I venture to say that the phenomenon I am describing derived chiefly from an emotional hunger whose cause was first of all deeply American.

Be that as it may, the wave of enthusiasm spread from the writers to actors, directors, even producers. It struck starlets and top executives, so that when later all sympathizers and contributors to the Loyalist cause were smeared with the comprehensive Red label, a grotesquely incongruous assortment of names from

Shirley Temple to Walter Wanger (who for a short time displayed an autographed picture of Mussolini in his office) made copy for the cockeyed world to contemplate.

The economic crises and conflicts of the early thirties were now broadening to a social-political struggle on an international scale. Our community life was centered in the various parties given at the home of this or that writer, actor, or director and at dinners or mass meetings to greet personalities active in the Loyalist cause. For a while the cultural life of Hollywood revolved almost entirely around these parties. They were in effect veritable beacons to lighten the sleepy evenness of Hollywood nights.

Perhaps the climax of these occasions was the meeting at the huge Los Angeles Shrine Auditorium, the chairman of which was the German poet-playwright Ernst Toller, and the main speaker André Malraux. Malraux's eminence as a novelist and his participation as a flier on the Spanish government's side made the evening a memorable event. The relatively small Hollywood picture colony mingled with the larger number of the Los Angeles population — a contact that is rarely effected except at such special social or musical occasions. It was as if the motion-picture people suddenly had the opportunity to behold there what was going on in the world.

What was going on was a bloody encounter between the predatory power of a greedy minority and the simple humanity of a whole people. In this conflict the bearers of culture, the true representatives of a nation's conscience, intellectuals, artists, even a good part of the priesthood, found themselves directly involved as participants in the fight for the humble man. Not everyone may march or fly, as Malraux did, but that such a man should find himself not above the battle but in the midst of it acted as a symbol of our own desire to bring ourselves in some way into the main stream of the true life of our time.

The mediocrity of so many relationships in Hollywood, the inner indifference to much of the studio routine, the flatness of the whole atmosphere in terms of any spiritual connection between one's job and one's real needs as a person, were set off by the metal of Malraux's personality and speech. Something stirred within the hearts of Hollywood's unrequited, and their large contributions in money were actually the poorest signs of it.

The current released by the Spanish situation did not immediately charge any of the Group to leave Hollywood by the next train for the firing line, which was what the theatre in New York was to most of us. In fact, I resisted every attempt to shake me from my resolution to wait. When the actors became particularly importunate, I told them they were at liberty to go ahead without me, to make plans in conjunction with Lee Strasberg and Cheryl Crawford, who showed no reluctance to proceed.

The actors in Hollywood seemed to feel that my participation in the Group was pivotal, and until I made some positive move no one else would be fired with the necessary enthusiasm or fortitude to take up the task. The best they could get out of me when I sought to appease their crying need was, "Something will develop; I know we will get together again."

Early in April 1937 Cheryl Crawford sent us a letter of resignation: she was not getting any collaboration from us. This was followed by another from Lee Strasberg. He added that in his view the Group had been a success, but his resignation was prompted by the feeling that the members of the Group had destroyed its leadership. I did not agree that the leadership of the Group had been destroyed by the actors; in fact it seemed to me such an accusation was itself an admission of incapacity for leadership. I accepted the two resignations with a kind of friendly fatalism, and no argument.

Shortly after the letters of resignation reached us, the *New York Times* ran the following notice: "Miss Crawford plans to become an independent producer, with a small group of associates. Mr. Strasberg will direct plays for her and other managers. . . . According to Mr. Strasberg, the nucleus of Miss Crawford's acting company will include some players now with the Group. . . ."

Only one actor bolted the Group. This actor, the *New York Telegram* reported, had resigned to join the Crawford-Strasberg

Theatre. But this theatre, as such, never got much further than making its announcements.

In the meantime all of us in Hollywood pursued a kind of treadmill course. Some of our Group altered their noses, but very little else. One studio executive asked Kazan to change his name to the more euphonious *Cezanne*. When Kazan pointed out that this was the name of a rather well-known painter, he was told: "You make just one good picture, and nobody will even remember the other guy."

Kazan returned to the East in disgust due to an inability to adjust his turbulence to the vacuous serenity of southern California. Luther Adler was very much discouraged to find Odets now at work on a new picture as if he intended to do nothing else the rest of his life. There were always moments in which Odets seemed to be planning one conquest after another in whatever field of work he was engaged in, and now that he was at a studio, he talked as if he foresaw infinite possibilities ahead.

Odets, it is true, now appeared only half awake. Even I grew passionately perturbed because I felt the world was going to hell when I read that Léon Blum in France was standing by his non-intervention policy in Spain, while Odets appeared utterly unaffected, at least on the surface. What Odets could do about Léon Blum I'm sure I could not say (nor was I of the opinion that he had to write a play about Spain), but in my frustration I connected the two through some mysterious subjective chemistry.

I was not doing much myself beyond my studio work, which was not in the least dull. When Wanger asked me how I felt about working in pictures as contrasted with working in the theatre, I fumbled for something pleasant to say. "Pictures," I remarked, "are an industry; the theatre merely an art."

The thought of the theatre plagued me at times like a bad dream. I had theoretic arguments about the theatre, which always became curiously violent. Nothing infuriated me more than the thesis so commonly advanced that the theatre had to cede its place to the movies as the horse and buggy did on the appearance of the automobile.

Molly Thacher, our play-reader, wrote me letters of a Puritan severity: if I was being seduced by Hollywood's glamour, then I was giving up my birthright for pretty small potatoes, and if I was being held in Hollywood by Stella Adler, then I was a pretty sorry Samson.

On the other hand, I received very disturbing letters from my father and brother, pointing out that I owed it to the family to remain in Hollywood and make myself solvent. It must have hurt my father to advise me as he did. I reminded him that it was he who had helped shape my character, had taught me the unworthiness of every consideration that blinded one to the ideal that our conscience sets up for us. William Dean Howells once wrote to his father: "It is a comfort to be right theoretically and to be ashamed of oneself practically." To me there was no comfort in this at all — only profound unhappiness.

One day early in May I received a letter from Elia Kazan saying he thought there were two alternatives before me. Either I could come back and risk setting up the Group again this summer, or I could wait a year or two, accumulate some money, restore my peace of mind, and start fresh with whatever materials were available at the end of this period.

When I read this letter, I answered as if there had never been any question of what I would do. There were no two choices. There was only one course: to begin work again next season with the Group. My ideas on the subject were clear; my will, energy, and faith unimpaired. I would be back in New York in August.

When I had acquainted the Group actors of my decision to reassemble the Group in New York the next fall, we held a few meetings. I set forth a policy for the next season. I would not guarantee a salary to anyone not employed in actual production work with the Group; there would be only one director, myself, and an appointed Council (Luther Adler, Roman Bohnen, and Kazan) to advise me. I could not promise to keep some of our old Group on a so-called active list, as I held little hope for their future. Despite this, I would do everything possible to maintain the bulk of the old company employed, since I still believed in the fundamental principle of the Group organization — the permanent company.

Our problem, however, was to find the first play. One evening Odets showed me a typewritten sheet with the bare outline of a play to deal with a boy whose father wanted him to be a musician, while the boy prepared to make a fortune as a prize-fighter. The very modesty of this premise (despite its strangeness) led me to believe that Odets could make it meaningful. I encouraged him to develop the idea.

I called a meeting of playwrights. "Like most theatre people," I said, "we in the Group theatre have had a hard time making things go smoothly. It would be much easier for all of us therefore to continue here in pictures. But we want to go back to resume our work in the theatre. We don't suffer here, we don't feel the work here beneath our dignity, and we find as many people to like out here as elsewhere. We think the technique of pictures is interesting, and we know that much can be learned from it. Yet we want to go back to our theatre. We don't expect to make as much money as we have made here, though we have nothing against making as much as possible. Perhaps none of you can make quite so much money in the theatre as you are making here. Your writing for pictures, we find, is clever, expert, and sometimes on a level that is not necessarily beneath what you have written thus far for the stage. Honestly, if you are satisfied with what you are doing now — and from quite a number of standpoints there is no reason why you shouldn't be — forget the theatre.

"If you feel that you are really represented by what you write for pictures — forget the theatre. But if you feel there is something more, something beyond, something essentially different that you want to say . . . if you feel that not enough of your imagination, invention, thought, or sentiments is being used in pictures, you must write for the theatre — carefully and patiently, since today the theatre needs the best you can give. If your need is as strong in you as it has proved to be in us, Hollywood will

not tempt you; you will have to return to work ever more actively
in theatres of your own choice. . . . But there is room today only
for the determined."

Odets and Luther Adler left for New York early in July. Odets
set to work immediately on his new play under the watchful eyes
of Adler and Kazan, who trembled lest some emotional eventu-
ality (the sudden return of his wife, for instance) might upset
the regularity of his writing schedule. A legend grew that Luther
Adler connived to keep Luise Rainer busy with odd jobs so that
Odets might have as much time as possible to be alone with his
work.

Adler and Kazan engaged in feverish activity in arranging for
new offices — to which I contributed from my personal funds —
and all the necessary preparation for the setting up of a functioning organization. One thing I had insisted on was that never
again would I be placed in the position of having to raise backing for our production; and my Council had promised that this
essential but debilitating task would be spared me. There was to
be a new corporation on a non-profit-making basis, and its officers,
aside from myself, were composed of the Council plus Odets, with
provision made for the addition of those other workers in our
midst who might prove their value and loyalty in the future. We
retained new attorneys, hired a new business manager, a new
secretary. My name was inscribed auspiciously on my office door
in the Sardi Building on Forty-fourth Street.

On August 23, 1937 I left for New York, and was greeted at
Grand Central by a small delegation of friends, like a hero returning from exile.

CHAPTER EIGHTEEN

Renewal

Two acts of the new Odets play, *Golden Boy*, were ready on my arrival. I read them and found they contained Odets's most clearly articulated writing.

Money for the play had to be raised immediately. Various people were approached. One manager offered to back the play if we would cast "outside the Group" — that is, with "names," actors whose stock on the theatrical Bourse was high. I cut off negotiations with this person at once. Other people thought the play too gloomy. A reading of the play to a group of wealthy merchants yielded only an offer of a $2,000 investment.

The problems of casting were serious, not alone from the standpoint of our would-be backers, but from our own. Odets had promised the central role to Jules Garfield — Odets, like many playwrights, had a habit of making promises to actors even before he had written a word of his script. Garfield was obviously the type, but he had neither the pathos nor the variety, in my opinion, to sustain the role. I wanted Luther Adler to play the part — a choice that shocked nearly everyone, since he seemed least like the fighter who was the play's leading character. But in my view this character was not a fighter — simply a sensitive, virile boy.

There were other disagreements over the casting. It was dangerous, Odets insisted, for Morris Carnovsky to play another Odets father, and Carnovsky agreed. Odets wasn't satisfied to use Phoebe Brand in the role of the sister, either. It became clear to me that Odets wanted a good Broadway cast, "the best cast money could buy." It was not my plan to shop for actors, but to carry on with the Group company. To do this I had to prove to Odets that the Group company made the best cast he could have under any circumstances.

It was not easy, because Odets was getting contrary advice

from practically everyone. The Group actors were themselves uncertain as to how I ought to proceed, while Garfield (still appearing in *Having Wonderful Time*) was thoroughly disgruntled by
my decision to use him in the comedy role of Siggie rather than in
the role he had been promised. There was a problem also about
the feminine lead. I was interested in Frances Farmer, who was
under contract to Paramount. My interest in her derived from the
conviction not only that she was suitable for the role in this play
but that she was an actress who might grow within the Group.

We went into rehearsal without money enough to produce the
play. This, of course, was contrary to my principles. I had to
choose between these principles and the knowledge that unless I
pushed ahead, the play would not be produced at all — at any
rate under Group auspices. There was no time to campaign for a
subsidy; there was hardly time enough to raise the little money
it cost to put on the play — $19,000. It appeared there was a busi-
ness recession in the fall of 1937: Wall Street was weak again.
Rehearsals continued vigorously, however, to the amazement and
admiration of my Council, who could not fathom my unperturbed
demeanor. I was not unperturbed — I was desperate.

Odets was displeased at my not doing anything to get money.
"When did Harold ever raise any money for the Group?" he cried,
forgetting even *Awake and Sing*. Ten days before the opening the
money had still not been raised, despite the fact that certain prospective backers were invited to fairly complete rehearsals. At last
Odets and Luise Rainer put up money of their own. Walter Wanger settled his contract with the Group actors by contributing
$2,000; two other people from Hollywood, Gary Cooper's mana-
ger, Jack Moss, the director Henry Hathaway, and my friend
William Melniker of the MGM foreign office completed the list
of backers.

Opening night, I was informed, proved a very swank affair.
The Group was almost fashionable now: a long line of big cars
drew up to the Belasco Theatre, and handsomely outfitted ladies
and gentlemen emerged to make a noisy, coughing, generally rude
first-night audience.

The press, though by no means uniformly enthusiastic, provided many "business notices." The production as such was almost universally admired. By money standards, *Golden Boy* was the greatest success in the Group's history. If the Group had been able to finance the play itself, this production alone might have provided it with a subsidy. At it was, because the Group owned a good part of the play's profits, enough money was earned to sustain the Group for two seasons.

The success of the play naturally released all sorts of forces. There was a great spurt of activity. Odets expressed the wish to be active in every phase of our work. He was added to the Council so that he might have this opportunity. Though I doubted that he would be as active as he hoped, I appreciated his desire to have a "home," in which at all times there was "housework" to be done.

This desire for some center around which one might build a complete life was basic, and almost all the people in and around the Group clamored for it ever more insistently. Bitter disappointment, even hate, developed within the Group itself when the Group failed to furnish such a center. Though no Group manifesto had ever promised it, there was something in the Group's attitude that made its members and even many outside its ranks feel it could be, should be, the focus of a world of activity that would make great actors of some, writers of others, directors, designers, teachers, organizers, producers, administrators, or a combination of several of these things of the rest. The Group's inclusive philosophy adumbrated a cosmos; therefore the Group's function, even its duty, was to become a cosmos. It had to provide what society itself failed to provide. Because somehow the Group's criticism of society implied that it was above society, it had to become a society within society, a protected unit, a utopia, an oasis within the city, in which one could work out one's life career and salvation.

Was all this contrary to logic, common sense, sanity? Hardly, since no one ever voiced these demands in so many words; no one even realized that that was what was being asked for. Yet in all the nervous complaints and the persistent hum of fervent grumbling, this was, willy-nilly, the leading motive. When there was no activity, the actors wanted to begin it "regardless"; when activity had produced some hope for the future, the emotional pressure strained toward the most ambitious vistas as if the whole face of the earth had altered and promised everything that had once seemed remote and visionary. What, in fact, did these people want? To lead full lives disciplined by a unified moral and intellectual code that would direct them toward smiling goals of spiritual and material well-being. Is that so much to ask? It is merely everything.

It is probably the objective of the whole world's struggle. It is certainly the unrealized American dream. It is that for want of which many years of heartache and passionate striving will still be our lot. Was it silly for some little people on a narrow New York street to cry for all of this? No doubt. But it was also their saving grace, even though in doing it they often weakened themselves and postponed their maturity. "I gotta right! I gotta right!" yells the impassioned little hackie of *Waiting for Lefty* in a tradition that is a hundred per cent American. The Group actors, ever dissatisfied, also felt they had a right to ask for more than just the privilege of appearing in a successful Broadway play.

What was incongruous in all this was that they asked so much of an organization which had the greatest difficulty in accomplishing even the little it did. What was dangerous as well as incongruous was that, in their quest for a total satisfaction in their work and life, they did not recognize that at times some of their demands were indistinguishable from the old push toward personal redemption and personal reward in which no idea beyond personal success is involved or needed.

Bobby Lewis had set up a small Group Theatre school, which offered ten free scholarships and a few half-scholarships, supported by some twenty paying pupils, whose tuition was a hundred dollars for a ten-week semester. The school, at which some of our actors taught, while special instructors in fencing, movement, and speech were called in, gave us an opportunity to train a few younger actors who were to prove quite useful to us. It also proved financially successful in a modest way.

The school could not continue for more than a season because the Group moved about too much on tours. With the passing of the Group School, however, many others grew up in its place. Group actors and directors took on either private classes or classes in various other schools all over the city. Thus many young actors to this day are indirectly Group-trained.

Our attorneys tried to engineer a deal with a company that hoped to produce motion pictures on Long Island. This, they thought, would solve all our money problems for the future. It could solve nothing, because one small company cannot act both as a film- and play-producing unit at the same time. It was one of those paper plans that, like so many solutions that take care of everything, simply eliminate a problem by suppressing its main factor.

I returned to Hollywood for a short time to see Stella Adler. She was happy and proud over the success of *Golden Boy*. This mood alternated with an ever mounting bitterness over the fact that the Group and I were going on without her. She had given so much to the building of our theatre, and now at the moment of its greatest material success she appeared stranded outside it. In a sense she could neither accept nor let go of the Group. She thought highly of its accomplishment, defended it staunchly against all attacks, but could not stomach its "pathological manners."

Franchot Tone took the success of *Golden Boy* as a kind of justification of his faith in us. He shared my pleasure and pride. He glowed in anticipation of the time when he would work with us again. Next year, he said.

I met Lawson again. He admitted that the Group's revival showed it had more life in it than he had suspected. But he seemed more entrenched in his new career as a screen writer than I had supposed he desired to be. I never attacked screen writing as such; but there were people who owed it to themselves, I thought, to continue writing for the theatre, for only in the theatre could they realize certain vital aspects of their talent.

Lawson now betrayed some skepticism even on this score. He held that the pressures of backers, real estate, press, and the $3.30

audience in the theatre made for restrictions on the dramatist that
equaled those on the screen writer. There was perhaps more to
this argument than I would concede at the time. In five years the
point of view enunciated here by Lawson was to dominate the
entire picture colony, and to appear incontrovertibly correct.

On my return to New York I found the theatre world divided
into unequal camps in regard to the Group. Broadway wiseacres were delighted that the Group now valued "entertainment"
above "propaganda." Partisans of "propaganda" were uncertain
and a little worried over *Golden Boy.* The play dealt with the
struggle of the individual ego in a society that tried more and
more to dismiss the subtleties of man's subjective needs as the
concern of "forgotten dopes." There was perhaps some social
criticism in this; on the other hand, the play dealt with no immediate political issue. The carriage trade liked the show and
did not question itself as to its meaning; and this too was a source
of some misgiving to those who preferred the Group when it was
least popular! Generally, however, there was a pleasant feeling
abroad that the Group had done its job well.

This was the Group's feeling too: it had not deviated in its
purpose or basic methods, but had made a sane synthesis of its
years of experience. For the rest, the Group people were active
in aiding such enterprises as TAC (Theatre Arts Committee for
Democracy), which was enlisting the co-operation of actors and
showfolk generally in the Spanish people's fight against fascism.

In a reconstructed beer-hall named Chez Firehouse on East
Fifty-fifth Street a kind of political cabaret under TAC's auspices was opened to foster interest in the good cause. It was a
lively place, lending the New York night scene a fillip of fresh
zest. The after-theatre shows given there smacked of a fine European tradition, but their content reflected an exuberant gaiety and
enthusiasm altogether American. 1937 was the year of hope and
confidence among progressives, and the songs, skits, and assorted
high jinks contrived by young actors and their composer and
writer friends added a special relish to their dreams. The folk
chants of Earl Robinson about Abe Lincoln and other home-

grown heroes were popularized here, and not only was the political folly of reactionary thinking mocked, but other symptoms of feebleness (like the preoccupation with death and other-worldliness that showed themselves in such current plays as *Our Town, On Borrowed Time,* and *Shadow and Substance*) were youthfully lampooned. "Our side" was sure to win, because lusty bright boys and girls like ourselves were rooting for it.

Besides members of the Group company engaged here as supervisors, directors, and performers, there were also many from the flourishing but threatened Federal Theatre Project and from the new organization that had recently opened house on West Forty-first Street. For the honors of the season were shared by the Group and the Mercury Theatre, or, more accurately, Orson Welles. Of the two, in fact, the latter possessed a more novel showmanship.

The Mercury productions — particularly *Cæsar* — had a dash of originality, a boyish zip akin to that of the TAC shows. I did not care for *The Shoemaker's Holiday,* which seemed to me much less bawdy than androgynously shrill, but the press liked it. The *Heartbreak House* that followed was not brilliant, but creditable as a revival of one of Shaw's most significant documents. The following season, after the failure of *Danton's Death,* the Mercury as a permanent theatre venture on Broadway vanished with Welles to the West.

I interrupt my narrative here on the subject of the Mercury Theatre and Orson Welles to make a point that has relevance to the whole theatrical scene in which the Group found itself during these years. The Mercury Theatre was an enterprise that the press was sincerely fond of; it was sensational but not controversial. It had the rebel air of a "hep" and hearty youth that suited the rejuvenated epoch of the late thirties. The Mercury was safe. It treaded on no toes, but rather kicked the seat of plays and traditions for which our reverence is more advertised than real.

When the Mercury folded, there were no regrets, no shaking of heads, except among its actors. The ebullient Orson Welles was off on another jaunt. An important New York reviewer, in fact, toasted the departed theatre with a blithe farewell. He demonstrated very cleverly that we had all loved the Mercury for its newfangled bohemianism, its fundamental lack of seriousness, its delightful capacity to turn easily from its presumed path with a genial "What the hell!"

The same reviewer — also a consistent champion of the Group — had admonished the Group some years earlier: "It [the Group] has been bound rather than liberated by its idealism; and it has needed more than anything else the counsel of a genial and skeptical mind."

What would "the counsel of a genial and skeptical mind" have done for the Group? Would it have prevented our doing a number of inferior plays? Hardly, since we have seen how skeptical and even harsh the Group itself was about many of its scripts. Would it have relaxed our actors in their first productions? Perhaps, but first steps are always the most difficult, and complaints against heaviness or over-tension became less frequent with the progress of our company. Would our testaments of faith have been less irate, our public relations sweeter? Unnecessary: because our occasional bumptiousness often called attention to what might otherwise have passed as negligible flops. I have a suspicion that "the counsel of a genial and skeptical mind" would have simply bid us quit altogether. "The counsel of a genial and skeptical mind" for a young man in the theatre is the quickest road to Hollywood.

Back of the reviewer's revealing phrase lurks that *theory-phobia* so characteristic of all our critical thinking. It is a fear of committing oneself to any method or goal other than "excellence" and its reward — success. The Group's theories were either descriptions of its actual work and technique or statements of a purpose that kept the Group going when its financial failure, not to mention personal difficulties, would under other circumstances simply have dissolved it. In other words, the Group's theory was actually its preservative; when the theory could no longer be translated into fact — that is, produce the results for which the Group was created — the Group ceased functioning, though its members had individually all reached a high point of competence.

Behind the fear of theory is the fear of being morally or intellectually trapped in an attitude that it might be convenient to drop quickly in a society where the test for everything is whether or not it pays. If, in our old pioneer days, "book larnin'" was scorned because what was most immediately useful was not headwork but muscle, so in our day — in the theatre at least — "theories" are out of place in a market that is increasingly fluid and unpredictable. A theory — that is, a reasoned idea, a firm belief, a method with a fixed objective aside from the box office — is something that may lead to your being caught with your pants down!

Worse than the Group's idealism or its theories was its lack of humor. To be without a sense of humor is indeed a sorry thing. A sense of humor bespeaks the ability to see all the facets of a subject; its lack betrays blindness or narrowness of vision. In the Group we were glad that our most serious plays were as much the occasion for deep gusts of laughter as for gravity.

But something else was meant by the reiterated complaint that the Group had no humor. I was often inclined to plead guilty, and to point out that if the complaint was true, there are no jokes in Jeremiah either!

But what was the meaning of this insistence on humor? Why was it so dismaying for me to write a preface to an Odets play or to make a speech on a theatrical topic in which I did not kid both myself and the subject discussed? Someone has written: "Ours is an essentially tragic age, so we refuse to take it tragically." That was not the explanation in this case. The sense of humor in question here — the sense of humor of our theatrical press, for example — is a method of advancing while making sure of the possibility of retreat. A straightforward statement made without an ambiguous grimace may be considered dogmatic. As dogma it is an affront to your listener (who may not agree) or it will embarrass the speaker should he be proved wrong. To defend it, you may have to fight, perhaps shame, your adversary; and if you are not strong enough to defend it, you will be held either a boor or a fool yourself. Any belief set forth without an evasive or apologetic grin is both bad manners and bad salesmanship.

Behind it all is the need to be free, to pick up or drop any notion
according to convenience, to avoid choice, lest one be caught in
the rigidity of a definite position, for in that lies difficulty and even
danger. The theatre in our slippery society has become very much
like gambling. The reviewers, like the financiers, hate to back a
loser. "The best and fairest way of discrediting any particular
point of view," a canny European has said, "is by not having a
point of view oneself."

During the summer in Hollywood, Irwin Shaw submitted for
my consideration a play with a Spanish Civil War background. I
thought it weak and unclear, and warned Shaw against his facility.
Naturally, he thought my judgment mistaken, as did evidently
Norman Bel Geddes, who accepted the play for production. When
Siege was about to open, Shaw realized it would be a failure and
was much distressed about the quality of its production. Those
who approved the supposed pacifism of his early work were now
shocked at his acceptance of violence and bloodshed. Others who
had hailed *Bury the Dead* as a masterpiece were now to pro-
nounce him "finished" (at twenty-four). I gave Shaw an advance
on his next play, *Quiet City*.

We went ahead with Robert Ardrey's *Casey Jones*. It was a
play with a sound theme: the enslavement of the individual by
his job in a society in which the job for the individual is uncon-
nected with any creative purpose. Better than that, it had a certain freshness of characterization in an authentic American vein
not often cultivated on our cosmopolitan stage. Our Council was
against producing the play. I realized some of the play's weaknesses myself, but now that it was the only script available, I
thought it reasonable to do it. It would give a young writer the
opportunity to see his play acted, it would provide a new director
— Kazan — his first chance at a major production, it might lead
to the strengthening of our acting company — we used Van Heflin
in an important role — but above all it would keep our organization active.

Accident rules in the American theatre. It proved much easier
to raise money for this weak play than it had been to raise it for

the highly effective *Golden Boy*. Miss Dorothy Willard put up $20,000 for the play's production. She seemed a lonely woman, and she wanted to learn about the theatre through young and sympathetic people. Five thousand dollars more was needed, but was never raised. The Group made up the difference.

No one profited through the production, not even Gorelik, whose design of a railroad locomotive was the hit of the show. In a successful season a failure such as *Casey Jones* does not hurt much. Even our actors — the most caustic of critics — were willing to forgive.

The actors were in a good mood, I repeat, because the air about them was alive with a feeling of activity, progress, hope. There were classes to teach or attend, funds to be raised on behalf of China in her struggle against Japan. Phoebe Brand and Frances Farmer wore lisle stockings as part of the boycott on Japanese silk, while the company agreed to give a Sunday night benefit performance of *Golden Boy* to help buy ambulances and provide medical aid for the defenders of democratic Spain. None of this was strictly Group business, since it was all carried out on the individual initiative of the actors themselves; but as the Group was the center from which these people proceeded, it was, in a manner of speaking, all Group work.

There was a kind of excitement in almost every event that took place now. For example, when the Theatre Treasurers in an effort to gain recognition as a union, threatened to picket all theatres, we arranged a settlement. When Brock Pemberton issued a petition against the Federal Theatre's invasion of the Times Square district, the Group, together with the Mercury Theatre and George Abbott, made a point of refusing to join in this move against the Project, just as the next season a number of Group actresses joined a general delegation to protest against the destruction of the Project by Congress.

Clifford Odets visited Luise Rainer in Hollywood. While there he tried to write another piece to supply the actors with a play to do for special matinees and Sundays. Perhaps the pressure of circumstances, but more probably insufficient knowledge of the

background, made this play, called *The Law of Flight* — based
on the life of a Cuban revolutionary leader — more or less of a
blank cartridge. I was looking forward to this play, and Odets
was eager to make as fertile a contribution now as he had to the
first season — 1935 — that marked his emergence as a playwright.
But when I read the play, I felt it would be a mistake to present
so unrealized a work.

Nothing — not even Jules Garfield's announcement that he was
leaving for Hollywood — lessened our sense of moving ahead.
Garfield had spoken to me about this possibility before I left on
a short vacation, and though I admonished him gently not to take
this step, I did not try to confront him with any implacable moral
barrier such as some of his fellow actors did. Morris Carnovsky
— nicknamed the "Dean" — who had taken Garfield under his
wing in a way he had with young actors, barely spoke to him
now. Lee Cobb's face lowered with wrath. The actors called for
a meeting, the object of which is no longer clear to me; I cannot
remember whether they wanted me to register their general disapproval or whether they thought they would be able to make
Garfield change his mind.

Some of his companions told him that he was still immature as
an actor and that he owed it to himself to continue to develop
with the Group before venturing into the wide-open spaces of
the screen. Some thought it fitting to tell him how monotonous
and mannered he had been in *Having Wonderful Time*. Others
simply told him how low it was to leave a production like *Golden
Boy* — which excelled through its ensemble — in the middle of a
run.

In Garfield's case, I wondered if the actor's wife hadn't exercised what was, from my standpoint, a mischievous influence.
I hardly knew Mrs. (Robbie) Garfield, but for some reason I
imagined she spurred her husband on to break with the Group.
She had developed a sense of justice or, at least, a stiff-backed
resistance to the thought of being taken advantage of, and she
felt — so I guessed — that Julie's innocence had been exploited.
In the first place, he had been promised a leading role, by Odets,
which instead had been assigned to Luther Adler by Clurman,

who may have been partial to the latter for obvious reasons!
Second, Julie had been earning $300 a week in the Kober play,
and he had left it before its run was over to take $100 and then
$125 in the Group, while Luther Adler, Carnovsky, and others
were getting more. If Julie might protest that the others (for instance, Adler and Carnovsky) had made their sacrifices in the past
— because the foolish husband would always defend the Group —
his wife could retort that while they were living in the humblest apartments, people like Stella Adler were luxuriating
on Fifth Avenue, so that there must be more (or rather less) to
these sacrifices than met the eye. Above and beyond all this,
Robbie Garfield wasn't sure that if the others had Hollywood
offers quite as attractive, they would remain quite so staunch. In
short, she felt bound to "wise him up." When this was done, he
might follow his conscience as he pleased.

All this, as I have said, was pure conjecture on my part, which
even if true I should not have taken amiss, since it was in the nature of things for such scenes to be enacted in the private places
where history is made. The reason I dwell on the matter is that I
knew of at least four cases where "Group wives" spoke of the
Group as they might of a corespondent in a divorce case. The
greater the faith the man had in the Group, the more virulent became the wife's attack on it.

Early in 1938 I appointed Stella director of the California
company of *Golden Boy,* where the play was to be produced by
Curran.

As I had directed *Golden Boy* with outstanding success in New
York, I received an offer from David Selznick to direct pictures
in Hollywood. I toyed with the idea of accepting the offer on a
six-months-a-year basis, and returned to California both to learn
if such a plan might prove practicable and to see what Stella Adler had done with *Golden Boy.*

I had not been away long when I came to the conclusion that I
could not be the director of the Group and at the same time pursue
a career in Hollywood. The Group demanded single-minded devotion. The fact that I considered even a six-months-a-year deal

(unacceptable in any case to most picture companies) was a sign that my previous experience in Hollywood had had some influence on me, as it had had, to some extent, on the entire company.

Not that there was a very strong temptation to remain in the picture business, but familiarity with it made it clear that Hollywood offered a way out of the economic dilemma for us as workers in the entertainment field. It is true that for the Group actors (or me) to enter the picture business was not to continue our career, but to change from a hazardous path of personal expression to generally lucrative employment in a craft that had to be approached in an altogether new way. Everyone in the Group sensed this and had made his choice; yet the fact that there was a choice to be made at all was enough to cast new light on all our thoughts. I do not believe that this played any crucial role in the future history of the Group, but to maintain that it exercised no influence whatever would be false. Something vague and disturbing was always, and increasingly, lurking in the recesses of our consciousness.

On my return to New York the actors were pleased with my reassertion to them of the need to stick steadfastly to our task. Our technical director, Michael Gordon, surprised me by saying that my speech had made him happy because he had had the feeling in the past few months that I had grown cynical. I really did not know what he meant, despite my faculty at times of seeming to entertain almost every kind of idea, including those most opposed to my true beliefs.

Yet the suggestion that traces of cynicism had been detected in my manner made me reflect that since the breakdown that followed *Johnny Johnson* something had changed within me. It was perhaps an increased awareness that the Group's situation was an impossible one, that we were carrying on a task that was almost against nature! Do not mistake me: I believed that this impossible task had to be carried out by us — since if it wasn't, by whom would it be? But, my idealism now did not preclude my seeing that in a very real sense we were fools. The point is, I believed in the value of our folly and, though at times I might laugh at it, I felt deeply that it was incumbent on us to persist in it. For not only did we find pleasure in what we were doing, but we were satisfying a need expressed by many people outside our circle.

At this juncture the immediate next step in our task was to undertake a London trip. Charles Cochran wanted to present *Golden Boy* with the original cast in London. He offered to finance the trip and the production if we would cross the ocean for an unlimited engagement. If we had been a company interested only in wringing the last penny from our profitable property, we should no doubt have accepted. But we conceived our function to be the continuous production of plays, not their exploitation to the death. We could not accept an unlimited engagement and turned down Cochran's offer.

However, an American actress living in London was anxious to play in *Golden Boy*. Furthermore, she was willing and had the means to finance the entire venture, even though we insisted we could remain in England for only a short period. Of course, we would not have considered such an offer if Frances Farmer had not been under obligation to return for the summer to do a picture in Hollywood. But as we had been informed that the actress in London was a competent player, I did not think it too mean a compromise to make the deal, though one or two people informed me in no uncertain terms that this decision betrayed a thoroughgoing opportunism on my part.

To my astonishment, I found a certain reluctance in some members of the company to make the trip. They admitted that if we were to close in New York for the summer, they preferred to use this time to line their pockets with more Hollywood gold. I argued gently that a London season would add prestige to the Group, that it would be something of an education for the company to go abroad, and that, in my opinion, this would probably be the last opportunity they might have for many years to come, as a European war was just around the corner. The company yielded to my persuasion.

Clifford Odets, Luther and Stella Adler, with her daughter Ellen (child of an early marriage), were to leave on the *Queen Mary* in order to reach London before the rest of the company, since our new leading lady would have to be coached by Stella before she could fit into the production as a whole.

Just before this we had had a series of conferences with Irwin Shaw. His play *Quiet City*, which he had brought to us in the spring, needed revision. At the last of our discussions Shaw told me that during the trip to Cuba we had taken together in March, he had thought of still another idea for a play, suggested to him by the memory of two old men in a boat he had once seen on a winter day near Coney Island.

On June 9, 1938 the *New York Post* ran the following pleasant item: "At 8 yesterday morning, Mr. Clurman met Irwin Shaw, who came in from Massachusetts; at 9 he met Stella Adler, arriving from Hollywood; at 10 he went to the sailing of the *President Harding* to say good-bye to other members of the Group Theatre; at 3:30 he sailed on the *Queen Mary*. Shortly after Mr. C. arrives in London, he will start his greetings all over again, for he will be on hand to welcome the Group members when they arrive in London."

CHAPTER NINETEEN

Era of Plenty

Golden Boy had run for 248 performances in New York to consistently good business. It was sold to pictures for $70,000, which meant that the Group share amounted to about $15,000. Despite this, when I left for London, I was broke. My earnings barely covered my living expenses, which included the partial support of a number of relatives. The Group itself was moving toward its one period of prosperity. By the middle of the next season the Group treasury showed a $50,000 balance. (Odets about that time told me he had $90,000 in the bank.) That this prosperity proved shortlived was certainly the least tragic aspect of our trials.

The London season was a triumph. I might have guessed it would be from the fact that at the dress rehearsal, which I thought very bad, the English producers under whose auspices we were appearing told me in almost the precise words used by James Agate of the London *Times:* "The acting attains a level which is something we know nothing at all about."

When St. John Ervine made priggish reservations about the play's values, or when Charles Morgan voiced a distaste for the milieu of the play's plot ("the hangers-on of the American boxing-ring are not the company in which one would choose to spend an evening"), other reviewers snorted with scorn, not so much because they thought the play beyond reproach, but because the play to them was an important occasion, apart from its own specific merits. The play was symbolic to the Londoners of something vital in America.

Whatever insurgent forces existed in the London theatre took heart from the Group's example, encouraged to see that a permanent company professing ideals of life as well as art had achieved sufficient success to cross the waters to England and to be acclaimed at a smart West End theatre.

A group of working-class amateurs that had built its own house – the Unity Theatre – was now carrying on valiantly with plays like *Waiting for Lefty* and *Bury the Dead.* This group (which at the outbreak of the second World War put on the most popular political revue in London) was much pleased with our presence in England and even looked to us for guidance.

The Group actors were guests at a Parliament tea, and one of the opposition M.P.'s alluded to the social meaning of *Golden Boy* on the floor of Commons.

I stopped at the Dorchester, chiefly because of Stella Adler's taste for the first-class. The Dorchester ("the very best people live there," an English press agent assured me) was full of heiling Nazis as well as spendthrift representatives of the Franco gang. The London *Times,* which ran an editorial assuring its readers that only the radical press of New York was pro-loyalist, was supplied to guests gratis by the hotel management every morning.

In Soho restaurants I heard table debates over collective security and a united front. But most people rejected these notions, asking with annihilating finality: "United front with whom?" Generally I had little time in London to observe much beyond the class-consciousness — that is, upper-class-consciousness — that appeared to be almost universal, except to note at a sitting in Commons that Prime Minister Chamberlain's mouth tightened when the opposition leader Atlee mildly indicated the shortcomings of fascist ideology, and to commiserate with a young English boy (now a decorated captain of the British army) who felt despondent over the increasing reaction that held his country in what seemed an iron grip. "London," the young man said in a defeatist mood, "is the dead heart of a dead Empire." When I left for Paris, he wrote me how much meeting the Group people had meant to him, how much it had renewed his faith in the future.

There occurred in London the first skirmish of a battle that was to continue with increasing virulence till the Group's dissolution in 1941.

Odets, it appeared, had harbored a number of dissatisfactions with the Group that he had not given vent to during the previous season. Now that there was little for him to do in London, he had occasion to tell Luther Adler, with whom he was sharing an apartment, what he found wrong with the Group. Luther enjoyed such tempests in the theatre as a sign that things were stirring and life was gay. He encouraged Odets to face me with his complaints. A wire was sent me, and another to the actors' council and our business manager, Kermit Bloomgarden, asking us to come immediately to the Odets-Adler flat to discuss matters of the utmost import.

When we got there, Adler, apparently speaking for Odets, opened the proceedings with the statement that now that the Group was in a strong position, we ought to make plans to run our theatre on a repertory basis. We had the actors, we could get the plays, and so on. A list of the best American plays of the past had been drawn up, and suggestions for Group casting were made.

All this was delivered in a rather defensive tone as if it might meet with strong resistance on my part. Why should I resist the idea of repertory? Perhaps success had made me stodgy; perhaps I had forgotten my early professions of faith in a popular institutional theatre. Nothing of the kind: I still believed this to be our proper goal. Some surprise and relief were expressed at my answer, but Adler caught an arch look in my eye. He wanted to know what it meant. I explained that while the plans he had drawn up so prettily represented what we all desired, he had not indicated how these plans could be realized. Even the most modest repertory program is much more costly than the ordinary single production setup, and thus far we had not had an easy time getting money on the less ambitious basis. What I wanted to know was how this repertory plan could be made to work in terms of dollars and cents, theatre rental, stage-hand expense, relation to new productions, and so forth.

At this there was an outburst of wild assertion, recrimination, and furious emotion signifying a dissatisfaction with far more than our theatrical plans past or future. It didn't make very much sense as argument, but the air was rent with such cries as "You're lazy. You don't respect your talent" (addressed to me). "I'm tired of the Group company; actors like Jimmy Cagney could do far more interesting things with our plays than the Group actors." (This from Odets, followed by a torrential roar of denial from me.) "The Group actors don't do anything to make artists of themselves," Odets ran on, and Kazan leapt into the fray, stunning everyone with savage energy as proof positive that he at least couldn't be accused of anything but high-powered vitality at all times.

Remedies for all the Group's ailments were tossed at me with reckless abandon. I was to fire our press representative in New York, to institute a limited repertory at any rate, to raise $100,000 at once, to act, not to talk. Luther Adler was happy now: "Yes, yes, to act, not to talk"; but the conference switched suddenly to a headlong attack on its hapless instigator, who was battered mercilessly because he "promised more than he performed."

Between London and Paris, Stella Adler and I conducted a running battle over the Group, for which she felt I had developed an exclusive, fanatical devotion. Her bitterness was aggravated by the presence in Paris of Odets, Bloomgarden, and Kazan, who had crossed over to Paris with us to spend a week prior to our return to New York.

Through the cover of my confusion I could see that Paris was still lovely. It gave evidences of a last flowering before the descent of the barbaric hordes and paralysis through its own diseases. I heard faintly anti-Semitic couplets at a Montmartre *boîte* where Blum's Popular Front government — already liquidated — was wittily defamed and Mussolini, "who after all is closer to us," teasingly chided. Just after we left, on the S.S. *Champlain,* Paris was getting ready to greet the King of England, a festivity that fizzled because the English government then was not popular in France with either the Left or the Right.

Stella Adler, with her daughter Ellen, went off to the Riviera, where she bade me join her. She was to return to London to stage the new *Golden Boy* production at the St. James's. This was scheduled to replace the Group when it returned home in September, to set out for the road and to rehearse the season's new productions.

Molly Thacher had sent me a play she liked, to read on the boat during my voyage home. It was William Saroyan's *My Heart's in the Highlands.* It was a play celebrating the purity of the poet and the humble. In the winter of 1937 I had sent Saroyan a note asking him if he would be interested to write for the theatre. His reply, pencil-scribbled on a penny postcard, admitted he had entertained the thought, but when he did write a play he would insist on directing it himself.

When I read *My Heart's in the Highlands,* I was captured by its freedom, simplicity, hobo charm, delicate sentiment, and humor. Kazan was surprised at my reaction. He imagined it would strike me, as it did him, as defeatist, weak, like "a flute's complaint." I found, on the contrary, that it struck a fresh note in dramatic writing. We would do it as an experimental show during the season.

Irwin Shaw had addressed a letter to me at the boat saying

that he had finished his new play, *The Gentle People*. He wanted an immediate reading.

When we landed, there was a great deal of work cut out for us. We had to assemble a new *Golden Boy* company and send it off to London without delay. We had to finance our next season and decide what plays we would put into rehearsal when our company returned.

Kazan was enthusiastic over *The Gentle People*. I liked it too. It worried me a bit, however, because it was both delicate and melodramatic, saying a little more than its simple fable indicated, yet not enough for the elaborate structure the production demanded. It was full of plot, yet somehow more narrative than dramatic, heavier than it was meant to be, lighter than the author's and the Group's reputation promised. After several days of hesitation I announced to Shaw: "It pains me to tell you I've decided to do your play."

I spent the summer with the Kazans at Henry Varnum Poor's house in New City. We came to New York when we had business to do. For a while Odets joined us, awkwardly maneuvering his newly bought Cadillac in sudden appearances and just as sudden exits between city and country.

He had begun work on a new play, the general story pattern of which he had outlined vaguely to me the previous spring. Before he began writing any specific play, new ideas for other plays would come to him, often acting as a diversion from the cruel necessity of buckling down to work. Shortly after *Golden Boy* Odets announced that his next play would be written as a vehicle for Luise Rainer and that he might turn it over to an outside manager for production because of Miss Rainer's equivocal relation to the Group. I said nothing to discourage this scheme, but waited to see what the Odets-Rainer home life would bring forth. When Miss Rainer sued Odets for divorce, I reminded Odets of the so-called "dentist play."

He was in a restless, rootless, uncertain mood that summer. One night he arrived in New City at about ten p.m., sat down in the living-room, and without preliminary explanation began a violent rebuttal of certain criticisms implied in my *Golden Boy* pref-

ace. The trouble with *Golden Boy* was not that he did not really
know the milieu of the play but that an adherence to story line
stood in the way of subtle and profound character creation. I did
not argue with him — I believe he was right — but my silence
pressed him back to work.

At this time I dreamed one night that I was to be confined to
an insane asylum. When I got there, aghast at my presence in
such a place, I was told by way of consolation that Boleslavsky
and Stanislavsky were also inmates of long standing.

This was a strange dream for this period because it was generally the steadiest era of the Group's history. There were not only
scripts in prospect and money in the bank, but a little leisure to
draft a practical scheme for the raising of the kind of fund that I
deemed absolutely indispensable for the conduct of a permanent
theatre institution. With the aid of our attorney, our business
manager, and other experts we drew up a plan guaranteeing the
production of at least four plays for the sum of $100,000. To the
investors we pledged fifty per cent of our profits, not only on
the block results of the plays so financed, but on all our productions for some years to come.

When we consulted with Odets on this scheme, he protested
that we were offering too much. With his own plays alone he
could obtain better terms from any manager; and we were making our offer for a series of plays, including his own and those of
writers like Irwin Shaw and William Saroyan. His argument was
convincing, but we decided to try our luck on the basis of our
perhaps unbusiness-like generosity. We should have no difficulty
now, since by this time we had produced fifteen plays, two of
them solid hits, several of them moderately successful, and only
one or two that might have been described as disgraceful. More
than this our production costs were comparatively reasonable,
and we had become a theatre of genuine renown.

Everyone we approached was interested. One gentleman was
sure he wanted to be in on the deal, but the day we came to his
Wall Street office he was very much perturbed. It seems he had
sold pound sterling short, counting on a decline due to an out-

Scene from *Golden Boy* by Clifford Odets, 1937. (Direction: Harold Clurman. Setting: Mordecai Gorelik.) LEFT TO RIGHT: Lee Cobb, Phoebe Brand, J. Garfield, Luther Adler, Morris Carnovsky, Frances Farmer.

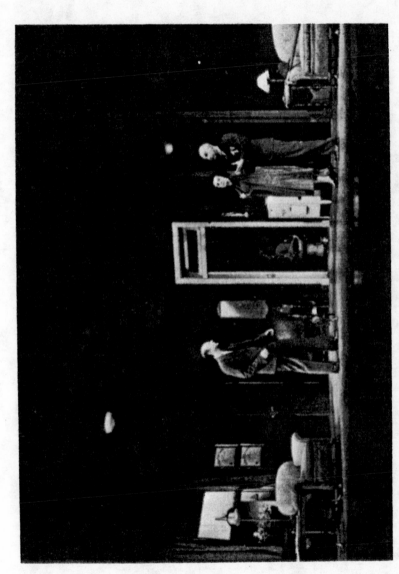

Scene from *Rocket to the Moon* by Clifford Odets, 1938. (Direction: Harold Clurman.

break of war, which appeared inevitable. But Chamberlain, the rat, was on his way to Germany to effect a compromise that would avert war. If Chamberlain succeeded, then our would-be "angel" would be broke. That week Chamberlain did us in.

Other candidates for the honored title of Group Theatre sponsors — some of whom had previously invested in us without damage — reflected that while we were a reliable outfit, our sense of responsibility might be impaired through the sudden security of a hundred thousand dollars in the bank. Still others wanted to judge our scripts before committing themselves. What had we to show specifically? The Odets script was not complete, but it sounded drab. Shaw's *The Gentle People* might prove expensive and it was really rather slight. As for Saroyan's little play, we hardly dared show it to anyone; it would have been like an admission of lunacy.

As an investment the play-to-play basis was still preferred to our long-term scheme. As for my feeling that there should be a sufficient number of people in New York to give us the designated sum out of sheer love of the theatre, for fun, out of cultural enthusiasm, for whatever reasons prompt people to support museums, orchestras, benevolent societies, I rarely expressed it now. Such talk might have been acceptable in some circles during the dizzy twenties; in the thirties it was no longer considered decent. For while it is true that a great orchestra or the opera, no matter how well attended, runs at a deficit that is paid off by patrons, such patronage for the theatre was out of the question because an orchestra or the opera can't possibly make any profit and is thus clearly a cultural institution, while the theatre can be profitable and therefore should be. If it is profitable, why does it need support as a cultural institution? And if it isn't profitable, then it must be bad. If the theatre is to make money, why choose plays that are commercially doubtful? And if the plays don't make money, isn't the theatre failing in its purpose?

The new Odets play, *Rocket to the Moon*, was backed by a few small investors who had earned a profit on *Golden Boy*, by Luther Adler (with the assistance of Sylvia Sidney), and by the author himself. *The Gentle People* was backed chiefly by Franchot Tone,

whom I tried to dissuade from entering into this side of theatrical
enterprise, as I believed it dangerous for him (and for us) to
confuse his concentration on the production as an actor with a
financial interest.

For the rest, we tried to extend our earnings through a road
company of *Golden Boy,* which was to follow us in towns the
Group did not play. This seemed a safe investment, but we lost
heavily on it because without our company *Golden Boy* was not
an attraction either here or in London.

As for our two experimental shows of the season, *My Heart's
in the Highlands* and *Quiet City,* no one was willing to discuss
them even on the rather modest basis we undertook for their production. We entertained no idea that they had commercial possibilities; we simply believed them proper material for our theatre.

One thing positive that our organization was able to accomplish
institutionally was the creation of a fairly regular audience. By
the season of 1938-9 a sizable Group Theatre audience had been
built up. This audience bought full houses or half-houses in advance (at a little below box-office prices) during the first four
weeks of our plays' runs. They did this through various charitable
or cultural organizations, schools, hospitals, political clubs, fra-
ternal orders, unions, and so on. Plays like *Rocket to the Moon*
and even *The Gentle People* could not have survived as long as
they did without the benefit of these audiences.

Yet playwrights and backers often shied away as a result of our
selling tickets in this way, as it meant a reduction of their potential
income, which they naturally anticipated in terms of maximum
success only. For the same reason repertory companies (such as
Miss Le Gallienne's company of old) always have difficulty in
acquiring new plays deemed "commercial" by their authors. And
what author doesn't believe his play "commercial" — prior to
opening night?

CHAPTER TWENTY

High Point

Isn't it shocking to dwell so long on money when our subject should be discussed on the high plane of culture, dreams, ideals, and noble pleasure? To be able to talk art with our company, we decided to guarantee the salary of about sixteen of our players fo; the whole season 1938–9. Freedom from money worry might stimulate other freedoms.

We anticipated a successful road tour of *Golden Boy*. Our anticipation was not vain: Chicago took to the play like a duck to water. We had nothing further to consider but our program for the season. It was ingenious and varied. I would direct *Rocket to the Moon* and *The Gentle People*. When the actors needed for the first of these plays had to leave *Golden Boy*, they would be replaced by others of our company; Luther Adler by Kazan, Carnovsky by Lee Cobb, and so on. When *Rocket* opened, I would begin rehearsals of *The Gentle People* on the road with Kazan, Lee Cobb, and others.

In the meantime I left for Hollywood to see Franchot Tone, who had announced his desire to return to the Group. The part I had in mind for him was the gangster in *The Gentle People*.

While business details were being settled between us, I warned Franchot that he might encounter disappointment in the Group. I had nothing definite in mind, but experience had taught me to be wary when anyone imagined our work and destiny in the guise of some theatrical Eden. There is no one so bitter as a disappointed idealist, no mockery so sharp as that which springs up in the breast of a frustrated utopian. I suspected that Franchot looked toward the Group with the fondness of youthful memory. "Franchot," I said, "promise me that you will stay with us for one year no matter what happens. Give yourself and us a chance." Franchot looked solemn and uncertain, but he promised.

On this trip I also sought an actress who might supply the very
special requirements called for by the central character of *Rocket
to the Moon*. It was my good fortune to come upon Eleanor Lynn,
who, just released by Metro, was unhappily marking time in the
sterile vacancy of the picture actors' "liberty."

The actors were impressed by *Rocket to the Moon*. It contained
some of Odets's most mature writing and two of his finest characters. The play as written, however, was thematically quite different from what had been implied in Odets's original sketch of
it. I did not realize till much later that this change — and deepen-
ing — of the play's theme made its structure defective.

As originally planned, the play was about a meek little dentist
ravaged through the love of a silly girl. Regardless of its object,
love was to give this man a depth of experience and thus a stature
beyond his normal scope. The dentist then was the central character, and the play was his play. In the actual writing of the play
the theme was transformed to that of the difficult quest for love
in the modern world. The person who embodied this quest was
the little girl, uneducated, childish, rattle-brained, and true. She
had become the center of the play, a person who despite her
"ordinariness" was what the author called a moral idealist, whose
pathos arises from an inability to find realization through connection with any of the representative middle-class men she meets
in the course of her quest.

Owing, I say, to the play's original premise, it was so con-
structed that it appeared to be about a man confronted with a
choice of women: his nagging wife and his trivial child mistress.
When the girl at the end of the play matured sufficiently to express the essence of her experience — and the playwright's thought
— a good part of the audience was bewildered by her transformation and the unexpected turn the play had taken.

Even the company was a little surprised by the play's development, since we never received the third act till ten days before
the opening. At the first preview the audience was cold and the
author puzzled. Why had the audience received the play so in-
differently, we wondered. Carnovsky was wearing a rather ro-

mantic wig, which, some suggested, belied his character. The wig
was eliminated (and restored some time later). The third act was
too long; it was cut ten minutes. Luise Rainer maintained — very
vehemently — that the little girl ought to accept the offer of marriage proposed by the play's old man. Very few agreed. Odets
himself concluded offhand that plays of any psychological com-
plexity were not made for the Broadway theatre-going public.
He expected a failure.

The play was not a success, but not the kind of failure we
feared. Certain reviewers thought it "better than *Golden Boy*";
others called it "the best of Odets's plays." The majority found it
brilliant in its first act but disappointing after that. Many had
difficulty in discerning the play's theme, though as a matter of fact
the theme was almost too insistently plugged throughout.

By now mixed receptions such as this were an old story to me.
In my opinion the play, for all its faults, was good; our stage offered very few that were better. That so many reviewers, however, could make so vital a point of the play's length was something of a curiosity to me. This new time-table school of criticism,
I mused, might turn in a very sour report on many masterpieces
of world literature.

The reviews, however, surprised me less than the reaction to
the play I saw developing within our own ranks. One or two
pointed out the obvious fact that if we had cut the play more
drastically, it would have met with a warmer response. After the
opening the play was cut another ten minutes or more, but later
audiences spoke of the play exactly as the first audience had. If
we had only opened the play out of town before its New York
premiere, it would surely have been a success. This of course was
an argument impossible to answer, even though it might have
been pointed out that the plays we opened this way were all
failures, while our more successful productions had opened without any out-of-town preliminaries.

More serious to me were the doubts in Odets's mind. A scene
in the second act, he said, had been directed without sufficient
story point. It was easy to change, and in my absence he changed
it. Then he wasn't sure whether our leading lady's physical frailty

did not weaken the last act. Of course, it would have been perfect if our actress could have been spindly and delicate for the
first two acts and robust for the last, but nature had held out on
her (and us). Finally Odets wasn't at all sure that I had given
him the proper guidance in suggesting that the dentist's wife,
who in the play's first version had appeared only once as a comi-
cally nasty character, should be developed along more serious
lines and reappear in both the second and the third acts. It is
true my reasons had been sound and had aroused no objections
— no one was to blame — but I had misjudged the audience's
psychology, for it was unable to accept the wife as anything but
a laughable shrew.

All these criticisms bewildered me, since they all contained
some truth. What I could not grasp was how all their irrecon-
cilable elements could ever be composed into a solution of constructive value for the future. All I could see was that Odets was
disturbed. But he did not seem able to fix with any certainty on
a definite point of dissatisfaction or arrange his disappointments
according to some scale of values.

On the road the *Golden Boy* company was doing excellent business in one town after another. Odets had not only "arrived" in
terms of public recognition; he was now virtually canonized
through a *New Yorker* Profile and through becoming the cover
boy on *Time,* with a special story to match. The *New York Times,*
reviewing our career, had just said: "In its eighth season, the
Group Theatre has become our leading art theatre by sheer persistence and hard-won ability. If Mr. Odets is its greatest asset,
it is just as valuable to him. It knows what he is writing about
and believes in it." But in its piece the Luce weekly insisted that
"actually Odets has most of the time carried the Group on his
back." If this was true, one might have added that he carried the
Group as a son carries his father.

What some of the Group actors were concerned about now was
defined in a radical weekly. "*Rocket to the Moon,*" its friendly
reviewer noted, "is a good play, a moving one, full of poignant
moments." Well? There was a But, a big But. "Now he writes

plays about problems people solved the day before yesterday. His dentist in *Rocket to the Moon* is today no longer worrying about the long sleep of his life. For the people of our country have learned how to be bold and brave in the last three years, and Clifford Odets has not. The dentist and his wife and his friends have been jolted out of their narrow vision of life by history, but Mr. Odets sees them today as they were long ago before the workers of Spain went out to fight Fascism before the workers of America organized to fight reaction in our nation."

Brave words. But can we say that everyone is entirely clear today about the relation of their personal problems to the world, that the subjective turmoil of small individuals no longer plays its part in shaping people's lives or even in the direction of history? How American is the rapidity with which this earnest reviewer counted the days of our progress. By her calendar the millennium will be overdue next year.

What mattered to me was not the superficiality of an isolated notice but its echo among us. Some of our actors repeated this pious mumbo-jumbo as others were influenced by the equally smooth chewing-gum of the less socially-minded wiseacres. Our actors' protests over the mildness of our program were now reinforced by *The Gentle People*. The latter was a fable illustrating the fact that the little people of the world often have no recourse against their tormentors but to meet violence with violence. Indeed, the more literal-minded were disturbed by the fable's immorality, since it appeared to condone personal vengeance, the gay killing of a gangster by two sweet old men who want to lead their lives in humble toil and peaceful play. The actors, however, feared that the play might be thought merely cute, and that by indulging in its tender humor and quaint melodramatics we were failing in our duty to help change the world.

When I grew impatient and asked them what I could do concretely to stimulate the writing of more important plays, my challenge was met with the suggestion that Odets be commissioned to write a Roosevelt-third-term propaganda piece! That at the time only made me laugh, but peculiarly enough I was less inclined to laugh when I remembered later that had such a play been written and produced in 1940, the same actors might have been quite critical of the project, for their political notions had changed.

Yes, every wind of doctrine was reflected in some corresponding ripple in the flow of our lives. Once the actors read somewhere that the theatre had become useless as a medium through which people's lives might be affected because the carriage trade sought only "escapist entertainment," while a theatre for the poorer classes was not economically possible. I had to point out that the Moscow Art Theatre — like some of the best literature and entertainment of earlier periods — had reached only a small portion of the people for whom it was presumably intended, yet its influence had not been inconsiderable.

Other doubts, far more insidious, assailed some of the company when people like Sylvia Sidney and Sam Jaffe were engaged to play with us, as there was a fleeting suspicion here and there that I was paying them more than the top Group salaries. This was not true, for these new actors understood the Group's particular setup. They came to us for satisfaction they did not often find where salaries were more attractive.

The Group people themselves had become reconciled, for the most part, to the truth of my repeated assertion that they could hope for little better than a decent poverty from our theatre. I always agreed with new actors who expressed shock at the salaries I offered them. Necessity, not avarice, dictated our budget. This carried conviction because it was known that I claimed no ownership of our properties or profits. My own salary now was $300 weekly, with no additional director's fee. It became our business manager's joke to say I was the only theatre boss who could keep his company together with the slogan: "You will be underpaid here."

When Franchot Tone finally reached New York, we began rehearsals of *The Gentle People* in good earnest, for we had not been able to accomplish much with an incomplete company on the road. There was little time left before opening; the play was prepared in less than three weeks.

Louella Parsons in her column reported that "Joan [Crawford] had told a friend that the only time Franchot was happy in Hollywood was when he was entertaining members of the Group Theatre at her Brentwood mansion." Now that Franchot had arrived, he was called on to make a speech at the Town Hall Club, which was quoted in the *New York Herald Tribune:* "I'd better not get started on the Group," he began, "because I'll get emotional about it and then I won't be able to talk at all." More striking than this is the following statement Franchot made in an interview at the same time: "The Group has a well-defined attitude toward human problems and affairs, and while I'm perfectly sure that such a formalized policy as this is by no means necessary to success in the theatre, it is necessary to me."

In the basement of the Belasco Theatre, the scene of so many Group meetings and rehearsals, Franchot threw himself into his work with an eager will. On the whole, he was well pleased with the conduct of rehearsals; his criticisms were affable and slight. When conferences on the progress of *The Gentle People* were held, I failed to invite him to join them, as it was not our custom to consult members of the cast on production problems of the plays in which they took part. That Franchot was not only one of the leading players but the play's backer gave him no special privilege in this matter. It was not my intention to snub him in any way, but Irwin Shaw pointed out that, whatever my intention, my behavior was tactless. Franchot, however, bore this with good grace.

The opening of *The Gentle People* brought out the movie fans as never before at a Group play. Since I was not present, because of my ancient detestation of Broadway premieres, I shall quote a reviewer who began his notice by remarking: "The movie fans in the gallery at the Belasco were happy last night. They practically held a club meeting when the curtain had lowered for a moment on an early scene. After all was not Franchot Tone (in person) returning to the Group Theatre? And was not Sylvia Sidney (likewise in person) also in the cast? Hence, of course, the autograph-seekers swarming the sidewalks, the extra cops, and the movie fans giggling and chattering in the balcony."

The press was not particularly perceptive about *The Gentle People*. Irwin Shaw had insisted in labeling the play "a Brooklyn Fable" in the theatre program, though I disapproved, for I thought the play made its allusions and meaning sufficiently clear without requiring any further editorial emphasis. Nevertheless a number of reviewers thought the play a comedy-melodrama about gangsters and wondered why Irwin Shaw had treated such a subject. When they heard that the play might have allegorical reference to fascism and the common people, they gibed: "Crystal gazers who can find such a meaning in this opus can surely find tongues in trees, books in running brooks, sermons in stones, etc., etc."

It didn't matter, however. The play and production fared moderately well. The first weeks brought a host of women to the matinees to admire the attractive pair from the pictures, while others liked the special glamour of Boris Aronson's settings and a sensationally hilarious scene in a Turkish bath in which Lee Cobb as a bankrupt business man played with a majestic Rabelaisian sweep.

The Group company was harshly critical of *The Gentle People*. Irwin Shaw himself was not altogether pleased with the results, despite the fact the play was the nearest thing to a commercial success he had ever had in the theatre; and I certainly was not sure I had found the correct style for the play, which required, it seemed to me, the appearance of realism with a simplicity that was not quite that. Perhaps a more frankly fanciful treatment might have served the play better. If Shaw had been a Soviet playwright, he might have been able to see his play in two or more interpretations at the same time, and everyone would be in a better position to pass judgment on these fine points of theatre art. But we were in New York, and if the production, as I suspected, wasn't all it might have been, I was still not at all ashamed of it.

When Bobby Lewis gave a party for the Group on the occasion of Stella Adler's return to New York from London, the atmosphere was positively frigid. I thought at first that Stella as the

Group antagonist was being rudely treated, but I soon perceived
that it was I who was being shunned for having done what some
of the actors deemed a second-rate job. I was ready to slap faces.

In retrospect that party takes on a very different significance
from that which I lent it then. I see in it the almost childlike trans-
parency of those people who, when they were miffed over something like their inability to praise me on my most recent work,
became socially helpless, unable even for a moment to dissemble
a cordiality they did not feel. They were kids without a trace of
worldly veneer. When they had a gloomy *arrière-pensée* they
were completely governed by it. They lacked the grace of hypoc-
risy, but at least they were saved from its vices.

Most of these kids were now over thirty, so something more
must be said of their naïveté. It was peculiarly provincial. This
provinciality the world-conscious Group, I am afraid, had helped
foster. How had this happened? When a society functions within
a society as a tiny minority that feels itself threatened on all
sides — as indeed it is — the smaller unit will slowly develop a
certain inbred quality, a peculiar spirit of retreat that, whatever
its philosophy, is wellnigh unavoidable. The small unit puts barriers between itself and what it fears, and these barriers shut off
more than is good for the natural life of the enclosed Group. It
becomes a little gauche, a little narrow, a little blind. In this
process it diminishes even as it had previously gained. The dimi-
nution will become altogether disastrous if the minority through
success does not merge with the majority or find some way of
establishing a healthy connection between the two. The Group's
provinciality was part of the price it had to pay for its long fight
and its independence. This is not to say there could be no cure
for it, but if the cure had been more easily available, the disease
might not have made so many inroads.

Franchot Tone was not present at this doleful festivity. He
probably was invited, but he did not mingle much with our people. His heart belonged to the Group between eight and eleven,
but after that his body belonged to the more sparkling environment of East Fifty-second Street. He liked to invite Kazan and me

to join him in after-the-theatre frolics, but neither of us was able to go his pace. Franchot, in full flight from Hollywood or from some internal discomfort, became the advertised habitué of New York's night spots. The *New York World-Telegram* ran a wickedly juicy story under the caption: "Try to Keep Up With Tone! — Scotch, French, 'Lovelies!' Franchot, Broadway's No. 1 Matinee Idol, Does the Town from Curtain to Dawn." Franchot, the story ran, spent a good deal of his afternoon "teaching French to lovelies." "After doing thirty-six pictures in six years without let up," Franchot queried of his interviewer, "a fellow is entitled to some fun, isn't he? I want to play a little."

I tried to persuade Franchot to take the leading role in Irwin Shaw's play *Quiet City,* which we planned to put on for special performances during the run of *The Gentle People.* Franchot protested that he was too tired to do anything more than one show at a time. When I insisted that he avail himself of the opportunity of playing more than his one role during the Group season, he consented to hear *Quiet City* read at its presentation to the company. He appeared to enjoy the reading, and he remarked wittily that the play would "achieve failure." Fear of failure is a corrosive that eats at the fiber of many good Americans.

Later I offered Tone the central role of Saroyan's *My Heart's in the Highlands.* He dallied with the idea; he made conditions, stipulations. He wasn't convinced we would do a good job with it; he wasn't sure he wanted to appear in special performances.

Irwin Shaw and one or two others insisted that we ought to make friends with Franchot, extend ourselves in his direction. After all, he was not only an excellent actor but one who had a most intelligent appreciation of the Group. We were eager to have real contact with him; and if we could not make it on his terms, perhaps we might appeal to him to make it on ours.

We invited Franchot to meet with us — Kazan, Bohnen, and myself — at Morris Carnovsky's apartment. We asked him to share our theatre life, since we had much to give each other. Franchot would hardly say anything open or direct. Finally he asked if we really respected him. "You are the kind of actor we need in our theatre," I said. "But you don't respect the reputation I have made in pictures?" he questioned further. "That is not why we want you," I rejoined. "But you are willing to exploit my name for its commercial values?" "Of course," I admitted.

Slowly Franchot built up a case against us in his mind. Perhaps he needed an inner justification for giving us up. He told people he was disappointed not to have come back in an Odets play, not to have been given the opportunity to act with Carnovsky, Stella Adler, Art Smith, and the others who had been his stage companions when he left. His friends and advisers had impressed him with the hideousness of our error in casting him in the gangster role, and now he resented the fact that we had done so. He suspected our business management. He doubted that I had retained my early sincerity and artistic integrity. He was annoyed that I had not held understudy rehearsals. The lighting of our production was not all it should have been.

To make matters worse, a person connected with the ownership of the Belasco Theatre had used a considerable part of the money from our advance box-office sale to pay off obligations incurred by his too extensive theatre holdings. When he was cornered, he confessed he had nothing to say in his defense, that we might do with him what we would. We made some futile arrangement with him whereby he might eventually return the funds he had misappropriated. Franchot, as the play's backer, had to share in this loss.

Toward the end of the season he dropped me a note severing all connection with the Group. Though next season he had complimentary things to say about one of our productions, he made many bitter remarks about us for another year or two till his soul and mind were clear of the onus that his long relationship with the Group had somehow put upon them.

During the run of The Gentle People John Howard Lawson had come to town with a new play named Parlor Magic. I read it with keen anticipation. The play had a remarkably fine scheme. Three brothers of a once stable New England family were confronted with a local situation in which evidences of a home-grown fascism might be discovered. One brother, in politics, was

slowly edging toward the astute racketeering that often provides
the fascist's training-ground; another was an aging Bohemian poet
weary of his wanderings; the third was a liberal lawyer motivated by a long tradition of idealism, now being crowded into
doubtful practices by the compulsions of a merciless epoch. In
the end the situation leads the politician into making the lawyer
conspire against the very life of their poet brother. Two other
characters — a boy and girl — represented the younger generation, in whom the hope of the future resides: the boy an intelligent worker, the girl a still uncontaminated member of the
stricken household. It is the poet who acts as the young people's
father confessor, bidding them go forward fearlessly to create a
better life than that which the decaying family now offers.

In this play Lawson took some of the subjective turbulence
and divided conscience of his earlier work and tried to order this
material with a rational, correctly contemporary (that is, progressive) point of view. The whole thing failed to come off. Qualities that had once been passionate and bursting with life were
now shadowy and insubstantial, while the author's point of view
was expressed with a carefulness and a propriety the mechanics
of which could not be concealed by efforts at a righteously lyric
fervor.

Lawson confessed himself bitterly disappointed at my reaction.
He returned to Hollywood, reconsidered his script, and decided
that it contained too many stories. Nearly two years later he had
revised it completely and had improved it from a technical standpoint. But it was still a mechanical job.

Lawson was now probably a much more practical, useful citizen than he had been from 1925 to 1935; he was no longer working as an artist. Had he "bottlenecked" himself through a too
strict discipline of moral self-scrutiny, a self-imposed censorship
calculated to make the old wine of his emotions pour properly
into the new bottles of his social sense? Had he tamed his unruly
imagination and inner drives with the self-inflicted rod of a stiff
ideology? It is not easy to say. One thing was clear, however: he
now had many more times the fifty dollars a week that he had
once declared sufficient for a concentrated pursuit of his career

as a playwright, but on no account would he now turn back to the theatre. Pictures provided his livelihood; their social possibilities provided their higher justification. For the rest, his spirit would find satisfaction in teaching, lecturing, and critical writing.

Since *Rocket to the Moon* was doing only fair business, had only one set, and used three important actors of the original *Awake and Sing*, it was suggested by Luther Adler that we revive the latter play and run it alternately with *Rocket to the Moon*. This would mark a step in the direction of repertory. I thought the suggestion a happy one and went about putting it into effect immediately.

Stella Adler did not wish to resume her original role, but recommended her sister Julia for it. Joe Bromberg, a little let down by Hollywood, was back in town, and we urged him to play his old part while he was rehearsing in our production of *Quiet City*. One of the actors from our Group School of 1937 was given Garfield's role. The original set had been held in our storeroom; even the original Tootsie (the bedraggled and tender canine life of *Awake and Sing*) was at hand. We were ready to open in a very short time.

The performance of our revival was relaxed to the point of glibness. The actors who had done the play before were altogether too sure of themselves. The production was distinctly inferior to the original. But the press was now far more enthusiastic. The complaints about hysterical direction, which several reviewers had leveled at the 1935 production, were entirely forgotten. In fact, the play and production were now accorded the reception of an honored classic. Brooks Atkinson of the *New York Times* asked me one day whether *Awake and Sing* had improved since he first saw it. "No," I answered, "you have."

With the revival of *Awake and Sing* not only the play and production but the Group as a theatre came in for its full meed of praise. "After eight arduous and sometimes desperate years, the Group has won its battle on Broadway very much on the original terms laid down on its grim visaged manifesto when the depression was first taking permanent hold in the country. Founded on an acting company, able, persistent and wisely managed, it is the foremost acting theatre of this country." Such was the tenor of practically every theatrical column in New York.

John Anderson pleased me especially when he used the word — implied in all the reviews — "continuity." The Group had fought to preserve its continuity, had insisted that no theatre was possible at all that did not maintain for itself and for its audiences a sense of continuity.

When I first spoke of continuity to our actors and playwrights and occasionally through the press or our programs to our audiences, many assumed that I emphasized continuity as a commercial asset. Continuity of effort to me signified the building of a tradition, the foundation of true culture. I had always affirmed that there was no lack of talent of every kind in our country, but our talent tended to thin out and droop with the years — not, as some imagine, because that is its nature, but because it is given so little to feed on, so little soil to sink its roots in, so little time to mature. For this there must be a permanent base that allows a continuity of activity along lines dictated by the first needs and creative impulses of the artist. To make the artist shift his foundations, to make his work discontinuous, as is practically the rule of our theatre, is to make him begin anew with each effort. The result is not only wearing and discouraging, but profoundly uncreative. The artist builds from the storehouse of his past strength, memory, training, and experience almost as much as he does from his present contacts and position. Without some dependence on his tradition, the tradition that he makes for himself and that others help him make, he starts his new work with an always decreasing stock, till he ends with a shadow or memory of himself, not a consummation. We lack memory. We cancel our experience. That is why for all our effort in the theatre, for all that of our predecessors, we proceed always on the basis of diminishing returns. And what is true of our theatre is almost equally true of our other cultural fields, so that almost all of us have lost a recognition of why so many years of promise and achievement are nearly always followed by a sense of frustration, of meager progress, of oblivion.

The alternation of *Rocket* and *Awake and Sing* at a two-dollar top favored the latter, so that first they divided the week evenly, later *Awake and Sing* took precedence, and finally *Rocket* closed. *Awake and Sing,* though possibly the most praised play of the season, did not run long, and *Rocket to the Moon* played a brief season in Baltimore and Philadelphia.

Before this and for many weeks Irwin Shaw's *Quiet City* had been in rehearsal under Elia Kazan's direction. The play, a mixture of realism and fantasy in unsteady relation, was replete with passages of fine writing and eloquent dramatic scenes. Its theme, the recurrent one of the troubled conscience of the middle class that cannot quite reconcile itself to its life in a distraught world — which, when it retains its honesty and sensitivity, it identifies with a life of sin — was here given full orchestration. Because of its unevenness of style, however, it was extraordinarily difficult to produce satisfactorily. It needed a very free treatment, while we were unable to give it anything but a skeleton production squeezed onto the stage of the Belasco, which still housed the massive *Gentle People* sets.

We had not been able to raise money for the play — it was too "experimental" — and produced it with our own funds. I agreed to this for two reasons: players like Frances Farmer and others had had little opportunity to do anything during the season aside from the early tour of *Golden Boy,* and I wished to see them continue their acting with us. I had promised Irwin Shaw a production of his play, and I felt it important to keep my promise.

Good motives do not assure artistic achievement. The director and company struggled earnestly with the script with indifferent results. We presented the play on two Sunday evenings to an audience as unconvinced as the company was unsure. We decided not to subject the production to further public scrutiny. All that remained of our hard work was a lovely score by Aaron Copland, which is not infrequently heard nowadays at orchestral concerts.

The upheavals and reforms of the thirties began to level off to a new norm. In 1938 the National Association of Manufacturers spoke lovingly of "a united effort of industry, commerce, agriculture, and labor in cooperation with the government." On March 28, 1939 Madrid fell to the fascists. Concurrently with this event came an almost unrecognizable change in the spiritual scene of American life. A certain flatness, a falling off of aspirational force, a kind of treadmill progression subtly characterized the environment from this time till after the outbreak of the war in September.

This atmosphere, I am sure, had nothing to do with the production of Saroyan's *My Heart's in the Highlands* in May 1939. But I have often wondered whether the sweet Saroyan note of loose affection and neighborliness (often resembling a benign indifference) which this ingratiating play introduced to the theatre was not eagerly seized upon as the dominant one in the first days of the forties because it filled the need for unity, good behavior, and humorous condonement of all our sins.

Because of its brevity, its ambling freedom, its lack of emphatic point, *My Heart's in the Highlands* fell into the category of the "experimental play." When we referred to *My Heart* as experimental we simply indicated to ourselves that the play — though easy and utterly successful within its framework — probably had a limited appeal owing to our audience's restricted habits in dramatic entertainment.

For this production I chose Bobby Lewis as director, because he had both a talent and a taste for fantasy and the non-realistic forms generally. Some of our actors thought the play was literary rather than theatre material; I disagreed. One wished to go on record as saying he thought it a "piece of cheese" — which was merely a rough way of expressing ideological disapproval. I disagreed with this as well. Finally one or two people, through a peculiar cliquishness that was rarely wholly absent but never dominated the Group's affairs, balked at Bobby Lewis as director. None of these brakes stopped me: I was determined to introduce Saroyan as a playwright.

Bobby Lewis chose a new designer for the décor, Herbert Andrews (who had done the sets for us at our summer camp in 1936), and Paul Bowles to write the score. The cast was to include our old friend Philip Loeb, Art Smith, and some young people who

Scene from *The Gentle People* by Irwin Shaw, 1939. (Direction: Harold Clurman. Setting: Boris Aronson.)

LEFT TO RIGHT: Roman Bohnen, Sam Jaffe, Lee Cobb, Martin Ritt.

Scene from *My Heart's in the Highlands* by William Saroyan, 1939. (Direction: Robert Lewis.

had never before played with the Group but who had sought this
opportunity for years.

When all the artistic arrangements had been made, I left for
a short vacation in Havana. After I had been there a few days, I
received a wire from our business manager: Council and attorney
stated that because of the loss of $17,000 suffered by the Group
at the hands of the Belasco Theatre's nervous official "it was felt
we should retrench as much as possible and stop production of
Saroyan's play. Please confirm our decision." I did not believe it
the Group's business to save money. I wired back immediately:
"The Group is not a bank. Proceed with Saroyan play."

Shortly after my return to New York I saw a rehearsal of the
play in company with the Theatre Guild board, which had been
called in either to contribute a part of the backing for the production or to provide for its inclusion among the Guild's subscription plays, so that a short run might be assured. I thought
the production enchanting. The Guild board liked it too, but
were worried that their subscribers might feel cheated by so short
a play. They did nothing. The production, financed out of our
dwindling funds, was announced for five performances only at
the Guild Theatre.

Most of the press reviewed the play in the vein of the *New
York Times:* "As a bit of virtuoso scribbling and acting, it is the
finest new play the Group has put on the stage this season — an
amusing, tender, whimsical poem which the Group Theatre has
translated into the lightest sort of beauty."

Some of the press were pleased to call the play "surrealistic" (a
rather helpless identification), others were glad it didn't have a
meaning, still others were sure it had the profoundest meaning,
and finally there were those who thought it pretentious gibberish
or a shameless bit of escapism and irrelevance to put on in the
trying times after Munich.

At any rate, it was an event, and John Mason Brown scolded
the Guild for not having taken the play under its wing. Brown
pointed out that the people who long ago had done *The Adding
Machine, Man and the Masses,* and *Processional* should have
found a place on their program for Saroyan's play. This may

have been valid critically, but under the material circumstances
of the late thirties to do plays like the present one or the equivalent of those mentioned would have spelled the Guild's ruin. Only
plays like *Caprice, Idiot's Delight,* and *The Philadelphia Story*
could keep the Guild going. In this connection, another relevant
matter of economics strangely enough always escapes the attention of most theatre historians. In the twenties it was possible to
do plays like *My Heart's in the Highlands* very cheaply. In 1939
to put this little play on in the most modest fashion cost nine
thousand dollars.

Nevertheless, prevailing sentiment as expressed in Brown's article hastened a change of the Guild's schedule. It adopted our
production of *My Heart's in the Highlands* and gave its subscribers a chance to see it. When the play failed to attract large
audiences despite its excellent press, the Guild could only explain
this anomaly on the grounds that we had made a mistake in casting an actor of conspicuously Jewish physiognomy in the central
role of the poet! Such an explanation does not bespeak anti-
Semitism; it is part of that weak-spirited rationalization for failure so characteristic of theatre people — the inability to accept the
plain fact that many good things can't make money in the theatre
— a fact, by the way, which calls for no complaint or bitterness

On a few occasions members of the Group who were enthusiastic about a production during rehearsals became severely critical of it when it failed before the public. With *My Heart's in the
Highlands,* a success with the reviewers, I heard little criticism or
comment on it within the Group. Most of the criticism of the production issued from Saroyan himself. He thought of his play as
virile realism, not at all as fable. He did not approve of Bobby
Lewis's delicate stylization, though he did not fail to borrow from
it later in his production of *The Beautiful People.* While there
may have been a point in Saroyan's strictures, he overlooked
throughout that the director as artist has a personality (as does
the actor) which in terms of the production as a whole may make
as legitimate and creative a contribution as anything in the written text, and there is ultimately no sure way of determining the

rightness or wrongness of a play's interpretation. It is certain
however that whatever limitation the quality of direction may
have had in relation to the present script, much of the play's success was due to it.

For the sake of æsthetic clarity it should be noted that the stylization of *My Heart's in the Highlands* was entirely compatible
with the fundamental Group approach to the stage interpretation
of its plays. All Group productions were "stylized," except that
when the stylization was, as in the present instance, directed toward fantasy and pictorial visualization, the stylization became
more evident. The Group's basic style consisted in forming a conception of the material at hand and so presenting it that it would
appear consistent with the quality of reality mirrored in the play's
text. Thus if the set for *My Heart's in the Highlands* was obviously not "true to life" it was because the director believed the
play called for a different type of stage picture to achieve the
reality of its author's vision, just as the sets of *Golden Boy* and
Rocket to the Moon (praised by many as "very realistic") were,
photographically speaking, quite remote from the actual places
they were supposed to represent. They were just as stylized in
their way as the set for the Saroyan play. Even plays as close to
traditional realism as *The House of Connelly* and *Awake and
Sing* were, in the Group's view, poetic plays and stylized as such,
though accepted as "realism" by the majority of the audience and
theatre commentators.

Critical or æsthetic considerations such as these, let us remember, had by this time become quite infrequent, as special and
old-fashioned as disputes about imagism, cubism, or "art for art's
sake." In the show world practical people spoke only of entertainment, "wows," or flops, while intellectuals argued only about
important themes, social significance, and ideology.

A few weeks after *My Heart's in the Highlands* opened, Saroyan
wrote *The Time of Your Life*, the most popular of his plays,
which made his mood of lyric anarchism and confused benevo-
lence the characteristic tone of the early forties. Saroyan brought
it to me on completion.

My rejection of this play was a serious error. It came about this way: During my reading of the script I was asked what I thought of it. "Every page of it has points of genius," I answered. It made me laugh; it touched me. Yet it annoyed me more than it amused me. There was about it a certain self-indulgence, a flagrant braggadocio of undiscipline, a thoughtless and almost cheap bathos that I could not abide. It was as if after the directness and simplicity of *My Heart's in the Highlands* Saroyan was seeking to popularize not only his message but his reputation — to say what he had to say and to call attention to his boldness and originality at the same time. This was much too severe a judgment, I am sure. The play, despite its blemishes, was an authentic expression of a true state of mind, both immature and generous, a state of mind not only personal to the San Francisco poet who is Saroyan but closely related to the wistfulness and humor of many Americans during this zero hour of history, when very few were quite sure what they thought except that they wished each other well, hated evil, sorrowed, wondered, and blinked. "No foundation; all the way down the line" (an actual phrase Saroyan had picked up in a bar) was at once the play's masterpiece of perception and the cause for my impatience with it.

When Saroyan discussed the play with me, I enjoined him to write with more precision and plot line. He answered quite truthfully that he wasn't able to do this. He was right about his method, and I was wrong about trying to correct it. In a few days I reversed my professional attitude toward the play and called Saroyan back in the hope that the Group might still be able to do it. It was too late; Eddie Dowling had just bought it.

PART VI

FAREWELL
TO
THE THIRTIES

CHAPTER TWENTY-ONE

Ebb Tide

I HAVE often thought, in retrospect, that the Group might have done well at the end of its 1938–9 season to announce its dissolution. In this way it might have called sharp attention to the fact that while its services had been acclaimed by practically all camps, it had achieved everything that could be achieved without the aid of any organized support. From this point forward, it might have proclaimed, either the Group would receive the kind of help its experience proved indispensable or it would quit at the height of its achievement.

But no one (save myself at odd moments) even dreamed of doing such a thing. We had lived so long under a low ceiling in the cavern of economic pressure that, though our backs were bent from it, we imagined we walked upright. In the course of its history, as a *New York Times* reporter put it, the Group had been accused of "artiness," "Leftism," and more recently "commercialism." None of these accusations was sound, but in the dim atmosphere that is the noonday light of the aforementioned cavern, how can anyone see clearly?

The League of American Writers, for example, at its 1939 Congress celebrated the victories of the "progressive theatre" as if it were at the beginning rather than the end of a great epoch. It pointed out that the Labor Stage production of *Pins and Needles* had been a huge success, that the Group Theatre had become the most successful producing organization in New York (just at the time when our till was emptied of its last penny), and such productions as *The Cradle Will Rock, Abe Lincoln in Illinois* and Lillian Hellman's *The Little Foxes* had won general acclaim. Plans for an even more ambitious future were demanded.

Alas, this whole movement in the theatre had already reached its apogee and was now on the decline.

I was not sure in May 1939 whether the Group people had better be permitted to accept Hollywood or stock engagements till the fall or whether to call them together for another work period in the country. When I consulted with my friends, they advised me to fortify the Group by adopting the latter course. They were in favor of this even if I had no definite play in view by July 1.

This may have been another one of those mistakes it is futile to be wise about through hindsight. Certain it is that most of the Group welcomed the call to come together again on July 15. I received a letter from Odets in Mexico that opened with the following words: "Dear Harold: What made me most happy in your letter of last week was the fact that the Group is going to have a summer. The news that we might do a picture over the summer was so depressing that I was unable to write for three days."

In other words, Odets felt a deep need to emerge from his isolation, caused by grief over his divorce, and to share life with his friends and co-workers. Nearly everyone else, in one way or another, felt the same need. With the assistance of Jules Leventhal, Broadway's road-company entrepreneur, we were able to hire Winnwood, a children's Christian Science school at Lake Grove, near Smithtown, Long Island.

Physically it was the largest and pleasantest place the Group had ever taken over for its summer work. The greatest number of actors, apprentices, and young playwrights ever assembled by us gathered to prepare for the new synthesis that we hoped our work in the forties would bring.

We spent the first weeks in an attempt to clarify some of the contradictory elements that had disturbed Group living and Group thinking. There were confusions, it seemed to me, that had made the active season we had just gone through far less happy than it should have been. Every issue was now a subject of dispute, no steps had been taken that had not been called into question or served as a cue for head-shaking and worry.

Many causes were ascribed to this peculiar state: we lacked new blood and had made no artistic progress for two years, we had poor business management, we were all now seeking personal success, we were allowing many commercial considerations to stand in our way. Harold Clurman was too easily distracted by personal problems, he was not clear or steady on social issues, there was insufficient democracy in the matter of Group decisions, and so forth and so on.

Finally Odets brought us *Silent Partner*. As far as I could remember, it had been revised very slightly. It had the same striking virtues — moments and scenes of extraordinary power and scope — and the same ruinous defects as in 1937. The actors were both anxious to do it and troubled by it. When I sat down to study the script with an eye to revision, I realized that the play still needed work so fundamental that it might take months to do it properly. More serious than this was the fact that the play had lost most of its topical value. Its message — the need for greater maturity in the mass base of our society to replace the decadent but none the less fierce enemy elements that seek to dominate it — was still appropriate, but the play's mood and plot pre-dated the progress in legislation of the past five years.

I told all this to Odets. I assured him that if he insisted, I would proceed with the production despite my misgivings. Odets had many reasons for desiring the play produced; one of them was that its appearance now might answer and rebuke those of his critics who after *Rocket to the Moon* had pronounced him "out of touch" with the people. But he agreed with my analysis and once again promised that some day he would take up the theme of this play and make it his most ambitious work. In the meantime he would turn to a subject he had had in mind since 1937 and had mulled over in Mexico.

Odets's volume of collected plays had just been issued on his thirty-third birthday. When he gave me a copy, I was deeply moved, for it seemed to contain in little the sum of our experience for the past eight years, which in our fantastically paced times had so soon become history. Giving me the little volume with its acknowledgment of the Group's collaboration and services was a small tribute. Odets felt impelled to do more: he bought me a car, an act that rather stunned me. It, too, told a kind of story.

We waited now for Irwin Shaw's new play to save the perilous situation of the Group's summer. It was called *The Golden Years.* Though it dealt with the breakdown of a semi-prosperous middle-class family as the depression hit the twenties, converting it from the nondescript honesty of the golden years to criminal means of rescuing its lost position in the world, the play was a parable illustrating the origins of fascist mentality and practice in American life. It was not a good play, unfortunately, but it emphasized again the fears that possessed the minds of sensitive young writers at this time.

That fascism was an increasingly threatening reality in terms of America was strikingly evident to us during this summer. Not far from our quarters at Upton was a Bundist camp, and there was more than a trickle of fascist influence in the surrounding neighborhood. A juke-box roadhouse to which the Group people repaired at midnight for snacks found as many insolent Nazis among the guests as there were actors and writers.

The rejection of *The Golden Years* was a greater blow to us than to Shaw: it left us high and dry. This was the moment to produce the long-promised revival of a classic. Many Group actors

were particularly fond of Chekhov. I chose *The Three Sisters* as
the vehicle most appropriate to our company's requirements.
Odets offered to prepare a new acting version. I would direct the
play with Stella Adler's assistance. The cast seemed to me an especially fine one.

Rehearsals began well, but my work soon became halting, in-
decisive. I cannot say whether this derived from an artistic limitation in myself — the play being too delicate, perhaps, for my
rather violent approach — or from a loss of heart due to a fore-
boding about the future. The war in Europe had just been declared. I was not sure of money to back the production. There
was something of a loose-end feeling in the air.

Owing to an inner perturbation — worse than usual for lack of
definition — I was unable to control a feud that broke out between two important members of the cast. At any other time this
friction would have been reduced to its proper level. Now it took
on major importance out of all proportion to its actual significance. The actors took sides and called secret councils to deal
with the crisis, which resulted in a lot of worried and sometimes
acrimonious talk. All the while, though I seemed to be torn by
this family quarrel as if it were the source of my near hysterics, I
knew that the true cause was far less immediate. Luther Adler
found me one day in a secluded corner of our premises vainly
attempting to master my jangled nerves. For a moment he pretended not to see me, then thought better of it, retraced his steps,
and came directly over to me with the question: "Harold, outside of everything, what's the matter?"

The question was well put. Everything was the matter. It was
not this or that small problem that disturbed me. It was the
fundamental problem of our whole Group existence — the problem I had virtually forgotten even though I had grappled with
it and named it in private and public for nine years. There was
no ground for a Group Theatre in New York; there never had
been. There was the material, the need, the value, the chance;
all this had been amply proved. We had done the impossible.
Yet, at the zenith of our efforts we were as far from being a truly
established, rooted organization as we had been as unknown be-

ginners in 1928. I sensed this, but could not say it. It was so much a paradox that I could not formulate it without seeming mad even to myself. So my answer to Adler was the rather pointless suggestion that we return to New York immediately.

For years some of our actors had demanded that the Group prove its catholicity as a theatre by producing a classic. Friends, critics, educators, and essayists had held forth on our fatal shortcoming: the overemphasis on the contemporary in our play program. "You will never achieve true eminence," we were instructed, "unless you include the old with the new in your program."

The truth is that a first-class production of a classic can hardly be financed in New York without the support of a star name — Evans, Gielgud, Leslie Howard, Lunt, Cornell. Eva Le Gallienne's Civic Repertory Theatre had been supported by a wealthy patron (and that only in the prosperous twenties). Orson Welles's *Cæsar* was made feasible because it eliminated most of the scenic and costume problems usual in a Shakespeare production, and the end of Welles's first season, despite its unusual success, found him with no funds for a second. To put on *Danton's Death* Welles had to invest his own earnings as a radio star. Though the Group had an enviable reputation as an acting company, people who had been willing to back even some of our weakest scripts refused point-blank to put a penny into our revival.

Robert Ardrey had just completed a new play, in which Herman Shumlin had expressed great interest. Shumlin had hesitated about proceeding to immediate rehearsals. Impatient, Ardrey informed us that he would turn the play over to us if we would undertake its production without delay.

It was a difficult moment for me. I thought the play literate, interesting in theme, theatrically attractive; but it was without lyric inspiration. I had long since abandoned the notion that a theatre could sustain continuous activity on the basis of top-flight dramatic works alone; our theatre was now sorely in need of a script with which to begin the season. I accepted Ardrey's *Tower of Light,* which was shortly to be produced under the title *Thunder Rock.*

When the play was read to the company, their response was cold, almost hostile. I explained at once that I was aware of the play's faults, but that I thought its subject worth while. It was an expression in terms of metaphysical fantasy of the quandary in which many thinking people in our day found themselves. They had reached a state of despair because of a hopeful past that had turned to ashes and a present that was enveloped in a European conflict of uncertain issues and dubious tactics (this was the period of the "phony war"). It was a time when idealists began to wonder again whether retreat into a condition of honest self-questioning and watchfulness — a new "ivory-towerism" — was not preferable to a headlong rush into a tumult of brave sorties, the consequences of which had not been truly comprehended. Ardrey's point was that the impasse of the present was no greater than that which had confronted our forebears a hundred years ago, and that to lose courage now was as wrong for us as it would have been for them. We need not enter the war at once, Ardrey suggested, since there was much to be done at home to keep us abreast of the great events of our day. Though the play's protagonist at the final curtain was still neutral in regard to actual combat, he had learned that struggle is still needed.

Such a theme in the play of a young American during the fall of 1939 made it entirely appropriate for our theatre, I reiterated, and added too that as craftsmen we had to do the best job possible with the only material at hand. My argument met with a reluctant acquiescence in our company, and as I had already pushed aside my own doubts about the play in order that the Group might continue its work, I rather resented the difficulty the actors seemed to have in doing the same.

The play — directed by Kazan, designed by Gorelik — opened in Baltimore with respectful notices, and shortly after in New York with a less than lukewarm press. The consensus of opinion was that Ardrey "continued to promise rather than to fulfill."

The history of this play's reception was far more illuminating, however, than a mere summary of the morning-after notices can indicate. Certain of my friends who had scorned the "cheapness" of *Golden Boy*, the "irrelevance and inconclusiveness" of *Rocket to the Moon*, and the "triviality" of *My Heart's in the Highlands*, now came forward to congratulate me on having chosen so daring a piece as *Thunder Rock*, which they affirmed was in "the true Group tradition."

Some of the actors began to think better of the play now, and when the production showed signs of faltering health, they expected me to urge them to continue the play despite this. Once again in letters of praise addressed to the press people such as Elmer Rice and Philip Barry came to the play's defense, and fervent zealots in the audience cried out: "Don't close the play! Don't close it!"

How confused the critical standards of our time are was further emphasized when my friend Waldo Frank declared he suspected defects in my "spiritual wholeness" (or taste) because I had chosen to produce *Thunder Rock*, while the Playwrights' Company awarded Ardrey a special prize for the most promising play of the season by a young American playwright. Further than this, the play, which many had abused as subversively isolationist, while others had applauded it for its sanity on almost precisely the same count, became the outstanding hit of London the following spring just as England was subjected to its first severe tests of the war. For in that country the play was regarded as a message of hope, saying exactly what its people wanted to hear at that moment.

Odets finished his new play, *Night Music*, before the run of *Thunder Rock* had ended. As I did not have proper roles for all our actors in *Night Music*, I encouraged some of them to accept engagements in outside productions. I also encouraged our business manager, Kermit Bloomgarden, to produce Albert Bein's *Heavenly Express* with John (né Jules) Garfield as star, Bobby Lewis as director, and Boris Aronson as designer. This would provide work for many of the younger actors whose careers, I told them at Winnwood, were of real importance to us.

Luther Adler had just been offered an important part with the

Playwrights' Company, which I was glad to have him accept, as there seemed to be no fitting role for him in the Odets play. There was more money in it for him, and his wife (Sylvia Sidney) was pressing him to take every advantage to break from the narrow confines of the Group, an organization in whose legend, she felt, he had too long been snared. Despite all this, Luther was somewhat piqued that I had not asked him to play even a minor role in *Night Music* (as I had insisted he do in *Men in White*). He enjoyed the release into conventional prominence through his engagement outside the Group, but he was also worried by this freedom, for it might indicate a scattering of our Group forces that would ultimately leave him and the others naked in the windy desolation of Broadway's market.

I liked *Night Music* very much; so did the company. It might have been argued — and was — that the play lacked definite theme, logical plot progression, coherent passion. None of this bothered me; I liked it. It was continuously entertaining and constantly melodious. It was what Odets said of all his many scened plays: "a song cycle on a given theme." The theme here was homelessness. The American boy is in search of a home. He is lost in a tragicomic wilderness of explosive phenomena that have no more meaning than a side-show. The brilliant and dismal circus he wanders around in is the big city. Somehow all the busy little performers are as lost and homeless as he, although they seem to cavort and wiggle through their routines with astonishing energy and conviction. To the naked eye the show seems more fun than a barrel of monkeys; to the thoughtful it is as heartbreaking as it is wondrous. At the cynosure of the city's splendor, the World's Fair (then in progress), the boy vents his secret agony, fear, and confusion. He is an angry Pierrot, tender and quarrelsome, immature and profound, battered by the most versatile mechanism in all creation. This Pierrot is the essential Odets in naïve comedy terms.

An ambling lyric improvisation, *Night Music* was, far more than anyone suspected, a topical play. Its apparent aimlessness was descriptive of a moment in American history. The late winter and early spring of 1940 were as special a period as the days preceding the bank holiday of 1933. There was an unvarying low level of pseudo-prosperity and with it extensive unemployment. The mood in New York might have been characterized as one of intense stagnation. History was marking time. Progressive thought and action seemed to stand in shadow, tired and disheartened. Everyone seemed to be waiting. Everything was in question, and all the old answers rang a little false beside the darkening reality. The tone of the play was gentle and melancholy, as if the clarinet the play's hero tooted was his only weapon to combat the featureless chaos of 1940.

As *Night Music* was a comparatively expensive production, we could find no one in the beginning to put money up for it. We hawked it around a bit in the manner customary to a Broadway producer looking for a backer. Odets for the first time declared himself humiliated at this procedure. He believed he had achieved a point in his career when his work could be spared such treatment. I sympathized with his feeling, but I was surprised at its innocence. He really thought his position as America's leading young playwright absolved his work from the laws of business evaluation. If I had said this, he might have retorted that it was the Group's incompetence and lack of social connections that were responsible for his humiliation — nothing else. It would have been difficult to convince him otherwise, since Lewin and Loew (independent picture producers) offered to finance the production in exchange for the rights to the play and Odets's services as writer of the play's screen version.

Night Music was put into rehearsal with a cast that struck everyone as ideal. Everything proceeded smoothly and Odets seemed extraordinarily pleased with every aspect of our work.

When he delivered the script to me, Odets had said I would be unable to cut a word of it — an unusual pronouncement for him. Before rehearsals were over, at least half an hour had been cut, with Odets's consent. The only dispute that arose between us related to the direction of the central character. I thought him too raucous, complaining, unsympathetic. Odets assured me he wanted the audience to dislike the boy during almost the whole first act. "You are taking away a vital element of the character," Odets remarked, "the element of cockiness and sharp impertinence."

The show opened in Boston and played to miserable business in a season of intense cold and snow. Odets began to worry: he felt I was not doing enough to improve the production. He now suggested cutting entire scenes. I agreed that the play was too long, but I refused to cut any of its scenes. The structure of the play, such as it was, needed every scene, though the play's excesses were obvious. Still the general feeling in the company was good; whatever was wrong with the production struck no one as more than minor blemishes. Hanns Eisler, who provided the play's incidental music, kept bouncing and bubbling with fine European gusto and an almost American optimism.

Odets insisted that we present the play at the Broadhurst, a large house on a street of successes, rather than at the smaller Lyceum. When I protested that the Lyceum was more suited to the needs of this intimate play, he twitted me about my taste for old theatres. I also learned that he had given instructions to our business manager that opening-night tickets in New York be sold on a $4.40 sale, something entirely opposed to the spirit of our organization. I could not quite understand why Odets wished to make everything about this show have a "big time" quality.

At the final dress rehearsal in New York, Odets, in an access of generous feeling, told me: "Harold, I think this is the best play and the finest production in New York." "Yes," I answered, "that's what worries me."

We had a very poor press. Typical was this: "Now that Odets writes like Saroyan, Doomsday is near. . . . In Elia Kazan it [the Group] presents one of the most exciting actors of America. For good measure it offers Jane Wyatt and Morris Carnovsky and a brilliant Group Theatre production. . . . The best acting organization in this country is offering a superlative performance. . . . Mr. Odets has been around long enough to improve instead of to subside into mannerisms; and there is no reason why he should take comfort at this late date from a new playwright who has not yet learned how to use the theatre expertly."

Odets was like Saroyan! According to current talk, Odets was the playwright of the thirties; Saroyan the playwright of the forties. Each decade — really, each season — has to have its hero on our cultural mart, where the vocabulary of commercial advertising has come to replace the language of criticism. What I heard now sounded very much like talk about refrigerators or different model cars.

The morning the bad news about *Night Music* struck, Luther Adler rushed to the Group office to consult, advise, and comfort. Odets, his agent, our business manager, and one or two others were present. Luther Adler spoke as if everything that had been said in the reviews was gospel. He suggested that we withdraw the play immediately; Odets should not be made to spend any more of his money. I maintained, on the contrary, that Odets should lose his money if necessary to keep the play on the boards for at least three weeks. Odets agreed. But couldn't the actors take a cut? No, I said, they should not be asked to. I was willing to forgo my salary; the business manager and press representative would forgo theirs. But the actors' salaries were the least costly item of the production. Most of our actors had earned something like five weeks' pay since the preceding spring. To ask them to cut their salaries under such circumstances was mean. Well then, let us play without scenery, cut the music, move to another and larger house, and reduce prices to a dollar. If Odets agreed, I would not stand in the way; but, I pointed out, one couldn't simply remove the scenery from a production that was conceived in terms of its use. Odets concurred. As for moving the production to another theatre, it was shown that the expense of moving such a show, even a few doors away, would be a costly matter.

Odets now felt hurt by what he considered my apathy or negligence about making a campaign to fight the press. He was willing, he said, to spend his last dollar on it. He expected us to attack the press through articles, speeches, posters — something spectacular. He hoped for high-pressure salesmanship to put the show over, publicity on a grand scale, obstreperous, eye-catching, and ear-splitting. I thought this might offer him some moral satis-

faction or nervous relief; I doubted its efficaciousness in regard
to the play. The audience that would enjoy *Night Music* enough
to turn it into a popular success was not a large one at Broadway
prices.

Slowly, very slowly, in the actors' minds a new critical opinion
of the production was taking shape. It was not that of the weekly
reviewers, whose notices were much more favorable than those of
the dailies. No, it was an opinion compounded of expert inside
knowledge furnished by a microscopic examination of the production over weeks of rehearsal, try-out, and performance, plus a
general reaction to conversation at bars and *kaffeeklatsches*, in
addition to a further distillation of everything the reviewers had
said, implied, or had in mind. It was the criticism of the Group
itself as it was acted upon, more or less unconsciously, by outside
influence.

That the reviews had been disappointing had not distressed me
much; nine years of experience had induced a certain resignation.
But the "higher criticism" of my colleagues, of their close friends,
of Odets himself, that was strangely oppressive.

What had been wrong with "the finest production in New
York"? I still liked it; indeed, I liked it as well as anything I had
done. Kazan, it seemed, had been miscast. He was oafish, unsympathetic. Had I not told him that the character was a Pierrot?
Why had I not persisted on this tack? Kazan had not conveyed
the impression of a Pierrot. True! Then, the play was much
lighter than I had made it. It should have been given a René
Clair touch. Was my touch like René Clair's? Decidedly not!
Odets now believed that the big denunciation speech in the
World's Fair scene should have been spoken wistfully instead of
being delivered passionately, as Kazan did it. A very good idea,
perhaps! Furthermore, Gorelik's sets had been too large, heavy,
gloomy. I had told Gorelik the sets ought to have the miniature
quality of a postage stamp. Did they have? Not on the stage of
the Broadhurst. The characterization of my secondary figures was
too emphatic, overelaborate. Perhaps. The little man in the park
had been made a bit grotesque; he should have been pathetic.
Possibly. The play was full of sweetness; I had injected a note of

hate. Oh, miserable error! O vandal, O trifler with masterpieces, O heavy-handed fanatic, æsthetic lout — how dare you!

Odets brought these matters up not once but many times, and each time he forgot that he had made the same points at our last meeting. He forgot because I never responded: I listened. After being repeatedly treated to this refined analysis, I lost all perspective. I had very little idea of what I had done or failed to do. I simply felt a dull ache.

The remedy for this, from an organizational standpoint, was simple: I would not direct Odets's next play. But what I wanted to understand was what had wrought this change in Odets's opinion and in that of many others who had told me, up to the very last rehearsals, what a beautiful job I had done. I no longer wanted to explain to myself why these family critics were wrong; I wanted to analyze the process that enabled them to become so right.

For everything they had to say was keen. This was not like London, when Odets had shouted: "You do not respect your talent," and everyone else had blasted nonsense at each other. Or was it like London? Who was the devil there that wrought such havoc? What was the name of this thing that yapped at me and bit into everyone and everything, including the biters? I found a name for it, one that expressed for me a deep-seated disorder. It came from the dilemma confronting people who want to occupy two different places at the same time; I called it the desire for this-and-that.

Odets wanted to run with the hares and hunt with the hounds; he wanted to be the great revolutionary playwright of our day and the white-haired boy of Broadway. He wanted the devotion of the man in the cellar and the congratulations of the boys at "21." He wanted the praise of the philosophers and the votes of *Variety's* box-score.

This was understood by everyone in the Group, but what was not so readily understood was all the forms this desire for this-and-that could take, all the people it consumed. There was a desire for anonymity in the Group and eventually a desire for personal aggrandizement. There was a desire for freedom and a

desire for a discipline imposed from without to silence the devils
that the freedom might set loose. There was a realization of the
time needed to produce anything real and complete in the theatre, and there was a bitter impatience with anything less than
the "just right," though created in short order under hazardous
circumstances. There was a desire for humility, for tolerance, and
there was suspicion of almost everyone's defects. The conflict of
desires amounted to an impatience with life itself.

The Group directors had once practiced the art of self-criticism
on their own productions and had analyzed each of the actors'
performances for educational purposes. The actors were apt pupils: they did not necessarily become better actors; they became
shrewd critics. With this new instrument of criticism they made
deft incisions into each other's work, into that of the playwrights
(who came to loathe them for it) and all other actors outside.
After a time almost everyone in the Group worried over everyone else's performance. At times there was an invisible silent
slaughter going on among the Group actors. Almost everyone indulged in it, not necessarily through mutual fault-finding, but by
asking me as director what I was going to do about X, Y, or Z.
At night I was wakened by solicitous telephone calls from some
actor who couldn't sleep because of another actor's performance,
and by day I received friendly letters from fellow workers ad-
vising me on how I might overcome the defects revealed in my
latest productions, listing them with remarkable patience.

It became evident to me at this point that Odets no longer intended to be burdened with the impedimenta of other people's
shortcomings. In the future he would get the best of everything
— actors, royalties, business management, publicity — for he had
suffered sorely from lack of these things for years.

CHAPTER TWENTY-TWO

Collapse

RIGHT after *Night Music* Odets was sore, the Group was sore, and I was sore. Odets, as we have seen, began by being sore about the reviewers, then about me; the Group was generally sore while seeking a way to fix on the party responsible for its condition — with a sidelong glance in my direction, where at the same time they hoped to find an emollient. As for myself, I tried my best to be objective and understanding.

At a talk I gave for all the Group and some of its friends on the closing of *Night Music*, I tried to convey a sense of my satisfaction with that production and some confidence in the future. I believed in the Group, I said, and the possibility of its continued life because in my view the Group was no longer an idea confined to our membership, and its development from this point forward need not be envisioned in terms of ourselves exclusively. I hoped that the Group next season and henceforth could become the association of the strongest creative forces in the American theatre.

My speech failed to impress. For one thing, the actors hoped I would beat my breast a bit and that I would declare myself in favor of giving the membership greater powers in the running of our affairs. This, they believed, would save us. If only I would be the leader who carried out the will of the collective — in other words, their will!

Just before *Night Music* I had issued a statement telling the actors that henceforth I would run the Group alone, with the advice and collaboration of whomever inside or outside the Group I saw fit to consult. "If the theatre is truly my theatre, you will find that it is yours as well," was the position I took. The actors were distressed at such wrongheaded high-handedness but believed that my ukase was the product of pique and that a few weeks of calm would modify my battered and swollen ego. They were mistaken as to both the cause and the meaning of my attitude.

Their reaction to my latest speech was to make them determined to do something on their own — to clarify their own position, consolidate their forces, and present me with a counterproposal as to the proper running of the Group. They called several meetings without me, which everyone attended. At one of these meetings Molly Thacher read a letter of resignation, saying the Group was no longer a group but a one-man theatre, and she treated her fellow actors to a lengthy analysis of the causes that had transformed me from a true leader into a would-be dictator.

A committee was finally elected to draw up a kind of new Group constitution that would establish a *modus operandi* for the organization as well as a program that conformed to their collective vision of the theatre as they wished to have it.

I bought a new play for the coming season: a dramatization by Victor Wolfson of Erskine Caldwell's novel *Trouble in July*. It was a tragicomedy of social indifference, in which a lynching occurs in a Southern village, not so much because of anyone's viciousness but rather because everyone is too shiftless and lazy to assume responsibility for stopping it.

Just then Kazan was making an attempt to raise funds to provide stipends for the encouragement of new plays and playwrights. The scheme fell through. A lady with connections in wealthy circles where art was still spelled with a capital A was to be engaged to work exclusively on the raising of a Group subsidy. Unfortunately we did not have enough money to spare for the lady's salary.

For myself I planned to get a job in Hollywood for the spring and summer. Before leaving I had a few conversations with Odets. He was quite tense with me. One day he took the bull by the horns and said that our fundamental disagreement now centered on one matter: he believed in *creating* the conditions for our theatre, I believed in adjusting to existing conditions. I had once talked of a "popular theatre," he said, a low-priced theatre, a repertory theatre, and so on. Had I given up this dream as impractical? I did not answer that it was precisely this we had been working on for almost ten years now, and that a few things had been accomplished in the attempt. I merely pointed out that to do what he asked, someone or a small group of people would have to give up at least a year simply to lay the foundation for such a theatre, and that this person or group would have to be supplied with enough money to sustain them while doing this work. Odets thought this could be arranged for me. His friend Billy Rose, he said, would surely be willing to lay out thirty-five dollars a week for this purpose.

An important picture agent had a job all sewed up for me in Hollywood. The agent and I went to see an MGM executive. He began with what must have been a usual speech, stating that I had to realize that pictures were a medium different from the theatre, and that I ought to spend a year on the lot serving a sort of apprenticeship. Nothing he said was in the least unexpected or unreasonable, but suddenly I found myself on my feet shouting about the ten years of the Group's accomplishment and full of scorn for the notion that I had to "learn the business" like the now successful boys he had mentioned. My harangue made quite an impression: Sam Katz wished never to see me again.

When I recovered from the shock of my insanity, I tried to fathom its source, for I was ordinarily tight-lipped outside the circle of my friends. With an inner shamefacedness I acknowledged to myself that I had unfortunately combined the desire to clinch the job (and had succumbed to a fit of strange "salesmanship") with a desire to be accepted on my own terms — that is, the terms of my Group record and reputation. The scene I had made was my unfortunate way of tracing the familiar pattern of an unresolved duality.

I returned to New York as Paris fell in 1940. For a short while I experienced a curious sensation of nervous exhilaration, a species of rational delirium. The outside world in its crack-up ap-

peared to justify the sense of breakdown within me. Up to that
moment I had favored a vigilant neutrality. At this point I
changed my view and favored all aid to Axis enemies. I quarreled with everyone who still allowed his suspicion of Toryism in
England and his fear of the "war-mongers" to lead to an opposition to Lend-Lease and conscription.

During the summer I spent some time at Cape Cod with Irwin
Shaw, who was at work on a new play. He had completed a comedy during the previous spring and had sold it, without notifying
me, to George Kaufman. When I first heard this, I spoke to him of
his "betrayal" of the Group.

I read the play now. In *Retreat to Pleasure* Shaw had attempted
to write a drawing-room comedy with social significance. It had
some good scenes and pleasant writing, but above all it seemed to
me to mirror the soul of the young middle-class intelligentsia and
the gloomy, rootless jauntiness of our society generally just after
the outbreak of the war in 1939. The play was a little *Heartbreak
House*, but unredeemed, despite dexterity, by either a sure hand
or a clear spirit. I liked it nevertheless as a kind of document of
the day: it evoked an escapist mood that looked toward no even-
tual release from its underlying disquiet. Shaw was pleased that
I could read the play's theme through the froth of its playful
verbiage.

When George Kaufman decided to relinquish his rights to *Retreat to Pleasure*, Shaw agreed to let the Group do it. "For heav-
en's sake, Harold," Shaw begged, "let's do a good job this time."

I expected to go ahead with this production unhindered either
by financial commitments to the Group actors, since I could not
even hope to meet them, or by the obligation to cast exclusively
from our regular company, a limitation that at this time the author
would not have accepted. I was free, then, to work untrammeled
by considerations of duty or ideology. Such freedom was not an
ideal with me. Like many other freedoms it was a sorry thing,
entailing a kind of dissolution far less creative than the planned
restrictions inherent in the methods previously employed by us.
But I had very little choice now.

If I had any hope, it was that, by admitting the wretchedness of our situation and defining it both publicly in the press and privately to our actors, some spark might catch on somewhere and fire new energies. The hope was vain. The article I published in the *New York Times* had too disconsolate a tone to inspire much confidence.

The cardinal fact about the Group, I pointed out, was

"that it had to operate all these years on the hit-or-miss system that characterizes Broadway. For a theatrical enterprise which has any other view outside the necessary one of making money, it is utterly destructive at every point . . . you cannot plan for continuity. Play scripts are measured by backers in the light of a single gamble, and only plays that are believed to have box-office appeal or offer at least the possibility of a movie sale can be conveniently done. . . . It should be pointed out, in this connection, that the habit of judging plays from the standpoint of their immediate box-office draw spreads insidiously from the backer to the producer to the company to the critics and finally to the audience, whose tastes and minds are thus unconsciously but progressively debauched and then made indifferent to the theatre generally. . . . If we fail to carry out to the full what is still our real program, the failure will be as much the failure of our theatrical environment as the fault of our abilities. . . . I believe that the task is extremely difficult, but if more people will realize the nature of the task, an organization like the Group Theatre . . . can function and thrive even as a business in this art which dares not speak its name."

I called our company together. During the summer they had drawn up a paper reiterating their age-old desire for an institutional theatre, insisting it be provided them, as if they were addressing someone who had the power to hand it to them but who perversely refused to do so. I began by stating what should have been obvious: that their demands had been mine for ten years, that they were merely a restatement of what I had hoped to achieve ever since we had come together at our first meeting in

1928. The actors' paper offered a blueprint with no provision for the materials in time and money to realize its design.

I had had enough of hearing this agonized echo of my own words hurled at me in accents of accusation. I was doing what I could: I would produce *Retreat to Pleasure*, the only play available then, which would employ only four or five of the old Group, and if possible would follow it with *Trouble in July*, which also called for a cast for which our company yielded very few candidates. Beyond that, I pleaded for help.

I had to carry on at this point as if I were an independent producer, but I was willing to step aside for any person or combination of people who could carry out our common task in some way that I might not understand or recognize as the correct way. If anyone else, I said, could make a Group Theatre with or without me, I begged him to do so. I not only would not stand in his way, but would apply as a worker at any job for which I might qualify.

This offer went unheeded: it was regarded as a challenge that smacked of disdain or mockery. Instead of my words being taken at face value, there was an outcry in which were mingled the boast that the actors were capable of going on without me and a passionate wail that I was abandoning my wards in midstream.

In this melee, however, I was increasingly disturbed by the sense that many of the people were crying for the Group as a force outside and above them to provide protection and care in a cruel world. But no one could say how such protection could be found. Words flew wildly. As at Winnwood, I lost self-control, and in my desire to make the basic situation clear my emotion burst forth in a deluge of angry sounds, desperate exaggerations, wild objurgations. Some of the actors turned from me as from a man lost. Luther Adler summed up the scene by saying sardonically: "Harold wants a divorce."

It was all much simpler than anyone would admit. There was no need for anger or for shouting. When you cannot do anything about an objective situation and you are unwilling to face this fact, all the subjective furies will be unleashed to wreak havoc. But the facts are not altered.

For ten years I had been an idealist. Despite my knowledge of the facts, I had been impelled by the feeling that if one's will is strong enough, if one's desire is sufficiently hot, these alone can mold events. When will and desire, however, no longer correspond to facts, when facts do not provide them a sufficiently substantial basis, when will and desire become isolated forces, they induce a kind of madness, cause pain without grace. My will and the collective will of my fellow workers were not sufficient to establish a Group Theatre that might endure despite the jungle life, the drought and famine, of the Broadway theatre in the early forties.

Odets was not present at this last big meeting of the Group Theatre. He did not have to be. He was brewing a special consciousness of his own, which, because of his privileged position as a playwright with greater opportunities for independence than any director or actor can hope for, caused him less distress than either the actors or I experienced. Nevertheless Odets's inner line, far more than he knew, resembled that of the actors, since it sprang from the same sources, the same contradiction.

In August 1940 Odets and I had a long conversation in which he imparted to me his most recent conclusions about the Group situation. Without dwelling on the whys and wherefores, he asserted bluntly that he was tired of the Group actors — he had described them as "minor Parsifals" — and he had no intention of allowing a lingering loyalty or the occasional resurgence of personal affection to stand in the way of his development as man or artist.

I assured Odets at once (though he asked for no comment) that I considered his state of mind perfectly natural. I remembered Waldo Frank's once telling me that a man has a crisis in his life every ten years, and now Odets was going through a kind of crisis that called for a change. He had to discard his old skin and grow a new one. The process was a healthy one.

Two days later I bethought myself and decided to write him a long letter in which I would point out to him that, while what I had said was true on the positive side, there might also be a negative side to his present attitude. My letter emphasized two thoughts. He must not allow his present reaction to his past blind him to the fact that the Group, for all its faults, had helped create him just as he had helped create it, and that a denial within himself of his past would be injurious to his spirit and thought in the future. Far more important than this was the paradox that followed from the premise of his present position. If he wanted to cut himself off from the old Group, it became deeply necessary for him to attach himself to a new one. This was more than a personal matter: it was his all-round human and artistic problem. As a man and artist he would grow no more unless he found people, a cause, an idea, or an ideal to which he could now make the gift of his love (that is, his talent) to replace his old enthusiasms, loyalties, fervor. Such men as he could not live and mature alone. Such as he must be forever attached to a body of people and a body of belief greater than themselves. They alone could offer nurture to his spirit, serve as the recipient of his passion, the counterweight of his ego.

There was nothing unusual about the difficulties I had in getting *Retreat to Pleasure* on the stage. Compared with stories any number of New York managers can tell, ours was a routine affair. Carl Laemmle, Jr., in Hollywood agreed to put $20,000 into the show, which left us with $5,000 to raise. Laemmle, or "Junior" as his friends called him, wanted to approve the casting of the two leading roles, but he would not come to New York to witness or assist in any phase of the production. He chose his friend John Wildberg to represent him in New York.

Besides this, Laemmle wished his lawyer on the coast to draw up very careful contracts between us. While the contract was being negotiated — as much time was spent over each item as it might have taken for Shaw to write another play — no money could be delivered, so that little preparatory work could be done.

This delay, which embarrassed me in my interviews with actors, designers, and others who were to contribute to the production, made me seek backing closer to Broadway. The producer Dwight Wiman was interested and wanted to associate himself with the

Group in doing the play. He raised his money among friends, and some time passed before they could arrive at a decision. After two weeks I was told that the backers of my would-be backer felt the play and its rather sour ending (the boy leaves the girl he has been pursuing throughout the play after the girl has rejected her other suitors) was a bad investment. A happier ending, on the other hand, would not have been honest. These backers, therefore, were obliged to retire because they could neither countenance a bad investment nor contemplate artistic trickery.

Another manager, Vinton Freedley (in conjunction with Gilbert Miller) was equally interested in the play. He had tried to persuade Shaw to let him have the play without any Group association. When Shaw refused, Freedley was eager to accept my bid for his help. He listened to my plans for the production, approved most of my suggestions, and then asked what I was willing to give in return for his backing. I offered him sixty per cent of the profits, credit as associate producer (even "first billing"), and the privilege of interference or "editorial advice." The Group was to retain artistic control and produce the play from its office. This was not acceptable. He wanted seventy-five per cent of the profits, artistic control, sole billing; and the production was to be supervised through his office. The deal was not made.

Since Junior was still reluctant to brave the rigors of a New York winter, I had to fly to Hollywood, where besides the opportunity of meeting him I thought I might find a suitable leading man — to my mind, the pivot of the production. I had told my colleagues that I would not do the production at all unless I found the right actor: someone sufficiently brilliant as a performer and beguiling as a personality to compensate for the insufferable egotism with which the leading character was beset. I found no one available who answered these requirements.

By the time Junior and his attorney were ready with the contract, and the precious check for $20,000 was ready for use, I found that to withdraw from the production might be unfair to Shaw, who, though warned and worried about the leading-player dilemma, wished me to proceed. I had spent so much time on these phantom negotiations that I was even more horrified at the thought that all of it might prove a total loss than I was at the prospect of the production's failure.

We went ahead with a cast that was weakest where it needed to be strongest, with sets and costumes hurriedly prepared. The actors did not see that I was dispirited as we rehearsed on the cold dirty stage of an abandoned theatre. There was little time left now for the mere matter of getting the play on.

Just before opening night Odets invited me to dinner in his new apartment on Beekman Place, lavish and dismal. There was something he had to tell me. I knew what it was, but I pretended ignorance. He had some difficulty in coming to the point.

He proposed to produce his new play, *Clash by Night*, with Lee Strasberg as director and Luther Adler and Sylvia Sidney in the leading parts. "Good," I said. He would produce the play under the Group Theatre official auspices, though he planned to own most of the show and to cut Lee Strasberg in on the profits. The Group offices, in other words, would be the center from which the production activities would issue. This fitted in perfectly with my own plans. I had just been offered a six-month contract in Hollywood. I would accept this now and leave Odets and Strasberg in charge of Group affairs. They could take over and conduct the Group Theatre without interference.

The production of *Retreat to Pleasure* was worse than bad: it was weary. It had its pleasant moments, it looked handsome after a department-store fashion, it was not too poorly played, but its origins in dreariness and discouragement were discernible to the naked eye.

On opening night Vinton Freedley during the intermissions explained to several reviewers how badly the play had been muffed. If he had done the play, Katharine Hepburn would be playing the lead, et cetera. In the audience Stella Adler was heard saying in reference to the production: "Sad, isn't it?" I sat alone at the Royale downtown, knowing that such goings-on were routine to the atmosphere in which plays see the lights in the vicinity of Forty-fourth Street.

The divisive forces of the New York theatre, which through indifference, casualness, need for excitement, malice, and a miserable competitiveness dog the coherence and stability of all organic effort, were enacting their final tired gestures in relation to the Group. For ten years talk of the Group's dissolution had been constant. When this dissolution was more apparent than real, a certain glee greeted the possibility of this catastrophe in many quarters. Disaster is always good news on Broadway. Now when the *coup de grâce* was actually to fall, there was neither weeping nor satisfaction in it. It was hardly noticed at all. The last official Group Theatre production closed "not with a bang but a whimper." The inertia of a seat on the aisle had triumphed.

No dirge was sung over our graves, because we did not announce a funeral, and even our death was a matter of opinion. Many a time the crows had cawed over a corpse that was soon to show renewed signs of life. Even now I did not assume that all was over merely because my energies were depleted. I wrote short notes to all the actors telling them I was leaving for the coast and that for six months at least they were free to do what they would or could in regard to the theatre's affairs at home. The Group Theatre was now *Clash by Night* with complete supervision in Odets's and Strasberg's hands.

When Odets ventured out to find backing for his new play, he encountered interested buyers, but their prices were depressing. He had to hawk it about a bit to find a good offer. Soon after I reached Hollywood I received a wire from Odets saying that Billy Rose was going to back his play, but that he wanted so large a percentage of the profits in return for his investment that there would be none left for the Group Theatre as such. What did I say? I said: "Go ahead." Another wire followed shortly after, informing me that Billy Rose did not wish to use the Group Theatre's name in billing the play. What did I say? I said: "Very well."

The play was not produced till November 1941. By this time it had become a vehicle for Tallulah Bankhead, Luther Adler and Sylvia Sidney having disappeared from the original production scheme. Of the Group company only Art Smith and Lee Cobb were included in the cast.

I did not see the production. I read the final draft of the play, which Odets sent me before rehearsals began. What interested me in this reading was the mood of despair that informed the play. The peculiar depression of the early forties — wistfully humorous in *Night Music,* flippant and wry in *Retreat to Pleasure* — had turned grim in *Clash by Night.* True, there was a sound young couple to be found in the noxious atmosphere of the play — young people intended as portents of a clearer future — but their presence represented a kind of ideologic afterthought rather than the creative center of the play, which, no doubt about it, was pessimistic. Odets's feeling seemed to be weighed down here by the sense of a working class that was basically homeless, racked with inner tension, ignorant, baffled, pathetic, and dangerously close to that breaking-point of "mystic" hysteria and violence that often provides the spiritual soil for the seeds of fascism. One might regret that Odets should be more aware of this aspect of our life than of others, but that this gloomy sentiment should prevail in his soul at this time was far more significant than anyone took pains to observe. The play had a brief run and was totally forgotten as the shock of Pearl Harbor silenced everything that wasn't entertainment or a contribution to the war effort.

For me the closing of *Clash by Night* marked the end of that literary-theatrical epoch begun in 1931 which reached its high point between 1935 and 1938. In the theatre its impetus had run down slowly but none the less perceptibly; in the novel it had boomed its farewell salute in Steinbeck's *Grapes of Wrath.*

Not that the epoch of the "social" play or novel left no traces. On the contrary, this whole trend in the theatre was absorbed by the high-school academicism of the Playwrights' Company, whose characteristic works were Robert Sherwood's *Abe Lincoln in Illinois* and Sidney Kingsley's *The Patriots.* Plays like Lillian Hellman's *The Little Foxes* and *Watch on the Rhine* showed the theatrical movement of the thirties become adroit, efficient, wholly acceptable. What had been "propaganda" in the thirties had become a forerunner or an echo of "national unity" just before and immediately following our entry into the world conflict.

The movement that centered specifically in the Group Theatre from 1931 to 1941 was not content to die. The passion that motivated the Group and a host of younger players and writers influenced by the Group did not wane in 1939. The steam that poured forth from our home controversies showed that there was fire somewhere on the premises, even though it could not be used to make our engine run. Hardly anyone attached to the Group between 1931 and 1941 had abandoned its ideals or lost faith in its hypotheses or practices. When Morris Carnovsky was asked how it felt to be in a success (he had just opened in *My Sister Eileen*), he answered: "I have been with a success for ten years."

Nor were these merely gallant words. I have already related how at our last meeting I had pleaded with the actors to continue with the common task, despite my exhaustion, since that is what they most desired. Many tried to take me at my word. Early in 1941 a meeting was held between Oscar Serlin, Lee Strasberg, Morris Carnovsky, and Clifford Odets to organize some sort of Group organization, without the blemishes of the Group's "religiosity." Nothing came of it, however.

Odets and Strasberg at about the same time made efforts to interest Billy Rose and other sources of needed cash in a new theatre under their guidance. This went no further than *Clash by Night*.

Those who felt the Group had wandered too far from its implied promise of a "people's theatre" at popular prices with a strong social accent also got together to set up such an organization. Nothing happened.

Finally, and most seriously, Elia Kazan and Robert Lewis took steps toward the founding of a Dollar Top Theatre. It looked very much as if this were to become a reality. The Dollar Top Theatre bought a script, issued a bulletin, published a preliminary article of faith, and disappeared. Despite every effort to make it work, it proved financially unfeasible even before it got started.

CHAPTER TWENTY-THREE

And Now ——

I NEVER officially called quits or formally ended the Group. There was no more need for such action in 1941 than at any other time in its past. Though the Group coffers were empty, the situation was no worse than it had been during the winter of 1932 or the spring of 1937. From a purely practical standpoint, indeed, the situation in 1941 was far better: the Group's reputation was established, its personnel well known and highly esteemed.

In an article in the *New York Times* in May 1941 I pointed out that "while on the one hand I still believe the Group type of organization the kind most conducive to solid, satisfying and truly representative work in the theatre, I also believe that to continue operating our Group on the old basis would be artistically misleading, financially disastrous, personally heartbreaking. . . . The basic defect in our activity was that while we tried to maintain a true theatre policy artistically, we proceeded economically on a show-business basis. Our means and our ends were in fundamental contradiction. Our past — the past which brought forth what I strongly believe was the most important theatrical accomplishment of the thirties — has shown what could be done in the worst circumstances. This compromise (running the Group on an unsound basis) was forced on the Group for ten years. But it is a compromise I no longer desire to make."

The Group Theatre, then, was not played out in 1941. It suffered from neither defeatism nor slothfulness. It had not lost its inspiration. The Group could not sustain itself as such because it was isolated. The Group Theatre was a failure because, as no individual can exist alone, *no group can exist alone*. For a group to live a healthy life and mature to a full consummation of its potentiality, it must be sustained by other groups — not only of moneyed men or civic support, but by equally conscious groups in the press, in the audience, and generally in large and comparatively stable segments of society. When this fails to happen, regardless of its spirit or capacities, it will wither just as an organ that is not nourished by the blood's circulation through the body. I knew this from the first, but frequently forgot it. For not only were my will and desire great, but every false reason for the Group's weakness was advanced inside the Group as well as outside. It was said, for instance, that we were failing for lack of sound business management. No doubt grave errors in this respect weakened us from time to time, but the fact remains that no proper business management was possible in a set-up that was topsy-turvy to begin with. Others asserted we should not have operated on Broadway. But Eva Le Gallienne's company sustained itself for five years not because it played on Fourteenth Street but because it was subsidized. This was equally true of the Neighborhood Playhouse on Grand Street; and the Theatre Union, taking its stand on Eva Le Gallienne's site, drew what strength it had from something quite different from its location.

Classics were recommended to fill the hiatuses of our insufficient modern program, but we have seen that, since we lacked a star, practically the only play we could not raise funds for was a classic. Our misjudgment of the value of such scripts as *Winterset* and *The Time of Your Life* unquestionably harmed us, but similar misjudgments did not kill off the Theatre Guild or any organization of the kind. Our selection of plays may have revealed certain limitations (accidental as well as deliberate), but its effect on our destiny was slight, for the general theatre public was quite satisfied with our successes without relation to past performances, while our special public never decried us for having neglected to do more comedies.

Within the Group itself personal failings of the directorate or of individual actors were often held to be of paramount significance. The personal certainly counts in all artistic enterprises, but one director's fuzziness of mind, another's harshness, or a third's combination of every fault — including laziness and doldrums due to trouble at home, dictatorial proclivities, egocentricity, excessive paternalism, distrust of inferior brains — did not conspire to do anything but make the life of the Group difficult, interesting, and not very unusual. If actor A was too hammy, if actress B was too artificial, if player C was too dry, if leading lady D lacked sex appeal, and so forth, the same might be said of every company that was ever assembled in any country. It was true that Lee Strasberg proved weak with certain scripts, it was true that both Strasberg and I were too prolix and that I frequently conducted myself with as much poise as a Holy Roller, but we developed new talent in the directorial and even executive field all the time — Stella Adler, Michael Gordon, Sanford Meisner, Elia Kazan, Robert Lewis — and none of these or any combination of them was able to carry on after 1941 on any major collective basis, nor was any other organization able to establish itself at that time. No, the waning of the serious theatrical movement of the thirties was not primarily a question of personal deficiencies or lack of smart showmanship on anyone's part.

Its cause lay in the peculiar economic-moral condition of our society today, especially as it affects the theatre and kindred cultural phenomena. I am not employing the term "economic-moral condition" as a euphemism for capitalism; as I have pointed out, there have been flourishing theatrical cultures in several capitalist countries. Yet there can be no doubt that the almost absolute emphasis on the profit motive in relation to the theatre — intensified rather than diminished in the past few years — has impeded all progress in this direction. This is significant not only for itself but also in view of the fact that in the thirties there developed to a high point of consciousness the hunger for a spiritually active world, a humanly meaningful and relevant art. However, the peculiar social-economic development of the thirties, successful at first, only to lead to a crisis in the outbreak of the war, brought about the dissolution of that movement of which the Group Theatre was one of the outstanding voices.

There was no group or combination of groups — private or civic, economic, artistic, social or political — interested enough, conscious enough, strong enough to give consistent support to organizations such as the Group Theatre. The government was able to maintain its theatre only for a short while; the ILGWU produced only *Pins and Needles;* the Theatre Union received inadequate aid from labor audiences; and though the Group in its later years had developed a reliable audience for theatre parties and the cheaper seats, it could by no means live on this alone.

The fundamental economic instability from which the Group suffered, its piecemeal, bread-line existence, accounts for much of its hectic inner life and explains more about its real deficiencies than any analysis of the personal traits of its individual members. There was hardly a single personal problem within the Group that could not easily have been absorbed in the normal functioning of the organization if it could have seen its path clear to the preparation of four or five productions a season undisturbed by acute economic worry, which not only disturbed its people as individuals but made proper planning of its productions very difficult. None of the Group people themselves, though individually aware of their money problems, ever quite realized how this pressure shaped their opinions and feelings. Thus one actor claimed that "Harold cannot afford to possess any human frailty; he must be perfect." When it was pointed out that this was a rather extravagant demand, the actor conceded the point but insisted none the less that the leader of the Group just had to be without blemish or the Group would be done for!

If an actor or director or writer has marital difficulties in an ordinary theatrical company, it may be a subject of innocuous or malicious gossip. It rarely becomes a matter of organizational importance. In the Group Theatre these things were likely to constitute a threat to the company as a whole, or at least so everyone imagined; and people's private troubles were subjects of general speculation and collective concern.

There was an emotional tug of war constantly going on between members of the Group and forces outside it. The Group felt itself menaced by the wooing of the outside world as much as by its attacks; hence the fanatic, almost hysterical clinging to the ideal of Group unity and antagonism to every possible force that might threaten it.

Criticism of artists outside the Group may be set down to dif-
ferences of taste and to an understandable desire to defend —
through opposition — one's own way of work, but criticism of
fellow workers within the Group itself was in many respects
sharper than anything directed against outside people; for a play
poorly directed might prove the massacre of our material hopes
for the season, a faulty performance by one or two individuals
might spell penury for all of us. Thus an artistic deficiency or
blunder — which should be every artist's privilege — often produced the same atmosphere of venomous distrust that hovers
over a political or military group in which the presence of a
traitor is suspected.

This is not a phenomenon peculiar to the people who have
been the subject of our story. Prolonged isolation within a society breeds a bitterness inevitable in any community that is
forced into the position of feeding on itself while actually living
in expectation of being fed from the outside. The leaders of this
particular group in the first formative years had to insist on an
absolute loyalty, a rigorous adherence to the principle of unity,
since an easygoing looseness would quickly have dissolved the
Group altogether. This insistence was welcomed by the Group,
was indeed a source of strength in an environment so free that
it lacks almost all elements of cohesion and clarity. But such a
strict discipline must be followed by a period of relaxation, usually made possible by the achievement of the aims for which the
group undertook to discipline itself in the first place. This happened in our case to some extent too, but at no time was our success sufficiently complete (through the acquisition of a large
sinking fund or a guarantee of continued support from any depend-
able source) to justify a real release of our tension, to sweeten
our mood with genuine confidence in the future. A tolerant attitude is the prize and flower of a secure society.

When I saw the effects of our isolation and inbreeding, I tried
to dispel them with pleas for generosity, common sense, rational
analysis, and humor. These entreaties were only temporarily useful, not because our people lacked the qualities called for, but
because the source of their trouble could not be removed by talk.

Indeed, my very plea for greater liberalism within the Group was regarded at certain moments with misgivings. In a jeopardized society strong discipline provides the greatest safety. "Discipline, of course," I would say. "But do not always seek to have this discipline imposed from without." A discipline imposed by strong leadership or a fear of common censure or both is more reliable as a weapon than the discipline of the individual conscience. Thus part of the Group tended to prefer the former, for they feared themselves — that is, their own weakness or the equivalent of their own weakness in the next fellow. They wished to eliminate all weakness within themselves, which they knew to be the tremulous reflection of the outside world's attraction for them.

If one wished to take a patronizing attitude, one might say of many of the Group that they were crying for a new papa and mamma to take care of them, to scold them, to lead them, and to be responsible to — a papa and mamma who would be all-knowing, strong, forever reliable, and infinitely resourceful. They were seeking moral guidance as much as economic stability; they were seeking something they could truly respect, believe in, and devote themselves to.

Our people were not peculiar in this search. On the contrary. The desire to make sense of our experience, to unify the elements of the world's apparent chaos, to live within a context of integrated thought and action, is one of the central needs of the healthy person. What often lent our people certain attributes of eccentricity was their inability to accept the anarchy of our times as their norm, and their demand that the Group by itself supply what the rest of the world could not.

We were thus in the strange position of being organized to bring society — or its ideals — closer to us, and at the same time of combating it. This anomaly made us both yearn for and fear the outside world, while at the same time it ended by making us cling to and struggle with one another.

This inner contradiction claimed some victims. A list of Group casualties was often thrust in my face. "These are the people you *ruined.*" Some people, it is true, after a few years' contact with the Group were neither able to live within it nor able to make their peace with the world outside. The Group had failed them as a haven and had both destroyed their faith in the theatre outside and incapacitated them for their continuing struggle with it. They were stranded. To this day I meet people — many of them still young, many of them people who had only a casual connection with the Group — who tell me bitterly that the impact of our doctrine and our example has left them with a desperate sense of emptiness and desolation. The world has somehow become spoiled for them, or they for it. The Group's failure to build further, to grow stronger, strikes them as a personal betrayal.

These people probably would have arrived at such an emotional impasse even if the Group had never come into their lives. Some of those who came to the Group, though disappointed that it was unable to sustain them in their struggle, nevertheless were left with a sense of a fortifying experience, not to mention a profound education in their outlook and their craft. Others who came to "cure" themselves found the cure the agent of even greater ills than those they sought to escape or to heal. The Group's high altitude of aspiration and endeavor stimulated their inner conflicts and wrought havoc with their whole being, just as certain select atmospheres chosen to kill the germs of disease often serve only to multiply them in the constitution of some patients who may not even be sure they were sick in the first place.

One of the most serious reflections on the Group's failure is the almost philosophic observation made by such people as Robert Ardrey. The Group was destined to fail, he believed, because its premise went against the American grain. The Group aimed to cultivate the individual through a collective discipline and a collective approach to the individual's problems; and America's culture is fundamentally individualistic.

The history of our country in the early processes of its development placed great emphasis on the solitary individual. From the first, however, there has been in the deeps of American consciousness the intuition that the independent individual as a permanent self-sufficient entity must ultimately prove inhumane, self-destructive. Every effort — including all sorts of religious teaching from our pre-American past — was made to balance the immediate demand for individual self-assertion with a sense of the more basic need for a collective harmony of men within the whole context of life.

When the American individual had built his house, made his machines, enriched himself with every comfort and finery that he could bear, he found himself more nervous than proud, more lonely than certain, more wistful than mature. He did not wholly understand the things he had wrought, which saddened and frightened him somewhat, even as he boasted of them. He did not know himself, he did not know his fellow man. He reached out with some suspicion and fear (reaching out may not *pay*), but reach out he must and will even if his first reachings are tentative, shaky, and spasmodic. His need for a co-operative interdependence (which is what I mean by the term "collective") is slowly becoming greater than his slogans of self-preservation and self-aggrandizement. He begins to realize that his competitive sense tends to kill off not only his competitor but himself. He is no longer sure his isolation spells strength or that his power means security. The enormous structure he has built is not yet a home.

The realists of the early twentieth century (Dreiser, Norris, et al.) had reflected this uncertain state of being with a sense of fateful doom. In the twenties most writers had become cynical, bitter, or maudlin over it. In the thirties some thought they saw a way out. If it was still true as Ardrey himself wrote, that "America is a highly individualized people, few of whom know each other," there can be no question that there has been growing for the past fifteen years at least the urge to remedy this situation, to bring Americans together in a greater understanding of the imperative need to fashion a life in which the individual is conceived not as a world unto himself but as part of a whole world. This movement — of which young Ardrey's plays themselves were an expression — manifested itself, not always consciously, not always clearly, not always maturely, not alone in the theatre, the novel, the arts generally, but in our whole social-economic-political life. It can hardly be said to have triumphed or come to full fruition in any field, but that it was the central factor of the past decade is now beyond dispute.

Most impressive to me in the years that followed the Group's career was the yearning on almost everyone's part to revive it in one way or another. Now that I denied all rumors of its resurrection, many who had been severe with it found its passing had created a serious gap in the theatrical-cultural scene. More significant than this is the fact that constant efforts were made by many Group people to find some substitute, no matter how modest, for what the Group had given them.

I have called the thirties a period of "spiritual activity." Actually, however, the thirties were almost as scornful of the very word as the twenties had been. "Spirit" smacked of mysticism and was therefore anathema. In the thirties the demands of the spirit for the younger people could only be satisfied by action that in some way became social and political. Hence the appetite for meetings, collections, demonstrations, petitions, and parades on behalf of some cause in which a specific social issue was at stake.

It was among the intellectuals, the artists, the world-conscious (as much as class-conscious) workers that this appetite was most strongly felt. These people made articulate the universal need that the depression — hitting capital almost as much as it did labor — brought to the forefront of attention and thought. Thus the intellectual in his dark corner formulated what the people as a whole expressed in the elections of '32 and '36. For the worker the nub of the question may have been a job or a few pennies more in his pay envelope or the right to bargain collectively; for the capitalist it may have been protection against the quicksand insecurity of banks and stock market. The intellectual and the artist were willing to accept these matters as concrete symbols of the world's disturbance. They espoused all measures that promised a happier situation with a fervor that they had hitherto reserved for such supposedly abstract notions as truth, faith, and beauty. The rock-bottom material needs of the worker and the complex fevers of the middle class were objects they seized upon to express the always present and universal hungers of man.

When Roosevelt's remedies had allayed the people's worst fears, reaction set in. Many who still sat in the saddle of power began to notice that the artists and intellectuals were clamoring that they wanted "more" before they would sing songs of satisfaction. A new worry crept into the strong men's hearts. Too many writers, actors, teachers, professional people of all kinds, had taken to habits that might spell mischief. Too many of these innocents were protesting against the progress of fascism, beamed on the Soviet experiment, approved of the CIO, and, after a fashion, entered the vulgar arena of politics. Thus these arose malevolent allusions to "Left" writers, "foreign" ideas, "un-American" ideals and other spurious epithets that serve to confound everyone so that the world may more easily be set back on the old anarchic path that people of power find normal and pleasant.

The term "Left movement" in the arts, though perhaps convenient, was actually a misnomer. It was a form of loose talk that misrepresented the true nature of things. The so-called "Left movement" in the arts was not "Left," "Right," or "Center," but was for our day the main movement of the American consciousness in the process of its growth. It was the focal expression of the American genius between 1931 and 1941. Its basic inspiration was not akin so much to the sources that produced the muckraking work of the Upton Sinclair and Lincoln Steffens era as it was to the humanistic tradition of the Emerson, Thoreau, Walt Whitman epoch. The end that the artists of this movement had in view could not be summed up or conclusively defined in a few political-social reforms. The end was man and his relation to the world or life itself on all the planes that the concept implies.

This was not understood by those who spoke fearfully or contemptuously of the "Left movement." Neither was it always understood by those who were its advertised champions. On one phase of the subject the estimable Van Wyck Brooks has written what strikes me as a definitive statement:

> Young people, all people, for that matter, need faith as they
> need hope and action. They need, above all, romance — one
> may smile at the word, but this is the word I mean and I use

it precisely. Young people are courageous, and they wish to be asked to use their courage. They are gallant, and they wish to be asked to fight; and you cannot say, Peace, Peace to them when they know there is no peace — they know that life is a fight from beginning to end. All they ask is to feel they are needed; and you may say if you choose that modern young people are not romantic. I say they are still more romantic for denying the word. For what is romance? In 1776, in this country, the romance of the young was revolution. In 1850, this romance was the cause of abolition. Later, our romance was money-making; and since every romance produces its heroes, who have been our heroes? The patriot fathers once, then Garrison and John Brown; later Pierpont Morgan and the builders of railroads. The young, in every generation, have followed these leaders, but the romance of money-making wore away, and after the first world-war we entered an epoch in which this country seemed to have no ideals. That is not true, of course, but what is true is that our only ideals were those of the past. . . . Our idealism subsisted on its own fat — and what happened to the younger people? The more they went to the devil, the more honest they were, for they could not believe in ideals that were long since played out. Well, during these years, a new romance rose in a faraway land beyond the sea; and while a few went to Paris, more went to Moscow. It is of no importance what the Russian leaders were: they became John Browns and Garrisons for our young people who had no Browns and Garrisons to contemplate at home. They seemed to be reliving the lives of our patriot fathers; they seemed to be translating into action the words of our Declaration of Independence. They were founding a great new civilization, just as our forbears did, that answered the needs of the world they lived in. Whether or not the Russian leaders were all they appeared to be — this is quite beyond the question; for no one whom we were producing seemed to be great, on this heroic scale of greatness. We were producing advertising geniuses and President Harding. We Americans are the most romantic of peo-

ples. More than any others, we need heroes; and we cannot
make heroes of people who only make money. Not for long, not
for a dozen years; and Russia was the world's romance for
fifteen years because the search for social justice is the romance of our time.*

The young people of the thirties were seeking the "good life."
They were eager not only to find it, but to fight for it. When I try
to summon a single phrase that might stand as emblem of their
desire, I think of the boy in *Awake and Sing* as he exclaims: "We
don't want life printed on dollar bills." Nearly all the Group
plays may be said to stem from this sentiment. Nearly the whole
impulse of the thirties — whatever its more limited aspects — was
fed on that fire. Men who failed in life — failed, that is, as men —
were (to quote the hero in *Night Music*) "those harmony boys
who mighta been." "Make this America for us!" they cried. Our
America could be so made if life wasn't "printed on dollar bills."

The world was and still is run by people for whom, whether
they admit it or not, know it or not, life is printed on dollar bills.
They are the people whose impulse and goal is power, the specific symbol of which is possessions and money. This is their supreme ideal, their philosophy, their religion. For the rest of the
world, whether they confess it or not, the impulse and goal are
one of love. There is a deep struggle forever in progress between
the representative of these two impulses, just as there is a corresponding struggle in the hearts of most individual men. Nowhere
is this struggle more crucial than in America, where the devotees
of power as well as their apologists are strongly entrenched and
where the potentialities of the other force are both so great and
so muddled. Perhaps no country in the world today has greater
resources of good will; no country in the world is culturally so
poorly prepared to use them.

The young men of the thirties achieved certain positive results,
most importantly of course in the domain of re-employment, labor
relations, and social security acts. The gains of 1933 to 1939, how-

---

* Van Wyck Brooks, *The Opinions of Oliver Allston* (New York: E. P.
Dutton & Co., 1941), pp. 128–29.

ever, did not perhaps penetrate deeply enough into the American imagination. The early forties, particularly that period which preceded our entry into the war, represented a kind of stasis, pregnant with possibilities for both good and evil.

The arts reflected this peculiar slowing down of tempo in the movement between 1937 and 1939; so that by 1940, though the theatre could look back proudly to at least five years of creative ferment, it was actually far behind the achievements of the twenties. Hollywood — the sheer business of money-making in the entertainment business — had depleted the theatre's forces (although Hollywood itself was not the cause of the depletion), and while the movies may have gained in the process, the gain, culturally speaking, did not entirely compensate for the general loss.

The Theatre Guild, so typical of the progress made in the twenties, struggled desperately but with decreasing grip in the thirties to the point of virtual dissolution. The forties have revived the Guild because, after the first shocks of the war, the forties have brought a flush of prosperity to Broadway of a rather hectic and indiscriminate sort. In this atmosphere the opportunistic Guild could regain lost ground. The word "opportunistic" is here used without invidious connotation. It stands for a policy that is guided by an adaptability to the trend of the times on the level of average good taste. In this sense the Guild was hardier than the Group or any other organization of its kind. It was a truer reflection of the middle current of American theatre-goers in that it borrowed from everywhere and used everything to sell to the broadest Broadway market for buyers of honest wares.

What is the trend of the day as mirrored in our theatre? We might call the present moment the Billy Rose and Michael Todd period on Broadway. It combines the feeling of the World's Fair with a rather garish night club, a library of nicely flavored "culture" with Coney Island. It produces the very pleasant, calendar-pretty pastiche of *Oklahoma!* — light, fresh, reminiscent, smart, and somewhat abstract, a national unity cocktail for absolutely every liver. It produces classics like *Othello* with no originality of approach save for the inclusion of a first-rate Negro personality. It adapts *Carmen* amusingly and attractively in an arrangement that can arouse nothing but plaudits from every quarter. It produces rather coarse vaudeville at unblushing inflation prices, creating the effect of a vulgarity frank enough to become disarming. Perhaps anything stronger would be doomed to failure.

The early forties combine elements of the twenties and thirties. As in the twenties, we have a feeling of good times over a volcano; a period of spending (though we are told to save), a time of heedless gaiety (though we are told to worry), a time of rather agreeable feverishness. But specifically, Americans today feel that something they expected from the thirties may come to a true issue after the war. We are in a fallow period in which the crop that we have been planting or are about to plant is strangely uncertain. At this point then, it is wise to look back and try to understand the road we have traveled. If we do not know precisely to what ultimate end it may lead, we should at least form some idea as to where we should like to go. The thirties were important because we learned from them that there were different roads and different goals and that there was need for and some possibility of a choice. We were sometimes confused about the names, we got mixed up in our geography, but there is no excuse for our being lost in our minds.

The worker in the thirties demanded life free from fear of unemployment and insecurity. The artist in the thirties like the artist in all times was driven by the hope and desire for a fullness of life. He made common cause with the worker. He found new matter for his art, he brought a new understanding to old themes, he related himself more completely to the world as a whole.

All this was more than useful. Something else frequently happened that was less good. Through his admiration for the man of decision (the progressive statesman, the enlightened labor leader, the heroic worker) the artist began to think of his work as an instrument for the propagation of their ideas. In doing this he often sacrificed his birthright, the particularity of his own vision. He forgot that only by preserving his own special sight — the more individual the better — could he best serve whatever causes he had come to believe in. The artist to be of value in any capacity must always proceed from what is — from what *he* is in the first instance — rather than from what he believes should be. The latter will offer him an angle of vision, but only if he keeps his eyes on what is — that is, on the object — and by being honest with it and with himself can his work achieve any lasting significance. It is more than dangerous for him to force his vision to fit a preconceived pattern (no matter how "correct" that pattern may appear to his intellect). As soon as he begins to exert his will in relation to what he sees, as soon as he allows any value beyond his actual sight to shape his creation, a distortion will set in that will end by betraying even those he hopes to help. When the artist is sincere — true to his own observations and impulse — even his mistakes may be useful; when the artist obeys considerations foreign to his own truth, however worthy his motive, he will fail even in terms of that motive.

The reason for this is simple. The objective of all our creative forces today must be — what it always was — to make man's hands work in conformity with the movement of his free spirit, to make his active life the reflection of his noblest dreams, to make the deeds of all his days rise from the springs of his love. The tragedy of modern life is the forced separation and contradiction between the "way of the world" and the "way of man," between the power motif of our external machinations and the love motif of our subjective desire.

This ideal — to unite the world of spirit with the world of fact so that one is the mirror or consequence of the other — is thus both æsthetic and social. If this ideal lay at the roots of the artistic and social movements of the thirties, then both artist and man of action have a common ground from which to approach the great problems of our time.

The man of action must know the material he is working with and for in his social struggle, he must know the individual man who provides the basic integer of all his work. The artist's job is to provide the report on the true nature of this man as he reads it through his own sensibility and perception. If the man of action fails to understand what manner of being he is dealing with and working for, how can he perfect a social and political technique that will be relevant to his task? If the artist falsifies his report — no matter what justification he claims for doing so — he invalidates his whole function both in terms of himself as an artist and in terms of his social responsibility.

One of the misfortunes of our history is the cleavage between the artist and the man of action. Our men of action (in social services or statecraft) will always have something amateurish and unripe about them until they have become more aware of those intimate human factors which are basically the province of the artist and the intellectual. In the same way our artists and intellectuals will always remain not only immature but positively impotent until they have learned on the one hand their organic role in life's essential problem and on the other that they must exemplify the fact that *every man* must work according to his own integrity, that is, in the spirit that the artist has always claimed as specifically his own. Until this comes about, our arts and our politics will function with only half their potential power.

The movement of the thirties that sprang from the depression and was on the surface merely a period of agitation and reform, was more truly a time in which our youth sought to bring the heart and hand closer together for the ultimate release of man. In this movement the Group acted the part of "primitive surveyor." As such we made many mistakes of calculation. Some of us fell out of line, grew suspicious of the others, shifted in our march from right to left, from left to right. None of these shifts, no matter what they are called, were so significant or clear as the main drive that gave the whole whirl of events their unity. The follies, absurdities, confusion, cleverness, or failure of our Group are far less important than what brought its people together, made them struggle, and kept them on their hectic course for ten years. The career and collapse of the Group were an episode. The thing that gave it birth is part of an epic of which the Group history is but a brief gesture. Those of our friends who deplored what seemed to them a needless preoccupation with social and political matters were right in so far as some of our conduct may have been hasty, superficial, juvenile; they were wrong in so far as they misinterpreted the source and goal of our preoccupation.

The partisanship of the thirties was good; the sectarianism bad. The world did not change its nature just because we had changed our minds. The world had to be just as difficult for us who thought we were right as for those we thought were wrong. The laws of the universe did not yield to us just because we thought we understood them better than some others. Though we stood for unity, we were too impatient with those who did not seem to be on our side. No matter! The lesson for today and tomorrow is that a truer synthesis must be achieved. No true politics, statesmanship, or general external activity can exist that does not stem from the heart of man, from the hunger of his soul as from the requirements of his body; no valid spiritual life (art or religion) can be maintained that does not make central the state of the body, the facts of the external world, the well-being of man as a social animal. Man's fundamental need to work with his hands in terms of his spirit, to feed and clothe his body, to live with his family and fellow men in the peace of a sound physical relationship sanctified by the consent of his heart and highest aspiration, must be the touchstone of every art and craft, of poet and "practical" man alike. We cannot devise methods to help man unless we learn to love and understand the individual. We cannot do good "in general." To be truer collectivists, we must be more deeply individual.

The state of the theatre by itself is no major matter. The superiority of one medium or another, of one place of residence or another, seems to me today of little moment. I hope chiefly that we do not "destroy our sight with a handful of facts." Victory in the war is indisputably our first need; for the time being, it must dwarf every other consideration. But this war and its peace must be seen as the focal point of all the conflicting tendencies of our society. The basic struggle of which the war is simply the most startling and overwhelming scene will go on when arms are laid down. There is no place today for black pessimism, no reason for blind optimism. There is only the problem.

In this struggle for life itself — this struggle for the moral and material world — our battle cry might well be that of the children's game: "Come out, come out wherever you are." Wherever you are, whoever you are, no matter in what profession, art, craft, job, your task will be fundamentally the same: to proceed in such a way that your sense of yourself at its finest and strongest be somehow converted to the uses of your own work, which shall reflect an ideal for yourself that is conjoined with an ideal for your friends — that is, the rest of mankind. Without such an ideal no sane life is possible.

Today there is much confusion and in the world of the arts almost a state of collapse. Let us admit, for the minute, that we have been stopped. In that case, let us say with Walt Whitman: "I think it is to collect a ten-fold impetus that any halt is made."

EPILOGUE: 1945–1955

As I REREAD my book—written in 1943–44—for the first time since its publication I am struck by two challenging statements: the first, which may be found in the original foreword: "The Group Theatre, in my view, was a symptom and an expression of a profound impulse in American life, an impulse that certainly did not begin with the Group Theatre, and did not end with it"; the second is the last sentence of the book, a quote from Walt Whitman, "'I think it is to collect a ten-fold impetus that any halt is made.'"

The questions I am chiefly concerned with now are: first, in what way has the impulse which the Group Theatre represented been carried on and, second, has there been an impetus forward after the "halt"?

The answer is: just as I originally wrote that I believed the Group Theatre to have been both a failure and a success, so I now believe that since those days I described as "fervent" we have both advanced and retrogressed.

That we have advanced is something that hardly needs elaborate demonstration since a great number of people whose first efforts are recorded in the preceding chapters may be said to have become the dominant figures of the American stage, certainly they are the people who have exercised the greatest influence on the younger generation of playwrights, actors, and designers today.

It is no exaggeration either to say that the Stanislavsky "method," once considered a foreign excrescence in the American theatre, has developed, in one form or another, into the prevalent method for training the young actor in drama schools, "studios," and colleges, and that the majority of the best young actors (actors between the ages of twenty-five and forty-five) are actors trained more or less in the Stanislavsky method—either through former association with the Group Theatre or through directors and teachers who were fostered by the Group Theatre. The Group Theatre now has "grandchildren"!

Some of the most significant successes of recent years (1945–55) —A Streetcar Named Desire, Death of a Salesman, The Member of the Wedding, The Teahouse of the August Moon, to mention only a few—were directed by men whose careers began with the Group. Such actors and actresses as Marlon Brando, Eli Wallach, Julie Harris, Kim Stanley, Maureen Stapleton, and Uta Hagen, who never were members of the Group itself, may be fairly claimed as the Group's offspring.

Sometime in 1947 an actress who had never been part of the Group—though she had studied with Sanford Meisner—told me that she had had a troubling experience during a rehearsal with an "old-time" producer-director. She had asked him why she had to make a certain move in the course of a scene. The director exclaimed: "Don't ask me any of those arty Group Theatre questions!" When I heard this, I remarked that the director in question was at least ten years behind the times since he, who had been successful in the twenties, had not had a hit in years, while the Group—through the majority of its former personnel—had become the *commercial theatre.*

There is another side to all this. The members of the Group Theatre had rendered the American theatre a valuable service and had prospered as individuals. They had brought what they had learned from the Group's collective effort to bear on their work outside the Group. This was progress—and all to the good. But it was not precisely the kind of progress they had once envisaged as members of the Group.

To fulfill the Group's dream of success it would have been necessary not only that its policy of a permanent company accomplishing ever more ambitious tasks (including the development of an enlightened audience aware of and eager to follow the aims of its dramatists, actors, and directors) be continued, but that more than one such company be developed both in New York and in the rest of the country. Since no such company now exists anywhere—although one always hears rumors of the formation of such companies—and since our theatre is still run entirely on a hit-or-miss basis as a series of unrelated triumphs or disasters, the true purpose of the Group cannot be said to have been achieved and hardly seems likely to be achieved for some time to come.

Is there really a need for such a theatre—a theatre, that is, which might become the equivalent of the Old Vic in England, the state or civic theatres of Sweden, France, and Germany or even of such companies as the Barrault-Renaud troupe in Paris? Rather than answer this question directly (I might note at once that most theatre people feel this need acutely, though there are some who deny it) I shall proceed to a closer inspection of the overall theatrical situation as it presently exists—for the answer to the question should be sought not in any theoretical statement but in the actual state of our theatre since 1945.

The American theatre in this period, it may fairly be said, flourished. I do not speak of economics, because in this regard a statistician might easily prove my premise wrong by pointing to the diminishing number of productions from year to year, the increasing shortage of playhouses available for "live theatre," the decimation of the "road" and its touring companies, the disappearance of most resident stock companies, the large percentage of unemployment among members of Actors Equity, and the great losses from unsuccessful plays every season. (It is true that while "hit shows" these days gross great sums of money compared to such

shows in the past, there are many more plays which lose their
entire or a large part of the money invested in them than formerly
when many more plays could unblushingly be termed "moderate
successes.")

When I say that the American theatre has flourished in the past
ten years I mean that the quality of production has been comparatively high, that new playwrights and actors of significant talent
have come upon the scene. Many Europeans—particularly the
English and the Germans—readily admit nowadays that the most
interesting contemporary plays come to them from the United
States.

The outstanding new playwrights of the thirties were Lillian
Hellman and Clifford Odets; in the early forties there was Thorn-
ton Wilder and William Saroyan. In the late forties Arthur Miller
and Tennessee Williams emerged; men who kept alive—this is
particularly true of Miller—some of the impassioned social conscience of the thirties. Both these men and younger ones—William
Inge, Arthur Laurents—as well as those of the twenties who continued their serious writing efforts in the theatre—all of them still
relatively young in years and achievement, all of them in a sense
beginners—have contributed to the liveliness of the contemporary
drama to an extent, I repeat, envied by many foreign observers.

I make no reference to the excellent musical comedies of this
period, for it is well known that in this field the ingenuity, energy,
and resourcefulness of the American theatre have no peers—although I am inclined to believe that, just as the *commedia dell'arte*
which had a deep influence on the theatres of the seventeenth and
eighteenth centuries left no one enduring work, it is not any single
example of musical comedy which will prove historically outstanding so much as the aggregate phenomenon.

In the fifties there has been some tendency to move away from
"realism"—of both the traditional Ibsen-like kind and the more
propagandistic sort—and our theatre as a result is becoming increasingly receptive to the work of such dramatists as T. S. Eliot,
Christopher Fry, Jean Giraudoux, Jean Anouilh; their influence
may prove broadening. The aesthetically aware have also given
visiting troupes such as those of the Old Vic (particularly when

Epilogue: 1945–1955

accompanied by Laurence Olivier and Ralph Richardson) and Barrault cordial welcomes. All this promises much for the future widening of our theatrical frame of reference, a larger sense of the theatre's scope.

Nor have the so-called off-Broadway productions been entirely without interest or results. ANTA (American National Theatre Association)—an organization founded to promote the idea of a national (state-subsidized) theatre and to stimulate theatrical activity outside New York—in its Experimental Theatre productions and later at its own playhouse (formerly the Guild Theatre) made respectable efforts to provide room for intelligent revivals of valuable plays of the not too remote past (O'Neill's *Desire Under the Elms,* for example) and for some new ones. Something of the same thing, minus the sponsorship of new plays, has been done for several years now at the City Center. The "arena" theatre known as Circle-in-the-Square has done admirable work, chiefly in the revival of fine plays which had been somehow neglected on Broadway—for example Tennessee Williams' *Summer and Smoke* and Eugene O'Neill's *The Iceman Cometh* (originally produced in 1946). Most recently commendable productions of both new and old plays have been given at the (Norris Houghton—T. Edward Hambleton) Phoenix Theatre.

What then, if anything, is lacking in our theatrical scene? What is missing now—aside from volume and dissemination of production, playhouses, and easier material conditions for the production and enjoyment of plays—which was once ours? Certainly it is not a question of talent. Just as there was as much talent in our theatre in the twenties as in the thirties (in fact, one can safely hazard the statement that no period of our theatrical history was as productive as the twenties) so there is as much talent available today as at any time in the thirties or forties. Is there really anything at all wrong?

I once heard a well-known American painter address a conference of graphic artists in which he remarked with wry humor that while many of the artists present had become as well-known and as affluent as serious American painters and sculptors were ever likely to be, they all tended to look back to the period in the lamentable thirties when many of them had been enrolled in the government

Federal Art Project, and to speak of those years as "the good old
days." Everyone laughed. None of these artists preferred the
penury of the Federal Project days—although at the time they
thanked God and Roosevelt—to their recently acquired security,
nor were any of them more sentimental than need be about the
struggles of their youth. But "the good old days" was a reference
to the fervor and faith in the collective effort characteristic of the
thirties in their best moments.

That the faith was often nebulous or sometimes foolishly employed in directly or indirectly mischievous ways seemed less
important at the conference (held in 1947) than that those artists
still felt the need to believe—as they did in the thirties—that they
were working toward some valuable artistic, social, humanly significant goal.

The Group Theatre's purpose was artistically and culturally
sound—and as we have just seen has nourished almost every
branch of the American theatre. That purpose, as very simply
stated in the early pages of this book, was "to combine a study
[and practice] of theatre craft with a creative content," or, to put
it another way, to make the production of stage plays actually
mean something in the lives of the participants.

The play did not have to have a "message" in the sense of a
demonstrable, "practical" point or to substantiate a defined ideology: it had to effect a spiritual union between those who played it
and those who saw it in terms of their common joys, pleasures or
misgivings. (The delicate lyric plays of Chekhov are far more
illuminating—even socially speaking—than any of Gorky's later
plays, not to mention the more recent Soviet plays. The bitterness
in Tennessee Williams' plays, their "negativism" if we are prone
to think of them in such a light, are as valuable as expressions of
our times as plays presumably written in the spirit of *Waiting for
Lefty*.)

What has happened to the *"excitement,"* that enthusiastic sense
of struggle which infused even some of the minor productions of
the Group? (Though many of the productions of the last ten years
which I have cited have been brilliantly proficient, none, I sincerely
believe, surpassed or perhaps even equaled in sensitive inner flow

and ensemble magic such productions as *The House of Connelly,
Men in White, Awake and Sing, My Heart's in the Highlands*.)
One can go even further and ask: What happened to the inquiry,
curiosity, reading and discussion around and about the theatre,
beginning in the twenties—see the books of Macgowan and Jones,
the criticism of Stark Young, the old *Theatre Arts Monthly*—which
extended with added dimension into the thirties? Where are the
controversies, the ardent credos, the hot championship of this or
that "school" of production, the philosophic or "mystic" elucida-
tion of plays and performances, the sharp points and barbed quips
of disagreement which marked the theatre of those days?

The theatre was as much a business in 1925 and 1935 as it is
today, and people then were not morally superior or aesthetically
more refined than they are today. What is lacking now is a sense
of purpose, of an ideal—something to be achieved over and above
a smash hit, a fat salary, rave notices, more fulsome billing and
more frequent mention in the columns.

Men like O'Neill never lost that sense of purpose, which is one
of the reasons—and not the least—of his eminence among our playwrights, nor did Robert Edmond Jones or even the far less knowing or craftsmanlike producer Arthur Hopkins. I recall these
names not only because they stand outside any contemporary
"competition" but to indicate that when I speak of "purpose" I
intend no narrowing interpretation—political, social, or religious—
but use the word in its largest spiritual and artistic sense—which
may include all the others.

The answer to my queries you may think is that with the passing
of the Roosevelt regime and the temper it reflected a sharp reaction set in which made everything that smacked of a departure
from the status quo more than a little suspect. There is considerable truth in this.

The political constriction which began to make itself felt around
1947 and which mounted in frightening tempo to reach a sort of
climax in 1953 made almost everybody disinclined to commit
themselves to any opinion that suggested anything specific beyond
"loyalty." (Perhaps the only value in all of this was that it made
a good many people less dogmatic and less glib.) But what began

as a kind of political terror inducing a political hush gradually deteriorated to a cessation of all serious discussion of any kind whatsoever and to a large extent even of thinking. There was nothing left, it seemed, but for us to drop dead.

None of this would have been too alarming, if the change of mind or heart in the country meant a conversion on our part to some fruitful idea other than that previously held. The rebel who turns conformist is not necessarily a sorry person if what he chooses to conform to is something deeply rooted in him and can give him the strength to become creative in a new orientation. A quietist may be socially constructive, a disillusioned romantic may turn his pain into a useful ingredient in the making of a fresh synthesis. Even uncertainty, deep doubt, nihilistic bitterness may acquire creative value—as witness the work of the so-called existentialists in France who attempted to make a positive humanism out of their prewar disgust and postwar despair.

What happened to most of us was that we came to desire nothing more than to be inconspicuous citizens, with no other thought than "to get on," no other ideal than celebrity or success—and in this area, one kind is as good as another.

I cannot overlook the incidents of the public admission in Washington by several former members of the Group Theatre that at one time or another they had been affiliated for shorter or longer periods with the Communist party. In the body of this book I have already discussed some of the circumstances and motivating forces which led to the political embroilments which these people apologized for, were defiant about, or tried to explain away in Washington. It will therefore be understood why I was always made unhappy by their statements, no matter what form they took, because they could not—given the place and time the questions were put to them—present a true picture of the emotional and psychological situation which had led to their "mistakes." They could not and did not tell the truth—because, strangely enough, they did not understand it.

The truth is that none of them had anything but the most rudimentary, naïve understanding of politics: they were all essentially apolitical no matter what they may have once argued, or clamored about—no matter what cards, documents, statements, they may have signed. They were *yearners* seeking a home—a home in the theatre, a home in the world of thought and action, something that would call forth their most selfless efforts in behalf of some concrete cause. If what they chose to do momentarily was to join a party which spoke tenderly of the humble and ardently of human brotherhood, one can only say that while they were childishly deluded in this specific political instance, their motivation had health and virtue in it; a health which many of them—having lost some of the impulse and having no particular Group, artistic or social, to make use of what remained of the impulse—may never quite recover.

So the Group people like many other of this generation, and the generation which followed in the fifties, entered upon a period of spiritual stalemate. All they hoped for now was to find work that paid well and prayed that things would get no worse, that they might prosper in the way the radio, television, pictures, popular magazines, assured us was the best, perhaps even the only way, to prosper. This was not an atmosphere conducive to creation. "He who desires nothing, hopes for nothing and is afraid of nothing, cannot be an artist," Chekhov once wrote. And to hope for and desire nothing but the luxurious comfort of success is to desire and hope for little.

But, the so-called practical man will ask, "What has all this to do with the state of the theatre?" If the theatre is doing well and, if further, the particular sort of theatre you espouse has added to itself in numbers, stature, and popular acceptance, why should there be any mention of "failure" or retrogression in connection with the Group Theatre idea?

The admirable actors of the teens and twenties—most of them trained through years of consistent work in stock companies, road tours and frequent engagements in new plays on Broadway—are now all but gone from the theatre. Alfred Lunt, America's finest actor since John Barrymore, has played nothing in the past fifteen years even as ambitious as Sherwood's *There Shall Be No Night* produced in 1941. Most of his vehicles have been shallow jobs which offered him no challenge. (Contrast this with Laurence

Olivier's Malvolio, Macbeth, Titus Andronicus, in one season—
and his appearance in plays by Fry, Shaw, Rattigan, just before
that—not to mention the Shakespeare films he directed and starred
in.) Ina Claire acts only occasionally. Helen Hayes, more active
than most of her contemporaries, prefers short engagements in
revivals of the old successes. Katharine Cornell awaits the safety
of another popular vehicle. Tallulah Bankhead has altered herself
into a legend of grotesque hilarity having little to do with acting.
Fredric March, the best actor of the "middle" generation, is in
virtual retirement from the stage—though his two most recent
appearances in Lillian Hellman's *The Autumn Garden* (1951) and
O'Neill's *Long Day's Journey into Night* (1956) have been honorable.

The best of recently arrived actors, Marlon Brando, has im-
mersed himself in film activity. This is typical. The average stage
career nowadays—I do not consider a return to the stage every
once in a while a stage career—is five years. The reason for this is
that since the theatre has become less a medium of expression vital
to its workers as artists than a medium of self-exploitation in terms
of "name" and money, the theatre is regarded as too insecure to
be a good investment. Movies and television—which in addition
to other advantages are great for publicity—claim the major part of
the actor's time.

The better-than-average young actor who has been praised in
the press for his part in a successful play or two soon becomes a
"star"—that is, he claims star-billing (and "billing" has become a
kind of craze in the theatre). As a "star" the young actor demands
a star's salary—regardless of his actual "cash value" to a production.
The producers are bound to meet the young actor's price because
with the perpetual flight of promising actors from stage to screen
(or television) there always seems to be a shortage of "name"
actors. This in itself is hardly disastrous, but it is symptomatic of
what is happening throughout the theatre: each individual uses
the theatre for himself alone. Ultimately, this may bring about the
destruction of the theatre—that by its very nature is an art of collaboration or teamwork.

This disease of each man for himself—beginning with the owners of theatre buildings, stagehands, and ending with a host of agents who aggravate the process—is most striking among actors, but it infects playwrights and directors as well.

The director grows timid about undertaking any play which is financially hazardous, not only because of the losses to his potential income but because a flop may lower him in the esteem of the "business," degrade his price, diminish his chances of future employment in pictures or television.

Playwrights no longer regard themselves as serious novelists as the older generation did—as working writers with something they were committed or owed themselves to say. No, there is a great deal of money to be made in the theatre, and if playwrights fail to make it—and keep on making it (one must always remember the tax problem!), they seem to find themselves justified—they deem it honorable, in fact, to devote themselves to more remunerative writing—without relation to what they might have once dreamed of achieving.

When O'Neill's first plays failed to yield more than a humble income, he did not exclaim, as I have heard many young authors, "If my next play flops, I'm quitting." More and more theatre people consider a play to have little significance unless it is a smash box-office success. As a result audiences every year tend more and more to view plays in the same light.

All this has become the norm of the theatre today—partly because of pressure of high costs (the economic framework within which the theatre exists), but the depressing economic situation in the theatre is in some measure due to what we now take for granted as the norm. Only the conscious desire on the part of each person within the theatre to contribute to its existence as a whole, because of a personal dedication to the idea which that theatre represents, can preserve the theatre as an art. But if the theatre has no incentive or goal beyond that which prevails in any ordinary business, the theatre must lapse into the peculiar condition it is in at present. And if society itself eschews every ideal except that which is merely a matter of lip service—without roots in our deepest personal experience—it is unlikely that such ideals will ever find expression in the theatre. That our theatre has not disappeared under these circumstances—no one has failed to notice its *shrinkage*—is a tribute to the great fund of talent our country commands and to our permanent and ineradicable need and appetite for theatre.

The skeptical may still persist in asking what difference it makes how we go about producing our plays if what is produced is good. To put it modestly I must answer, to begin with, that we might do much better. The theatre functioning as it does now, as a series of disparate individual enterprises without even the ambition of organizing itself for continuous work, tends to waste its efforts, wear itself out, and creates no foundation upon which anything enduring may be built—so that in the end we are left exhausted and empty: so much strain to achieve so little. It is dispiriting always to have to begin over again from the beginning.

America, Van Wyck Brooks once said, is the country of first acts. We begin with great promise—energy, imagination, fresh impulses. We rarely fulfill ourselves. This is inevitable if we think of each creative act as the dazzling product of an isolated individual to be applauded, admired—and forgotten.

It is a law of life that man cannot live for himself alone. Extreme individualism is insanity. The world's problems are also our personal problems. Health is achieved through maintaining our personal truth in a balanced relation of love to the rest of the world. No expression is more emblematic of this relation than the creative act which we call art. No art by its very constitution typifies the social nature of that creative act more than the theatre. The theatre, to be fully understood and appreciated, must be seen as a manifestation of this process of interchange between society and the individual. It must be judged as a continuous development of groups of individuals within society, a development which becomes richer, acquires greater force and value as it grows within the society in which it originates. Only in this way can the theatre nourish us.

When we think of the French theatre, for example, it is not simply a matter of saying that Corneille, Racine, Molière, de Musset, were great French dramatists—big shots in their day!—we understand that they helped make France and the French people what they are, and in France, as in other European countries, such dramatists not only performed their life's work, but governments created institutions so that their work might continue to live and fortify their peoples.

It took a long time for the theatre to take root in our country. The first flower of a truly indigenous theatre may be said to have arisen only in the early part of the twentieth century. We are also right in acclaiming Eugene O'Neill as the prime example of this flowering. With him came others—I speak of actors as well as other theatre craftsmen—who worked as dedicated artists, though only a few of them displayed the pertinacity needed to establish a continuity of effort at the enormous task.

In the thirties such organizations as the Group Theatre set an example of what might be carried to greater maturity by a later generation. The Federal Theatre, through the social accident of a government desiring to increase employment in a period of economic distress, gave evidence of what could be accomplished even under the worst circumstances in spreading serious theatre production throughout the country.

When George Kaufman and Moss Hart in *The Fabulous Invalid* tried to dramatize the decline of the theatre to the low point of a Federal Theatre Project, they also introduced a character as a presumable "savior"—a character based on the personality of Orson Welles, whose first productions were sponsored by the Project. And Orson Welles, it might be added, exemplifies how a grand talent may be wasted when it deprives itself of every real connection with the theatre as a whole.

In the forties and the fifties *the line* seems to have become lost—for reasons I have tried to suggest—though talent has flowed on. The Theatre Guild, our oldest theatre institution, has become a distributing agency dependent to a large extent on other managements or "package deals" with small units of independent writers and actors. The Playwrights Company, an outgrowth of dramatists previously identified with the Theatre Guild, has now lost most of its character—and is largely sustained as a branch of Roger L. Stevens' activities—helpful and generous gifts of a "theatre-struck" businessman to playwrights who need a boost.

Some of the spark of that enthusiasm which emanated from the Group Theatre and kindred organizations has been transmitted to young people of today through the conversations and scene study of the Actors Studio (its directors are Cheryl Crawford, Elia Kazan, and Lee Strasberg, all familiar from the Group and now widely known throughout the theatre), but though it serves a praiseworthy purpose one wishes that general understanding of it would not be limited to a publicity which has willy-nilly been incorporated into the glamour-fetishism of the Broadway assembly line.

Several of our most prominent dramatists are, I repeat, serious writers, but by standards of the best which has been created in the modern theatre they are still beginners. Under the circumstances one may be excused if one worries whether the brilliant first acts of their careers will lead to mature last acts (Shaw wrote *St. Joan* at the age of sixty-seven). One also wonders where the gifted young actors we know will be when they are fifty.

I am no crapehanger or mourner. I am confident that the American theatre will somehow or other endure and eventually progress closer to the goals we esteem. There is too much creative energy in our country for this not to be so. We must also constantly remind ourselves that the theatre is more influenced by historical and social contingencies than any other art. The theatre cannot solve its problems alone. Perhaps our complaints are only another manifestation of that impatience which is a symptom of American youthfulness. We hope to accomplish everything more rapidly than life will permit.

I could not do my work in the theatre if I did not believe in the value of the effort in relation to the objectives I have delineated. But I also believe in the value of a certain dissatisfaction, what might be called creative discontent. In an environment in which every success is hailed as a triumph, any creditable piece of work is ballyhooed as genius, every impressive performance is dubbed great, and every momentary achievement is made to sound like the ultimate, it is useful to remember that the New York theatre does not cover the continent, and that the contemporary American theatre is not *all* of the theatre. Such a narrowing view—let us call it Broadway provincialism—tends to depress rather than enhance our standards of excellence and the fineness of our practice.

EPILOGUE: 1974

IT WOULD SEEM natural that after the rather pessimistic account of the course of the American theatre in the preceding Epilogue that now, almost twenty years later, my further remarks should sound like moans of utter calamity. *Variety*, the trade's weekly register of booms and busts in the entertainment business, proclaimed in the front-page headline of its June 5, 1974, issue: "Theatre Is Now a National Invalid."

The facts which appear to substantiate this report indicate that in box-office receipts and in the number of stage presentations, the 1973–74 season fell markedly below the figures of the 1971–72 season. The overall shrinkage in theatre production is, to say the least, disquieting. In 1899–1900, eighty-seven new shows were to be seen; by 1927–28 the number rose to two hundred sixty-four. During the depression years (1930–39) there were never less than ninety-eight plays on the boards, and in 1931–32 there were as many as two hundred and seven. But 1971–72 saw only fifty-eight, and in 1973–74 the total dropped to forty-eight.

Still, these statistics do not convince me that all is lost or that a taste for theatre is becoming extinct among us. *Variety* speaks only of *money* and, in its count of productions, only of Broadway. But other factors must be taken into account and other standards.

The general condition described in the Epilogue still obtains, with several more aggravating symptoms. These relate to the ever-increasing cost of production, the inflation of operational expense, and the consequent high price of admissions. As a business the theatre is no longer a reasonable risk; one prominent producer has declared it "not viable," though he still hopes to continue functioning in the disabled traffic.

The theatre will not disappear unless we are all done in! The theatre has never died, though at times it has suffered a partial eclipse. Even with the banning of the theatres in England between 1642 and 1660 there remained a theatre, underground.

The theatre never dies, because it is an art of *actual presence*. People, not their images, are in immediate contact. The impulse to celebrate and manifest themselves in close proximity with one another has from time immemorial been deep-rooted in human nature. "Broadway" is only a momentary and minute part of the theatre's history. In despondent moods I refer to it as the theatre's ghetto.

Variety's analysis represents the thinking of Broadway's theatrical professionals, including several of the critics and parts of the audience. Broadway is taken to be synonymous with the theatre as a whole. It is an entirely false premise. Hence, without having turned optimistic, I believe our theatre has made a certain degree of progress in the past ten years and may advance in the future to ever more valid contributions to our commonwealth.

If we look back to the yearbooks (first edited by Burns Mantle) which collect *The Best Plays* of each theatre season and list all of those produced, we find no mention of plays produced off-Broadway during the years of the Group Theatre's activities, 1931 to 1941, because, in fact, there were hardly any. Organizations such as the Washington Square Players, the Provincetown Players, the Neighborhood Playhouse, which marked our theatre's coming of age in 1915, were among the first to separate themselves from

the mainstream of our theatre life. Though they all occupied
houses below Fourteenth Street, they were not thought of as what
we now dub "off-Broadway." The little theatres of that period,
which later were to become known under the generic heading of
Regional Theatres (groups operating outside New York), were
hardly noticed by our metropolitan press until the founding of the
(old) *Theatre Arts Monthly* in 1917. As mentioned in the Epilogue, it was not until the mid-forties and early fifties that off-
Broadway and the Regional Theatres began to be given serious
attention as a vital element in our theatre world. Since those days
there has been a much wider and more important development in
the movement away from Broadway. For the original off-Broadway
impetus soon became musclebound and to a harmful extent impeded by the economic net which strangles Broadway productions.
The off-off Broadway enterprises—productions in cafés, churches,
cellars, warehouses, lofts, and so on, and with them entirely new
organizations in and out of New York—have brought new energies
to our theatre.

It is no longer news that Broadway has become ever more dependent on a few musical comedies each season, on the import of
a few London hits, and on plays originating with the Washington
Arena Stage, the Mark Taper of Los Angeles, the Shakespeare
Theatre Festival at the Public Theatre and elsewhere, as well as
with such off-off Broadway groups as the Chelsea Theater Center
at the Brooklyn Academy of Music and the Circle Repertory Theatre Company on upper Broadway and on lower Seventh Avenue.

Even this is not the whole story. Until the fifties there were no
free performances in Central Park, no Guthrie Theater in Min-
neapolis, no theatre at Lincoln Center, no Performing Garage
productions, none of the La Mama Theatre's work, no Long Wharf
Theatre of New Haven; very few of such forward-looking groups
as those of Boston, Hartford, Baltimore; no street theatres in various parts of the country, no Actor's Workshop of San Francisco,
no Mime Troupe, no Bread and Puppet Theatre, no American Con-
servatory Theatre, none of André Gregory's productions, no Man-
hattan Theater Club, no black theatre efforts. Then too, there
were rarely any ambitious theatre programs at the universities

such as are now to be observed at Yale, for example. All these, and probably many more I have no doubt overlooked, have made our theatre today something other than the disaster area which it is constantly declared to be. Even in a skeptical estimate, we cannot fail to recognize that all these manifestations have added fresh notes, suggested further possibilities in the growth of our theatre arts.

We should also remember that there are now various foundations which were not in existence in the Group Theatre days and which in recent years have played a valuable role in sustaining presumably worthwhile theatre activities of a noncommercial kind.

There are three main reasons why many commentators insist that our theatre is through. One is our mania for *bigness*, as if only what is immense in size, number, and profit is important. If this were so, most of the great cultural achievements of history would have been aborted. The second reason is that certain deep thinkers take pleasure in demonstrating that all the new activities I have just named have vouchsafed us very few first-rate works, no masterpieces. But masterpieces have always been scarce. At no time has the theatre been able to subsist on masterpieces alone. Ordinary popular plays and worse provide the soil from which masterpieces grow. To take *literary* masterpieces of the past as a criterion for judgment of a particular moment is to betray a museum mind and a faulty conception of the theatre as an art. But the most important cause of all for the fatal prognosis of our theatre's condition is our persistence in viewing our theatre as a business, something chiefly aimed at monetary profit.

The British National Theatre, to take only one recent example, is certainly *successful* without being *profitable*—nor does anyone expect it to make money (just as we do not expect this from our libraries, our schools, our universities, or our symphony orchestras). The cry for help in England and elsewhere abroad issues from the commercial theatres rather than from the others: the subsidized theatres on the whole possess the greater popular appeal!

Still, the heart of the matter, the essential theme and point of the story told in *The Fervent Years*, lies deeper than any of these arguments. To this day very few people who interest themselves in the stage understand what constitutes a true theatre. And since the Group Theatre, only three or four companies have attempted to create one or have pursued the effort to the extent that the Group did or for as long a time.

What is a true theatre? It is a body of craftsmen—actors, directors, designers, technicians, administrative staff—united on a *permanent* basis to develop its own technique, to embody a common attitude to life that an audience more or less shares. Such theatres may be socially, politically, or religiously motivated, but each of them must develop an identity, a style, a "face," a meaning of its own. (The Ancient Greeks did not produce Asiatic plays, nor did the theatre of the Middle Ages mount atheistic ones, any more than the seventeenth century French theatre lent itself to plays of anti-royalist persuasion! And in modern times, with heterogeneous audiences, even Germany and Russia have developed theatres of varying orientations in style and content.) Above all, true theatre sets itself a goal and plans its work as a lifelong *continuity,* very much as the individual artist does.

So long as theatre production is envisaged as a piecemeal endeavor—a series of disparate "good shows," organized by individual entrepreneurs or managers—the fruitless cry for theatre as a profitable business will persist and talk about the theatre's decadence or desuetude will continue, ad nauseam.

None of this implies an arty refusal to face economic considerations; the *avant-garde* groups are as in need of funds as the so-called commercial theatres. Each must construct its own efficiency in this respect. Still, I do not at all hold with those who maintain that the high price of tickets has little to do with poor attendance at Broadway theatres or with the swift collapse of many of its offerings. The Theatre Development Fund, a nonprofit organization established in 1968, has devoted itself to the aid of productions of special merit, whether on, off-, or off-off Broadway, and has proved that by the reduction of ticket prices, the life of many plays has been prolonged. And the enormous success of the tent on New York's Duffy Square, which sells "TKTS" on the day of the performance at half price to most of the theatre attractions in the area, provides unmistakable evidence that there are vast numbers of people who would be eager to go to the theatre if it were not so costly.

Government subsidy for the theatre is certainly desirable, but a true theatre may exist even without such subsidy. The Moscow Art Theâtre was privately subsidized from 1895 to 1917. But it is indisputable that true theatres simply cannot exist as profitable commercial ventures. To require them to do so is to deny theatre altogether. It should also be asserted that if theatre is merely a business for profit, as some would have it, its demise, though deplorable, would be no tragedy! As a business, such theatre would not fulfill its function.

Some glints of enlightenment have begun to dawn on our land. We now have a National Endowment for the Arts—which includes the theatre—and civic and state endowments. And certain public-minded citizens have contributed to the establishment of theatres in various parts of the country. But what frequently occurs is that these are founded by real-estate interests and other such enterprises (possibly for tax-deduction privileges) and are housed in enormous new edifices. They immediately reveal themselves as impossibly burdensome to all concerned, but especially to the artists for whom they have ostensibly been built. Original costs budgeted at three million dollars soon rise to over ten million; even empty, some of them demand as much as two hundred thousand dollars a year for maintenance. Productions under such circumstances are not very much less expensive than those at the commercial theatres.

Giant luxury constructions do not serve art. The British National Theatre up to the present occupied the site of the "Old Vic," situated in a poor, out-of-the-way neighborhood, a theatre which before 1914 purveyed melodramatic and music-hall entertainment. Brecht's Berliner Ensemble, which has influenced stage practice everywhere, found no difficulty in accommodating itself to an old-fashioned, almost Victorian, playhouse. Grotowski's theatre is a tiny place in a comparatively small Polish town . . . but why go on? An architectural face-lift and the most modern equipment offer no solution to the essential problems which the theatre confronts.

We are the problem, we and our ignorance of the theatre's very nature. For the theatre is not a business; it never has been basically that. It is an art of direct communication grounded on shared social and moral values. It is not, first of all, a condiment, a genteel pastime, an escape from reality, but like all art it is a resource in civilization's human treasury. It is, moreover, perhaps one of the most telling expressions of a people's innermost character, because it is an art composed of many elements, of which the matrix is the public itself. Everyone in the theatre is a vital communicant; each is responsible to the other. Theatre will always be with us, for better or worse, as there will always be admirable individual talents, plays, and performances. But to achieve its greatest efficacy and significance, the theatre must be organized and conducted in the spirit, if not the precise form, which the Group Theatre in its ten years of existence sought to exemplify. Every departure from that general ideal, no matter how tricked out by technical novelty, by advantageous physical means, even by endowments of huge sums of money and property, must of necessity diminish its most valuable function, its true reason for being.

Index